Rosemary Ingham is a freelance writer and costume designer and former assistant professor of Theatre at Southern Methodist University in Texas. She attended Yale Drama School as a special student in playwriting and design, and is the co-author, with Ms. Covey, of *The Costumer's Handbook* (Prentice-Hall, Spectrum Books).

Liz Covey has done extensive costume work for London theatres and is a New York-based freelance designer.

THE Costume

Designer's HANDBOOK

A Complete Guide for Amateur and Professional Costume Designers

Rosemary Ingham
Liz Covey

A SPECTRUM BOOK

Prentice-Hall, Inc., Englewood Cliffs, New Jersey 07632

Library of Congress Cataloging in Publication Data

Ingham, Rosemary.
  The costume designer's handbook.

  "A Spectrum Book."
  Bibliography: p.
  Includes index.
  1. Costume design. 2. Costume. I. Covey, Liz.
II. Title.
TT507.I46 1982   792'.026   82–20478
  ISBN 0–13–181289–0
  ISBN 0–13–181271–8 (pbk.)

Cover photograph: A scene from The Hartford Stage Company's
production of Galileo. *Costume design by John Conklin.*
Photograph courtesy of the Hartford Stage Company.

The Costume Designer's Handbook: A Complete Guide
for Amateur and Professional Costume Designers
by Rosemary Ingham and Liz Covey
©1983 by Prentice-Hall, Inc., Englewood Cliffs, N.J. 07632

A SPECTRUM BOOK

Printed in the United States of America

10 9 8 7 6 5 4 3 2 1

ISBN 0-13-181289-0

ISBN 0-13-181271-8 {PBK.}

Editorial/production supervision and page layout
   by Fred Dahl/Inkwell
Interior design and color insert design
   by Maria Carella
Cover design by Hal Siegel
Manufacturing buyer: Cathie Lenard

This book is available at a special discount when ordered in
large quantities. Contact Prentice-Hall, Inc.,
General Publishing Division, Special Sales, Englewood Cliffs, N.J. 07632.

Prentice-Hall International, Inc., *London*
Prentice-Hall of Australia Pty. Limited, *Sydney*
Prentice-Hall Canada Inc., *Toronto*
Prentice-Hall of India Private Limited, *New Delhi*
Prentice-Hall of Japan, Inc., *Tokyo*
Prentice-Hall of Southeast Asia Pte. Ltd., *Singapore*
Whitehall Books Limited, Wellington, *New Zealand*
Editora Prentice-Hall do Brasil Ltda., *Rio de Janeiro*

Contents

Reference

Foreword

My joy in the theatre is collaboration. I began my artistic life as a writer, but I couldn't bear the loneliness: the quiet room, the blank piece of paper in the typewriter, the desperate hope that the phone would ring. I am cut out for the frantic energy of the rehearsal hall and for the complex interweaving of sensibilities that mark a fruitful design conference. The designer supplements me more profoundly than anyone else in the production process, for my visual skills have had to be developed consciously over the years, and my teachers have been the fine design artists who have taken me in hand. None was more influential or more persuasive in the early years of my career than one of the authors of this invaluable book.

Rosemary Ingham helped teach me color, and certainly line, but more importantly how to enlist the actor's best instincts in reaching vital costume decisions. I have no patience with costume designers who view actors as pliable dolls on which to drape fabric. There comes a time in nearly every rehearsal period when a good actor will know certain things about the character to be played that neither the director, the designer, nor even the writer can possibly know. If asked to wear clothes that violate his or her own deep sense of reality, the actor will remain an actor in a costume for the run of the show. A bit of breath will have been knocked out of the character, and breathing—*life*—is what the theatre is all about.

Of course, a sensitive designer can guide the actors toward that very discovery of a character's inner nature, provided the director and the designer have between them a true, if sometimes unspoken, bond of understanding. I can't always speak to a designer in specific visual terms, although I have learned with the years a much larger visual vocabulary than I had when I started. Nevertheless, I have found that visual specifics are not necessarily the material of my most productive design dialogues. I must work with designers who have a genuine concern for text and for meaning, and who can express themselves in those terms. They must delight in the discoveries of rehearsal and be as flexible in their ideas as I try to be in mine. An admirable design is meaningless if the actor cannot wear it with conviction and if the director cannot help the actor find some grains of the character's identity in the clothes.

Relaxation is, for me, the key to all good work in the theatre, and I hope for the same ease in the costume shop or the fitting room that I attempt to preserve in the rehearsal hall. No one has to deal more with actor tension than the costume designer, and his or her ego must be securely in place in order not to exacerbate a moment of fury or despair. I like designers who are strong and confident enough to hang onto one of their most precious tools, a sense of humor, when someone may be trying to grab it out of their hands.

So the designers who function best with me are those with a sense of the whole, a sense of humor, and a sense of self. Of course, taste and visual genius don't hurt a bit. That's a lot to find in one person, but it's just such a confluence of remarkable individuals who can exult in sharing that provides me with the true excitement of collaboration in the theatre.

ARVIN BROWN
Artistic Director
Long Wharf Theatre

Acknowledgements

Frances Aronson
Mark Avery
Whitney Blausen
Veronica Ann Brady
Richard Bryant
Mary Aiello Bruce
Richard Casler
Bob Chambers
Martha Christian
Rosalind Heinz
Richard Ingham
Robert E. Ingham
Susan Medak
John Stefano
David Weiss
Arena Stage
The Costume Collection
Long Wharf Theatre
Milwaukee Repertory Theater
McCarter Theatre
Theatre Division, Southern Methodist University

And a special thanks to the designers who allowed us access to their portfolios and to their professional lives:

Michael J. Cesario
Susan B. Cox
Lowell Detweiler
Arnold S. Levine
Andrew B. Marlay
David Murin
Colleen Muscha
Carol Oditz
Susan Rheaume
Susan Tsu
Jennifer Von Mayrhauser
Ann Wallace

The Costume Designer's Handbook

DESIGNING

1
The Playscript

Each element has its own particular relation to the drama and plays its own part in the drama. And each element—the word, the actor, the costume—has the exact significance of a note in a symphony. Each separate costume we create for a play must be exactly suited both to the character it helps to express and to the occasion it graces.

ROBERT EDMOND JONES
The Dramatic Imagination

Plays are crafted. A playscript is an artificial construct, not a slice of life. It is structured experience, not random experience. However artless it may appear to be, a play is wholly artful. It is created, contrived, crafted, and shaped by its writer.

Plays are both more than life and less than life. Dramatic actions are packed with more meaning and more significance than most random life events. Plots organize dramatic actions into complete structures with beginnings, middles, and ends. Every dramatic event, no matter how small, influences and shapes play structure; in contrast, routine real-life occurrences seem to have little effect on the sprawling human story. On the other hand, dramatic characters are far less complex than living people, and dramatic

dialogue is a contrived arrangement of words, usually composed to sound like human speech but selected only to articulate the play.

Even when a play seems most realistic, when its characters appear to speak real conversation, sit on real sofas in real rooms and drink real coffee, it is not like life, only life-*like*. A play has far more in common with a painting, a sonnet, or a sonata than it does with life.

When you compare a play to a piece of music you can speak of its notes, its themes, its harmonies. When you say it's like a painting you can point to the elements of design within it—line, shape, color, texture, pattern—and the principles of composition with which these elements are combined—unity, variety, balance, emphasis, rhythm, proportion. Like sonnets, plays are shaped both by external and internal forms. They are closed systems, formal and interdependent, and they rely upon surprising combinations of familiar elements for their interest and power.

A playwright is a craftsperson, and a play may be said to be designed and built, unit by unit, action by action, word by word. Each play has a finite number of units, even when the multiplicity and complexity of the units seem to be infinite and to defy analysis.

FIGURE 1-1. A play has far more in common with a painting, a sonnet, or a sonata than it does with life. *The Ascent of Mount Fuji* by Chingiz Aitmatov and Kaltai Mukhamedzhanov at Arena Stage. *Set design by Ming Cho Lee. Photo by George de Vincent.*

Because plays are constructed from units you can examine, they are open to analysis. You may search for the nature and structure of a play by correctly identifying its parts and by perceiving the patterns in which the playwright has arranged the parts. But, because plays are creations of the human imagination, which is capable of combining dramatic events in an infinite number of patterns, each playscript analysis will require a different process and each play will contain a unique collection of facts and will have a unique structure.

How to Read and See Plays

Good theatre designers must be good play readers. This is not a skill that comes naturally to everyone. Children seldom encounter plays in their early reading experience. By the time a play does appear in a sixth- or seventh-grade literature anthology, the habits acquired from reading continuous prose narrative are well ingrained. Some of these habits may inhibit good play reading.

Plays make different demands on their readers than stories or essays do. Because you are given less information, every piece of which is vital to the structure, you must pay close attention to every word. You may not skim through passages that seem to stray from the theme or plot because plays do not allow for digression. You must not expect plays to describe or elaborate or reflect because plays are nothing but action. Plays exist in the present tense; therefore, the reader must learn to perceive the actions *as happening* rather than *as happened*.

Exercise Your Imagination

It's difficult to learn to read plays well if you have not seen many plays performed on stage. When you are reading a play well, you are seeing it in your mind's eye. There is an environment, there are characters, and there is movement. Only in live performance can you discover the means by which dramatic events in the playscript are brought to life by actors and by design elements. As you watch, you build up a store of staging and setting possibilities with which to fuel and excite your own imagination. You can practice applying these possibilities as you read plays.

Especially valuable experience can be gained when you see the same play in different productions with different sets and different actors. Even when the playscript is not altered at all, you will see how different choices in emphasis, color, rhythm, etc., make each production unique. You will realize that the goal of production is not doing the play *right* but making it *coherent*. You will begin to understand how to read the playscript as the blueprint rather than the description of a production.

Films and Television

Watching a filmed or televised play is not the same experience as seeing a play on stage. Film and television scripts are different from playscripts in two very important ways:

1. The most important structural element in the filmscript is the camera; and
2. A film or television script is intended to become a record of what has happened, not of what is happening (except in the almost extinct "live" television dramas).

In all filmed and televised play productions, the camera shapes the experience for the audience by selecting what is seen in contrast with what is heard. The audience has no choice; the selection is absolute. The larger scene, the other characters, the broader action, are simply eliminated from the picture and the viewers are carried through the story seeing precisely what the writer and the director want them to see.

Focusing Attention
Without the Camera

When dramatic events occur on stage, there is no way to make the rest of the setting, or other characters in the scene, disappear. There is no mechanism for zooming the audience's attention in on significant glances or gestures. Focus, which in film or television is imposed by the camera, must, in the theatre, be created and maintained by the combined efforts of playwright, director, actors, and designers. It is their task to make sure the audience is attracted to the right place at the right time in order to experience the significant event.

Playwrights manipulate focus through their choice of words and events and by the way in which they arrange them. A gifted playwright can capture the audience's attention by contrasting sounds or dialogue rhythms, by an entrance, by ringing the telephone, or by introducing an unexpected piece of information at just the right moment. Directors support and clarify the playwright's choices by staging and orchestrating the events in ways that make it difficult for an audience to miss their significance. Actors find physical and emotional ways to command focus at the correct times. Designers contribute to focus through their selections of set and costume elements, through area illumination and the use of evocative color. Creating consistent stage focus for the audience is the greatest challenge faced by those who work in live theatre.

Young theatrical designers whose main experience with drama has been through the media of film and television often have difficulty manipulating focus in their designs. They are used to seeing everything in detail, up close and selected for them. Their sets and costumes may, therefore, have too many areas of interest to allow for any focusing of attention or they may be uniformly bland. Such designs seem to be waiting for an outside eye, a camera, to select from them. The best way to solve this design problem is to see live

FIGURE 1-2. Designers contribute to focus through their selections of set and costume elements, area illumination, and evocative color. The Follet family in *All the Way Home* at the McCarter Theatre. *Costume design by Jennifer von Mayrhauser. Photograph by Cliff Moore.*

performances and notice all the ways by which your attention is directed. You will be surprised how often design elements figure directly in both successful and unsuccessful focusing of stage action.

Plays Happen Now

Stage focus is affected by the fact that plays happen in present time. Even though the production has been designed, built, rehearsed and "set" prior to its opening to the public, each performance is *now* and subject to change. Designs and performances must, therefore, be flexible enough to allow for a certain amount of variation from performance to performance. While a film director may do fifty "takes" of a scene until the needs of his or her visual structure are fulfilled, a stage director must seek ways of doing each scene that will be effective despite the changes in audience, atmosphere, temperature, and in the delicate emotional balance between characters that will inevitably vary from night to night. Designs must be, as Robert Edmond Jones called them, environments in which the play may live rather than decorative backgrounds that illustrate one static view of the play. A film is the same every time you see it, selected, spliced, and sealed in a can. No two performances of a play are ever identical.

If you have seen many more films than plays, you will probably visualize any playscript you are reading as if it were a filmscript. As you read, notice that you are perceiving most action in medium and close shots. If this is your way of visualizing, try to change it by taking a few moments at the beginning of the play to set the whole stage in your mind's eye. Furnish it, plant trees, erect walls. Place the characters firmly in the set, and every time you are inclined to zoom in on one or two faces for an intimate bit of dialogue, recall the set you have imagined and listen to the dialogue from the middle of the house with the whole stage visible. Learn to read playscripts as plays and not as movies.

The First Reading

Even though you're reading a play because you've been asked to design it, read it the first time for pleasure only. Try not to take note of what the play will eventually demand of you. Be the audience. Read to find out who falls in love with whom, which character murdered the king, and whether or not the young couple ends up happily ever after. Try not to make notes and, if possible, read the whole play at a single sitting.

When you have finished the first reading, stay put for a moment and experience your response completely. One of the basic tenets of good playscript analysis is the ability to suspend judgment and examine the text in objective terms, not through a haze of likes and dislikes. But, since all play readers, including designers, respond personally to the plays they read, make sure you have an opportunity to register your feelings about the play immediately after your initial encounter with it. Designers can do good work whether they like the play they're working on or not. Quality design does not depend on personal taste and feelings. But, if you allow your feelings free rein for a few moments in the beginning of the process, it will be easier for you to put them aside later on in order to proceed with the objective part of the work.

These are the goals of the first reading: discover what the play's about and what happens, meet the characters, and respond to the play as personally as possible. Having done so, accept the play on its own terms, without prejudice (prejudging), and prepare to find out what it's made of and how it works.

Additional Readings

Most designers will read a play straight through at least once or twice more in order to become thoroughly familiar with everything that happens. These readings are important steps in the process of establishing the play as a construct, an ordered system of parts. They often excite the first visual images that suggest the play's environment.

Choose a pleasant surrounding in which to read. Some people like music in the background while others prefer silence. Some read late at night and others early in the morning. The important thing about a surrounding is that it allow the reader to achieve a state of maximum concentration with minimum interference.

During the last of these general readings it is helpful to be armed with a transparent yellow marker, or "highlighter," with which to mark costume and character references in the script as well as entrances and exits if the play has a complicated movement pattern. These highlighted areas can be spotted quickly when you settle down to make charts and lists.

A Designer's Analysis

As soon as you feel satisfied that you understand what appears to be going on in the play, it's time to turn your attention to the process of *analysis*. In this process, you must examine the play in order to distinguish its component parts, separately and in their relation to the whole. Everything that is said in the play, everything that happens in the play, and everything that is described by the playwright must be scrutinized. The first part of the process is to correctly identify these script facts, and the second part is to discover how each fact functions within the whole play.

For many theatre designers, analyzing a text is a frustrating task, a necessary evil to be gotten through as quickly as possible. Their approach generally consists of gathering a few obvious facts about time, place, and number of characters, possibly drawing a rough chart to follow the characters through the action, and maybe making a few vague notes about atmosphere and feeling. Thus armed, these designers put away their scripts, attend production meetings, listen to and talk with the director, and, without consulting the script again, begin to draw and build.

Designers who work this way misunderstand the unique nature of plays and divorce themselves early from their most reliable and evocative source of information *and* inspiration, the script.

On the other hand, a designer who recognizes that the text should be central to the design process develops methods of using the playwright's words to discover how the play works and what its environment looks like.

Playscript analysis would be easy if each play were a simple construct with a single interpretation and only a few parts, clearly discerned. Such a play would make easy visual demands and require only one production to illuminate the script completely. But, if this were true, if plays were so simple and transparent, the theatre would have lost its vitality centuries ago. The fact is that even the smallest and most straightforward play is a construct of many meanings and, depending upon the angle from which it is viewed, many faces. It can be acted, directed, and designed in many ways and from many angles without departing from the text. One of the endless fascinations of a great and complex play, such as *Hamlet,* is the sheer density of its structural elements and layers. One of the greatest problems in producing *Hamlet* is choosing which face, or faces, of the play to show on the stage at any given time.

You must remember, however, that even in *Hamlet* the number of possibilities for production is not infinite. *Every play,* whether it is relatively simple or highly complex, *does have an inherent structure.* The playwright built the structure, for better or for worse, and it is as basic to the play as your genetic structure is to you. The structure is the play's potential; it tells you what it is capable of being and what it cannot be.

Limitations and Possibilities

Playscript analysis for designers functions in two ways which sometimes appear to be contradictory but are, in fact, complementary: 1. You discover many design possibilities within the script; and 2. You discover the limitations the script imposes on design choice. On the one hand you find information that allows you to see a character in many different guises, inhabiting several sorts of landscapes, all of which are allowed or indicated by the words of the text. On the other hand you find a structure in the play that imposes a set of guidelines you may use for choosing suits, hats, and architectural detail. In the process, you learn that many things will work for this play but not everything.

None of this discussion is meant to suggest that designers should limit their participation in the collaborative process or ignore the ideas of directors. This analysis is part of the designer's pre-conference preparation, and the primary aim of the analysis is to help designers be more active collaborators. Designers, more than any other members of the production team, need to discover the largest number of possibilities in every script and find many visual statements that are true to the play so they can absorb and assimilate all the ideas the director, actors, and other designers have about the play. The more complete a designer's analysis of the script is before the collaborative process begins, the more flexible that designer can be in the process of creating the physical production.

Fact Finding

The first step in playscript analysis is to move from an understanding of the play in terms of what appeared to be happening in the early readings to a rigorous examination of the facts that are contained in the play, facts that are there to tell you precisely what is happening. In your search for script facts, collect only what is there. Don't make assumptions. That is to say, don't add to the given or expand upon it. This is particularly important when you are dealing with plays set in well-known historical periods. A designer may know more about the period than the playwright does. It is usually counter-productive to add facts to a play when the playwright, either out of ignorance or because he or she was consciously limiting the scope of the play's world, didn't include them. It is not, for example, at all helpful to add what is now known about the good aspects of King Richard III of England's character to a production of Shakespeare's

Richard III. Such facts may be true but they are not true of Shakespeare's play.

Remember that a play is the sum of all its facts and no fact is, ultimately, more important than another. One may take up more stage time, another may be more interesting to discuss, and yet another may be more accessible to you, but the success of the play in production depends upon the balance created between all the parts within the whole.

FIGURE 1-3. Shakespeare's *Richard III* at the Long Wharf Theatre with Carolyn Coates and Richard Venture. *Costume design by John Conklin. Photograph by William Smith.*

Analysis for the
Imagination and Intellect

*The creative act is not merely a mechanical manip-
ulation of matter into form.*

BERNARD BECKERMAN

Design in the theatre is intellectual and imaginative, practical and poetic, mechanical and
magical. For playscript analysis to have broad
application to theatre design it must feed both
the imagination and the intellect. It is not enough
to use analytical tools to discover only what
physical things the play requires: How many
doors must the set have? Will the windows be
practical? What historical period should the
swords and shields convey? Which characters in
the ball scene wear masks? You must, of course,
know these things; and yet it is of equal importance to discover visually informing bits and
pieces within the script which translate from the
verbal to the visual in ways that always seem
mysterious even to those who repeatedly engage
in such translating.

No one can describe the process of creating
images or perceptions or explain why each one is
unique to the imagination that creates it. (And,
of course, no one has the vaguest notion why
some imaginations contribute to works of genius
while others foster works of smaller scope.) Yet,
unpredictable as it is, you must as theatre designers possess a responsive and well-exercised imagination. It is as vital to your work as your ability
to read and think logically.

Imagination seldom approaches problems
in a sequential manner. Instead it produces images, perceptions, and emotional responses
which may, on the one hand, present themselves
as fragments which seem to have little connection
with one another or, on the other hand, spring
forth whole and intact like Venus in the myth.
These imaginative products don't seem bound to
ordinary reality, and yet they may illuminate a

given design choice more brilliantly than "real"
facts, shedding entirely new light on all that you
have previously known.

Both the intellect and the imagination are
stimulated by facts discovered in the script. The
intellect uses these facts to define and solve
practical problems related to place, use, and
historical accuracy. Imagination uses the same
facts to reflect and evoke sensoral response and to
support psychological and emotional forces. The
intellect and the imagination work interdepen-
dently to create the play's visual environment.
The two processes illuminate and check up on
each other. A design that is all intellect may only
serve the play in mechanical ways while one that
is all image may be perfect for one moment in the
first act but wrong for all the rest.

Combining Intellect and Imagination

Fully realizing that examples are always
simplistic, here are three isolated facts from three
well-known plays and a brief consideration of the
intellectual and imaginative responses they might
evoke:

1. Big Daddy is dying of cancer.
2. James Tyrone is a stingy man in the eyes of
   his family.
3. Horatio describes the beard of Hamlet's
   Ghost "as I have seen it in his life, /A sable
   silvered."

Your intellect will make note of these facts, place
them in groups with related and substantiating
facts, and assign them to help solve the following
problems:

1. What does Big Daddy look like?
2. What does James Tyrone's house look like?
3. How "ghostly" is Old Hamlet's Ghost?

You will be led to ask additional questions, some of which can't be answered in the script—What does a man dying of cancer really look like? What color is sable?—and some which the script can answer—Which characters accuse James Tyrone of stinginess and under what circumstances? Does anyone who encounters Hamlet's Ghost have difficulty recognizing him? Consider all the questions raised by facts you discover but make it a rule of thumb to concentrate especially on the ones that can be answered in the text.

Your imagination, stimulated by the facts of Big Daddy's cancer, James Tyrone's meanness, and the sable silvered beard, is unconcerned with practicality and order; it responds at random with visual fragments, spacial constructs, sensory ideas, or with pure feeling. Because each imaginative reaction is unique and personal, it is difficult to find examples that don't seem contrived. But suppose, for the sake of this example, that the following visual images are produced by the facts discovered above:

1. Big Daddy's cancer appears to you as a body shape, drawn and lumpy with a tension in it that suggests a big man's body being drained from within.

2. You respond to James Tyrone's tight-fistedness by visualizing a bare room with only a clutch of skeletal furniture shapes crouched in the gloomy pool of light cast by a single burning light bulb.

3. Horatio's specific observation of the exact color combination in Old Hamlet's beard invokes a ghost that is vibrant, super-real, more minutely detailed and more accurate than life.

How can you integrate your intellectual and imaginative responses to the text and apply them to the choice of suits, hats, beards, ground plans, and furniture?

BIG DADDY'S CANCER

If you allow your intellectual response to Big Daddy's cancer to dominate, there is the chance that what you discover about the physically debilitating effects of the disease will inspire you to over-indicate these effects with detailed make-up and ill-fitting clothes due to weight loss. Before making that decision, consider the image your imagination produced; it was not specific but suggestive. Allow these responses to inform each other and perhaps you will come to "see" Big Daddy as a man who is dying, in fact, but whose disease must be perceived gradually by the audience and by the other characters in the play. His costume and make-up may help suggest that he is being ravaged from within; they must not illustrate it.

JAMES TYRONE'S STINGINESS

The room image created by the fact of James Tyrone's stinginess might well, if not tempered by rational questions, lead you to create a set that is far too shabby to be the summer home of a celebrated, well-to-do actor. In this case you must reassess your image in intellectual terms. James Tyrone is an ambiguous figure. Can you afford to emphasize one side over the others? To whom does he appear stingy and what exactly is the nature of that stinginess? Don't abandon the image, however, because it remains an important reaction. You may want to use it to inform the environment for the final act when father and sons are, in fact, caught in the bleak illumination of the single bulb James Tyrone will permit.

OLD HAMLET'S GHOST

Using your image of a "real looking" ghost that was stimulated by Horatio's detailed description of his beard, you can return to the script to check out the logic of such a choice. You discover that no one who encounters the Ghost has any difficulty recognizing him. No one describes him in other than human-appearing terms. You might also ask if young Hamlet is not apt to be more emotionally affected by a ghost that actually looks like his father did than by one costumed in a fearful ghostly suit? In this instance, image and intellect may illuminate and substantiate each other.

These are examples of how designers interrelate what has recently come to be called *left brain thinking* (intellectual and rational) and *right brain thinking* (spatial, intuitional, and image-producing). Both are essential. Both must be given equal weight. Both require facts to stimulate them into action.

An Outline for Playscript Analysis

The following outline will help you discover the important script facts in a relatively orderly fashion and suggest a way to examine the facts that will reveal something about the play's shape and structure. The wording of the outline and the order in which its parts appear are of little importance. Not all the questions or statements in the outline will apply to every play. When you encounter one that doesn't fit the situation, skip over it and move on. Playwrights don't write plays in order to have them fit into anybody's outline. Yet any outline for playscript analysis that is worth considering should be malleable enough to work for any play. Playscript analysis is only viable for designers if it helps them make discoveries about the play that have visual as well as verbal components. Results are far more important than slavish adherence to method.

I. Where are they?
1. Exact geographical location.
2. Note textural references and descriptions

II. When are they?
1. Day, month, year.
2. Note special significance of date or season.

III. Who are they?
1. Relationships and socio-economics.
2. Under what government?
3. In what religious environment?
4. Believing what about ethical conduct, sex, marriage, family?

IV. What happened before the play begins?

V. What do the major characters think about their world?

VI. What is the function of each character?
1. Who is the protagonist?
2. Who is the antagonist?
3. Which characters lead and which support?
4. Identify and describe stereotypical characters.
5. Identify and describe crowds.

VII. What is the Dialogue Mode?
1. Naturalistic dialogue.
2. Literary dialogue.
3. Poetic dialogue.
4. Sound and grammar.
5. Ambiguity.

VIII. What is the play's action?
1. Create an action chart.

IX. What is the play's theme?

I. Where are they?

1. Exact Geographical Location
2. Note Textural References and Descriptions

Most playwrights make a statement of place at the beginning of their scripts. These may range from a terse, "A country road. A tree." in Samuel Beckett's *Waiting For Godot* to George Bernard Shaw's detailed three-page description of St. Dominic's Parsonage in *Candida*—he identifies certain books on the shelves and tells us there is "a black japanned flower-painted coal scuttle" on the hearth. Jot down such facts (within reason!) but keep your eyes open for textual substantiation because it is usually what characters say about their surroundings that proves most evocative for designers.

At the opening of Shelagh Delaney's *A Taste of Honey,* you will read: "the stage represents a comfortless flat in Manchester and the street outside." A half-dozen lines into the first scene, Helen describes this flat:

Anyway, what's wrong with this place? Everything in it's falling apart, it's true, and we've no heating— but there's a lovely view of the gasworks, we share a bathroom with the community and this wallpaper's contemporary. What more do you want?

A few pages further on, Peter, Helen's boyfriend, sums up the neighborhood in three words: "Tenements, cemetery, slaughterhouse." These are the kinds of textural facts that excite the designer's imagination. "Comfortless flat" is too general. The more specific the fact is, the more resonant it will be.

II. When Are They?

1. Day, Month, Year
2. Special Significance of Date or Season

Note the day, month, and year if they are given. Note the time of day and the season. Make an additional note if the date has special significance. *Ah, Wilderness!* takes place on July 4, and you may be sure the playwright had reasons for making this choice.

You won't be able to discover a precise "when" for all plays. Some suggest timelessness, some project into an unspecified future, and some can be played in a variety of periods. Many of Shakespeare's plays fall into this last category, particularly the comedies.

The director usually chooses the period in which the play will be set but occasionally the costume designer will be involved in the production early enough to affect that choice. When you're reading a play that does not have a specified time, be aware of general time impressions you receive from the dialogue, small facts or an overall tone that might help locate the play in a particularly suitable period. If you are asked to design a play in a period that seems inappropriate to you, go back to your script and see if you can discover specific events or words in the text that seem to justify your response. Share these with the director. They may be things he or she has not yet discovered.

FIGURE 1-4 (above). Family dinner on the fourth of July in Eugene O'Neill's *Ah, Wilderness!* at the Long Wharf Theatre. *Costume Design by Bill Walker. Photograph courtesy of Long Wharf Theatre.*

FIGURES 1-5 & 1-6. Sir Andrew Aguecheek from *Twelfth Night* in two different centuries. Figure 1-5 (below left), designed for the Great Lakes Shakespeare Festival and Figure 1-6 (below right), for the Indiana Repertory Theatre, both by Liz Covey. Both sketches executed with technical pen and ink on heavy tracing paper. *Photograph by Frances Aronson.*

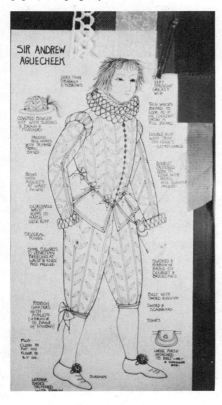

III. Who Are They?

1. **Relationships and Socio-economics**

2. **Under What Government?**

3. **In What Religious Environment?**

4. **Believing What about Ethical Conduct, Sex, Marriage, Family?**

Be certain you know who is married to whom and who their children are. Note all family relationships, however vague. Ask what economic relationships exist between the characters. Who is rich and who is poor? Are the characters coming up in the world or going down? Who has the money power? Who does not? Who is the employer and who is the employee? Who leads by birth and who leads in spite of it?

Always be aware of subtleties in social and economic relationships and remember that the playwright may be writing from a point of view and from life experiences quite different from your own. Learn to pick up clues to socio-economic identity. A female character who remarks that she attended Radcliffe is slipping you a fact about who she is. A character who says his father was "on the dole" gives another. Sometimes a speech mannerism will indicate a lower class background when everything else about the character obscures it.

Many Americans have little or no understanding of social class in the English and European sense and therefore cannot always see the difference between economic status and social class. Remember, although the level of economic affluence may relate to social class, it doesn't always. A character is not lower class simply because he or she is low on cash. This is particularly true in countries, and in areas of this country, where class status is more closely associated with family background than with money.

It is usually important to know what form of government is in power in the play's world. Is it a monarchy, an oligarchy, or a dictatorship? Who is the leader? Is there political stability or

FIGURE 1-7. Be certain you know who is married to whom. Family and guests in Noel Coward's *Hay Fever* at the McCarter Theatre. *Costume design by Robert Morgan. Photograph by Cliff Moore.*

political turmoil? Are the characters in the play directly related to the political structure? If so, how?

The relationship between characters and government may be implied rather than stated. Absence of specific dialogue about government or politics is, in itself, not enough reason to rule out the presence of a political climate. Playwrights often assume—particularly when they are writing plays contemporary with their own lifetimes—that the current political structure is an understood part of the play's structure.

Chekhov's plays cannot be called political plays; the government is seldom mentioned. Yet, when Vershinin rhapsodizes about the future in Act III of *Three Sisters*, he is speaking in a political as well as in a philosophical and sentimental framework. The more you know about that framework, the more you know about Vershinin.

And yet, in reality, what a difference there is between what is now and has been in the past! And when a little more time has passed—another two or three hundred years—people will look at our present manner of life with horror and derision, and everything of today will seem awkward and heavy, and very strange and uncomfortable. Oh what a wonderful life that will be—what a wonderful life!

Ask also if the play takes place in the context of particular religious perspective. Is there a national religion? Do the major characters belong to a distinct religious group? Is organized religion an important social institution in the play?

A religious component, like politics and government, may be present in a play's background even though little or no specific reference is made to it. In Frank Cucci's *High Time,* a play about a 40-year-old Italian/American widow adjusting to life without a husband, the Roman Catholic church plays a major role in the woman's world even though the play has no religious theme as such. It is a fact that demands some support, however subtle, within the design scheme.

There are, of course, some plays which have nothing whatsoever to do with religion, government, or politics. Accept the absence and do not try to impose any of them on a production when they are absent in the text.

The moral stance in a play is particularly important to designers. Study the script to discover the prevailing attitudes about ethical conduct, sex, marriage, and family. How are women viewed? Is ethical conduct valued? What social institutions exist to uphold community morals?

FIGURE 1-8. Formal attire designed for the McCarter Theatre's production of *Heartbreak House* by Andrew B. Marlay. The sketch is done in pencil, watercolor, and colored pencil on watercolor paper. *Photograph by Frances Aronson.*

Social institutions are the moral guardians of any age and they set and enforce behavior. They put pressure on people to dress themselves appropriately and to furnish their homes correctly. Adhering to correct modes of dress and submitting to accepted lifestyles have been moral yardsticks since the dawn of civilization. In some periods restrictions are many, in some they are few. They are seldom absent altogether. Costume designers in particular must understand the role of social institutions in regulating fashion, and they must be able to relate contemporary mores as they are expressed in clothing to the particular play being designed.

Many playwrights write about the struggle between free spirited characters and the prevailing moral stance of their day. Costume can add important visual support to such conflicts. A character who lives comfortably within the mores of his or her time projects a very different image from one who looks on contemporary mores as constraints and struggles against the institutions that try to enforce them.

The answers to these first three questions—where, when, and who—will provide you with a bulging and unwieldy bag of facts about the play, its world, and its characters. Some of them may be contradictory, others are sure to be confusing. Try not to jump to conclusions about anything until all the facts are in and have begun to take on a shape. For the present, simply collect.

IV. What Happened Before the Play Begins?

As soon as you are familiar with the play's present, begin to discover its past. Be sure you stick to the text, however, and consider only what is revealed there. Many designers fall into the habit of making up background facts that seem reasonable but which, if incorporated into the design, may give false signals and confuse the present action. For instance, it might seem quite plausible to assume that Stanley Kowalski played football in high school. But if the costume designer gives him a school jacket to wear with an athletic letter on it, the audience may expect him to be a former high school hero who is having difficulty adjusting to adult life. Such expectations, completely unsupported by the text, can obscure what Stanley is and does in the present. It is always a temptation to "fill in" what the playwright has chosen not to present. Be wary of such impulses.

V. What Do the Major Characters Think About Their World?

Ask if the play's major characters are representative of their world or in revolt against it. Are they insiders, part of the establishment, or outsiders. If they are outsiders, do they wish they were inside or are they outside by choice?

Contrast character attitudes at the beginning of the play with attitudes at its end. Most major characters move from some form of ignorance to some form of knowledge in the course of the play. Sometimes this knowledge is acquired by the progression of present dramatic events and sometimes by the revelation of a past event which then affects the character's attitude toward the present.

Perceiving changes in attitude can be especially helpful to a costume designer. Natasha, in Chekhov's *Three Sisters,* is in awe of Andre's house and of his sisters when she makes her appearance in Act I. By the second act she is Andre's wife and familiarity has replaced awe. In Act IV she has become the undisputed mistress of her environment, plans major changes in the landscaping of the estate, and criticizes the sisters' appearances as they once criticized hers. Such clear-cut attitudinal changes in a character undoubtedly demand visual support in her choice of clothing.

VI. What Is the Function of Each Character?

Francis Hodge, in *Play Directing, Analysis, Communication and Style,* defines character as what the playwright makes and characterization as what the actor makes. This is a useful way to separate script fact from rehearsal and production fact. In the following pages, all references to character will refer to what can be found in the play's text. Characterization will mean character *plus* actor, director, and physical production.

Much of a costume designer's work involves supporting a successful union between character and characterization. It is easier for the designer to affect this union when he or she has had enough time to get acquainted with the character before actors, director, and production realities appear on the scene. (This is *not* to suggest that costumes ought to be designed before a play is cast which is risky business, not unlike designing a set without knowing anything about the stage or the theatre that will house it.)

Dramatic characters are the moving parts of the play structure, the speakers and the doers. Their words and actions are confined by the play and they have no other life than the one given them by the playwright.

You have already collected many facts about the characters in the play. You know where, when, and who they are. You know something about their backgrounds and their attitudes. Now it's time to consider characters as units of dramatic structure. Ask what each character contributes to the play and how his or her function might be visually supported. It's obvious that an on-duty policeman in a play has to wear a uniform in order to perform his function on stage. The leading man, the villain, the innocent victim, and the crowd extra also have specific tasks to perform and must be dressed in ways that will help the audience see them do what they were created to do. This is an important part of creating stage focus.

The following functional labels often overlap. Use them to examine the ways in which characters perform rather than as character definitions.

FIGURES 1-9 & 1-10. Two Kates strike characteristic poses in two unusual costumes for productions of Shakespeare's *Taming of the Shrew*. Figure 1-9 (left) is Rose Pickering in the Milwaukee Repertory Theater's version. *Costume design by Susan Tsu. Photograph by Mark Avery.*
Figure 1-10 (right) is Leslie Gerasi at the McCarter Theatre. *Costume design by Liz Covey. Photograph by Cliff Moore.*

1. Who Is the Protagonist?

The protagonist is the leading character, the mover, the one who wants, the one who incites action. Lear is the protagonist of *King Lear*, Jimmy Porter of *Look Back in Anger*, Dolly Levi of *The Matchmaker*, and Vanya of *Uncle Vanya*. Protagonists are always wanting things, telling others what to do, hatching plots and shooting at people who displease them. Some plays may have more than one protagonist although it's unusual to have two of equal weight. The protagonist is

an important focal point for the audience who must see everything that character does.

2. Who Is the Antagonist?

This character stands in the way of what the protagonist wants. This is the adversary, the complication. In melodrama the antagonist is the villain, and in farce it may be the stupid servant who delivers the note to the wrong lady. Iago *(Othello)* is an antagonist and so is Banquo *(Macbeth)*. Traditionally, antagonists take focus periodically but must be able to slip into the background at other times.

3. Which Characters Lead and Which Support?

The terms "lead" and "support" in this context do not refer to Actor's Equity Association rules which govern pay scales for actors playing lead and support roles. A lead character in playscript analysis is differentiated from a support character, not by number of lines spoken or time spent on the stage, but by the function each performs in the play.

Lead characters advance from ignorance to knowledge, they go somewhere, they learn, they come to understand, they rise and fall, and, by doing what they do, they move the dramatic action forward.

Support characters do one thing, exert one force, or express one unchanging point of view. Their stance quite literally supports the actions of the leading characters, although that support often takes the form of resistance against what the leading characters want.

In Kaufman and Hart's *The Man Who Came to Dinner*, two support characters are Mr. and Mrs. Ernest W. Stanley, the couple in whose house the play takes place. These characters, whose attitudes never change, exert a constant—and very funny—resistance to virtually everything the leading characters want.

FIGURE 1-11. Halo Wines and Mark Hammer as Miss Preen and Sheridan Whiteside in *The Man Who Came to Dinner*, produced by Arena Stage. *Costume design by Marjorie Slaman. Photograph by George de Vincent.*

Miss Preen, in the same play, performs a lead function even though her role is a small one. Her character alters considerably as a result of her constant exposure to Sheridan Whiteside's insults. Her comic progression from ignorance to knowledge drives her to turn on Whiteside, to abandon her assignment, and to resign from the nursing profession.

It is far more useful for a costume designer to consider characters in terms of their functions than it is to think of them as big and little parts. Support characters often demand costumes that are single bold strokes, specific, to the point, and absolutely correct. Even if the character is only on stage for a moment to perform a single action, the physical appearance must support that action clearly and without ambiguity.

Lead characters are complex and multidimensional. They have many levels of personality and are capable of expressing different points of view. Even in such a relatively uncomplicated lead character as Miss Preen, there is room for some complexity. Her function is to change, and the potential for this will be part of the way she looks.

As you examine characters and their functions, make a list of the leads and one of the supports. Identify the protagonist and the antagonist. By each lead character note what change in attitudes (or actions, or whatever) occurs in the course of the play, and by each support character describe what task that character performs.

4. Identify and Describe Stereotypical Characters

Stereotype is not a derogatory word. A stereotypical character is not a character the playwright has neglected to develop completely. Playwrights depend on stereotypes and bring them on when they need to show the audience an immediately identifiable character type, using as few words of dialogue as possible. The audience recognizes them chiefly by dress and behavior: the Irish cop, the talkative New York City cab driver, the gum-chewing secretary, the salesman, and several varieties of private detective. Wordy introductions are not necessary. It is the first impression that makes the statement.

Sometimes the stereotypical character will remain just what the initial appearance showed him or her to be. At other times the stereotype will broaden into a more complex character, perhaps quite different from the stereotypical expectation.

Many costume designers, in an effort not to be thought dull and unimaginative, avoid choosing the obvious outfit for a stereotypical character: a slinky taffeta dress for the prostitute, a polyester leisure suit for the automobile salesman. They search for something more subtle, something different. Before you shun the obvious in these situations, consider the playwright's intent. If the structure of the scene depends on that character being instantly recognized by the audience, anything the costume does to delay that recognition will interrupt the flow of dramatic events. In these instances it is always best to support the character with clothes that speak louder, and more pointedly, than words.

5. Identify and Describe Crowds

The secret to costuming crowds is to perceive them as members of one functional group. A crowd is usually "the peasants," "the other inmates," "the mob." Imagine them as a single force and, without resorting to inappropriate uniformity, never permit crowd members so much individualization that their group identity will be lost.

VIII. What Is the Dialogue Mode?

Playscripts are virtually all direct discourse, which we call dialogue. Dialogue, spoken by characters, tells you everything that happens in the play and everything the playwright wants you to know about what happens. Because of the tasks it must perform, dramatic dialogue is carefully structured and therefore totally unlike most human conversation. It cannot ramble from subject to subject as most people do when they talk to someone else. Dialogue is the most artful building material in the dramatic construct and the play's most important structural element.

The first reading of a play will tell you what the dialogue says; you also learn what happens from moment to moment. An analysis of the dialogue introduces you to *how* the play says what it says.

There are three important modes of dialogue. Each one affects the way in which the audience perceives the play. In some plays dialogue is structured to imitate ordinary human speech as accurately as possible. In other plays it is much more artificial and only seems to sound like talking. Some plays are written in a dialogue mode which, when compared to ordinary conversation, is frankly fake. The choice of a dialogue mode is up to the playwright but it is strongly influenced by the historical period in which the play was written, the type of play it is, and its subject matter or theme.

1. Naturalistic Dialogue

In Paddy Chayefski's *Marty,* the dialogue closely imitates ordinary conversation. The words the characters speak seem to be exactly what you would expect to hear in reality. The mother says: "My son, Frank, he was married when he was nineteen years old. Watsa matter with you?"

Such dialogue is characterized by very careful selection of specific details, rhythms, pronunciations, particular grammatical structures. The visual worlds for plays such as *Marty,* often called naturalistic plays, are also careful selections of specifics, artfully combined to evoke a sense of reality.

2. Literary Dialogue

Literary dialogue never reads like ordinary conversation but, when it is spoken by actors, it becomes their mode of speech, fully accepted by the audience as such. George Bernard Shaw wrote masterful literary dialogue. The following example is from *Candida:*

MARCHBANKS
Misery! I am the happiest of men. I desire nothing now but her happiness. Oh, Morell, let us both give her up. Why should she have to choose between a wretched little nervous disease like me, and a pig-headed person like you? Let us go on a pilgrimage, you to the east and I to the west, in search of a worthy lover for her: some beautiful arch angel with purple wings—

MORELL
Some fiddlestick!

Playwrights who work in the literary dialogue mode create characters who are by nature verbal enough to speak in this somewhat heightened manner. It is the mode for plays of ideas and exploration. Within the literary mode the playwright is not expected to include all the conventional utterances that characterize real speech, the "uh-huhs," the "you knows," and so on. There is a freedom to allow the character to say exactly what is necessary in a highly articulate manner.

Designs for such plays are similarly freed from the demand for explicit naturalistic detail. Visual elements can be direct, suggestive rather than representational, the essence of reality rather than its imitation. *The Glass Menagerie* is a play exquisitely written in the literary dialogue mode. Look at the set design by Jo Mielziner for the original Broadway production of the play and examine the essential elements and the way they are melded into an environment for that play.

3. Poetic Dialogue

Dramatic poetry doesn't pretend to be common speech. Plays written in poetic dialogue tend to be particularly intense whether they are comic or serious. Everything the actors say is heightened by poetic devices: rhythm, rhyme, metaphor. Poetic dialogue is the richest ground in which the designer's imagination can work, cultivating visually evocative words and phrases and reaping powerful images.

JULIET
'Tis almost morning. I would have thee gone—
And yet no farther than a wanton's bird,
That lets it hop a little from his hand,
Like a poor prisoner in his twisted gyves
And wish a silken thread plucks it back again,
So loving-jealous of his liberty.

4. Sound and Grammar

Playwrights arrange sounds and manipulate grammatical structures in order to give dialogue more than simple sense meanings. Short words and uncomplicated constructions are typical of the dialogue spoken by forthright characters; sinuous sentences with a complexity of dependent clauses can reveal a sneaky nature. Short, clipped sentences and hard sounds are associated with sophisticated comedy, and romances may have dialogue with full, rounded sounds and many parallel constructions.

Most designers respond kinesthetically to sound. The feelings that are stimulated by hearing spoken words and rhythms engage the imagination in the production of visual images. Inspiration and information may come hand in hand from listening to the sounds and shapes of dialogue.

Notice, for example, that the Nurse and Juliet have a lot of direct, declarative speech in *Romeo and Juliet*.

NURSE
Will you speak well of him that killed your cousin?

JULIET
Shall I speak ill of him that is my husband?
Ah, poor my lord, what tongue shall smooth thy name
When I, thy three-hours wife, have mangled it?

In contrast, Claudius' dialogue in *Hamlet* has quite another sound and shape. Here are his opening lines in Act I, Scene ii.

FIGURE 1-12. Petie Seale as the Nurse and Valery Mahaffey as Juliet in the Milwaukee Repertory Theater's production of *Romeo and Juliet*. *Costume design by Susan Tsu. Photograph by Mark Avery.*

Though yet of Hamlet our dear brother's death
The memory be green and that it us befitted
To bear out hearts in grief, and our whole kingdom
To be contracted in one brow of woe,
Yet so far hath discretion fought with nature
That we with wisest sorrow think on him
Together with remembrance of ourselves.

Convoluted, dependent constructions continue for a total of twenty-four lines before Claudius can manage his first simple, declarative sentence on Line 24, "So much for him." Claudius is, of course, as slippery in action as he is in words.

Playwrights also manipulate grammar to protect information or to make points. Much dialogue is constructed in such a way that the important phrase, the actual point of the speech, is at the end. Human conversation seldom manages such precision, and information often gets lost. The playwright cannot afford to take chances; the dialogue is structured so audiences will be sure to hear the important parts.

These are George's lines in Act I of Albee's *Who's Afraid of Virginia Woolfe?*

I'm very mistrustful. Do you believe ... do you believe that people learn nothing from history. Not that there is nothing to learn, mind you, but that people learn nothing? I am in the History Department.

Not only does the important statement come at the end of the segment, but the "I am" is not contracted, adding emphasis to the sentence.

In some instances a designer may perceive the essence of a whole play through the shape of a few lines, not only through the information contained in them but also through their sound and shape. The following segments from a variety of plays may provide you with examples of the kinds of dialogue you might perceive as microcosms of the entire play.

THE CHALK GARDEN by Enid Bagnold
What I have been listening to in court is not my life. It is the shape and shadow of my life. With the accidents of truth taken out of it.

THE LADY'S NOT FOR BURNING by Christopher Frye
Poor father. In the end he walked in
Science like the densest night. And yet
He was greatly gifted.
When he was born he gave an algebraic
Cry; at one glance measured the cubic content
Of that ivory cone his mother's breast
And Multiplied his appetite by five.
So he matured by a progression, gained
Experience by correlation, expanded
Into a marriage by contraction, and by
Certain physical dynamics
Formulated me. And on he went
Still deeper into the calculating twilight
Under the twinkling of five-pointed figures
Till Truth became for him the sum of sums
And Death the long division.

HEY YOU LIGHT MAN by Oliver Hailey
Hey, Mayonnaise! Well, would you look at that. Roy Roca never let me keep mayonnaise. Never. He got sick on it once in 1947—a brand I got on sale for a dime a quart—and he never allowed it in his house again. Me, I love mayonnaise. I've missed it something awful. Not a sandwich goes by I don't think of it.

MURDER IN THE CATHEDRAL by T.S. Eliot
...living, living and partly living.

5. Ambiguity

Expository prose should be, insofar as the language will permit, clear and straightforward. Writers of books such as this one choose words because the meanings of those words are as precise as possible. Verbs should describe exact action and nouns should name specific things. Dramatic dialogue is not the same at all. Plays say many things at the same time, as you have seen. The simple conveying of information is but one aim of dialogue; other facets of meaning are equally important. Playwrights often choose words precisely because those words do not have

FIGURE 1-13. John Kani and Winston Ntshona as Vladimir and Estragon, with Bill Flynn as Pozzo, in Samuel Beckett's *Waiting for Godot*. Produced by the Baxter Theater, Cape Town and presented by the Long Wharf Theater. *Designer, Donald Howarth. Photograph by Gerry Goodstein.*

explicit meanings but are evocative of many meanings, in other words, *because* they are ambiguous. Characters are also allowed to make contradictory statements about themselves, others, and events in the play. They may be constantly guilty of saying one thing and doing another, as the following excerpt from Samuel Beckett's *Waiting For Godot* illustrates:

VLADIMIR
Well? Shall we go?

ESTRAGON
Yes, let's go.
(They do not move. Curtain.)

Meaning in plays is not simple. Listen to the following segment, also taken from *Waiting for Godot:*

ESTRAGON
So long as one knows.

VLADIMIR
One can bide one's time.

ESTRAGON
One knows what to expect.

VLADIMIR
No further need to worry.

ESTRAGON
Simply wait.

VLADIMIR
We're used to it.

Everything in the preceding passage is intentionally obscure. There is a suggestion of present tense meaning which has to do with the actual dilemma faced by the characters, yet every word seems to mean more than it says. Each line may be perceived on several different levels.

Not all dramatic dialogue is this ambiguous but you must expect most dramatic characters to speak more than simple sense. Usually, what is underneath the simple sense will speak to designers in ways that stimulate visual images. In Gogo and Didi's (Estragon and Vladimir) exchange it is the underlying tone of resignation and futility that allows you to *see* the characters in their world.

Many designers in the theatre are serious music lovers whose work is profoundly affected by all the qualities of sound. Those who design for the opera, the musical theatre, and dance use music as the wellspring of their work. There are musical components in all plays which, when perceived, can inspire design work on many types of plays. Practice listening to plays until you can hear the underlying rhythms, the contrasting tones, the different keys in which different scenes are played. Listen to plays read aloud and try reading them yourself. When you can hear *how* a play speaks as well as *what* it speaks about, you are a step closer to creating its environment.

VIII. What Is the Play's Action?

Now you know enough to begin to examine the play as a whole structure, which is another way of saying that now you can discover the play's central action. Francis Hodge defines action as the "life force of the play." Action is not plot, it is the reason for plot. Action is what causes audiences to laugh and to cry.

A play's central action can usually be expressed in a few words related to the attitude changes in the leading characters. The central action of *The Matchmaker* is Dolly Levi's pursuit and capture of Horace Vandergelder. In *Romeo and Juliet* it is the two young lovers' attempt to realize their love even though their families are bitter enemies. In *The Miracle Worker*, Annie Sullivan teaches the blind, deaf, and mute child, Helen, to communicate with the outside world.

Each central action is composed of many subsidiary actions and reactions. The continuous process of action and reaction advances the play. The end comes when an equilibrium is reached, when the energy for producing reaction is momentarily still, when whatever the central action proposed to do is done, successfully or unsuccessfully.

Whenever you speak about a play's dramatic action, be sure to choose strong, active verbs that state rather than explain the action. Amanda Wingfield *imposes* her will on Laura; Regan and Goneril *betray* Lear, Didi and Gogo *wait* for Godot; Macbeth *murders* the king.

1. Create an Action Chart

This is a good time to turn all your analysis into a tangible expression, a character/scene action chart that will provide you with both practical planning facts and a means by which you can discover the play's rhythmic structure.

Lay out the action chart on a sheet of paper wide enough to allow each scene in the play approximately an inch and a half of space across the top of the page. Draw vertical lines to create a column for each scene. (Using graph paper for the chart will save time.) List each character in the play, usually in order of appearance, down the left side of the paper, and divide this list with horizontal lines. These lines will intersect the columns and form a block in each scene column for each character. (See Figure 1–14.) Following each character, from left to right on the chart, place a mark in every scene block in which that character appears. Self-adhesive, colored spot labels are specially neat and handy for marking. The position of the mark within the block can indicate the portion of the scene in which the character enters. Some designers will add a brief description of each character beside the name: the Squire, a Franciscan brother, Arkadina's son, etc. Write in the actors' names when you know them.

In the blocks designating scenes, note the location, the time of day and date, or passage of time from the preceding scene, if that is pertinent. Some plays will respond better to charting if you divide them into French scenes (a French scene begins at each major entrance or exit of a character or characters) rather than conventional act and scene breaks. In this instance use script page numbers rather than act and scene numbers.

The action chart's main analytical function is to reveal to you at a glance the individual and group movements of characters through the play. Many times these movements occur in patterns—repetitive, parallel, alternating—that identify each play's unique rhythmic structure. Similar patterns may be perceived in scene locations—an alternation between Venice and Belmont, a progression from country to city or from public place to private place—times of day, and seasons of the year. The purpose of the action chart is to organize facts you have already found into facts with a design.

FIGURE 1-14. An action chart for G.B. Shaw's *Arms and the Man*.

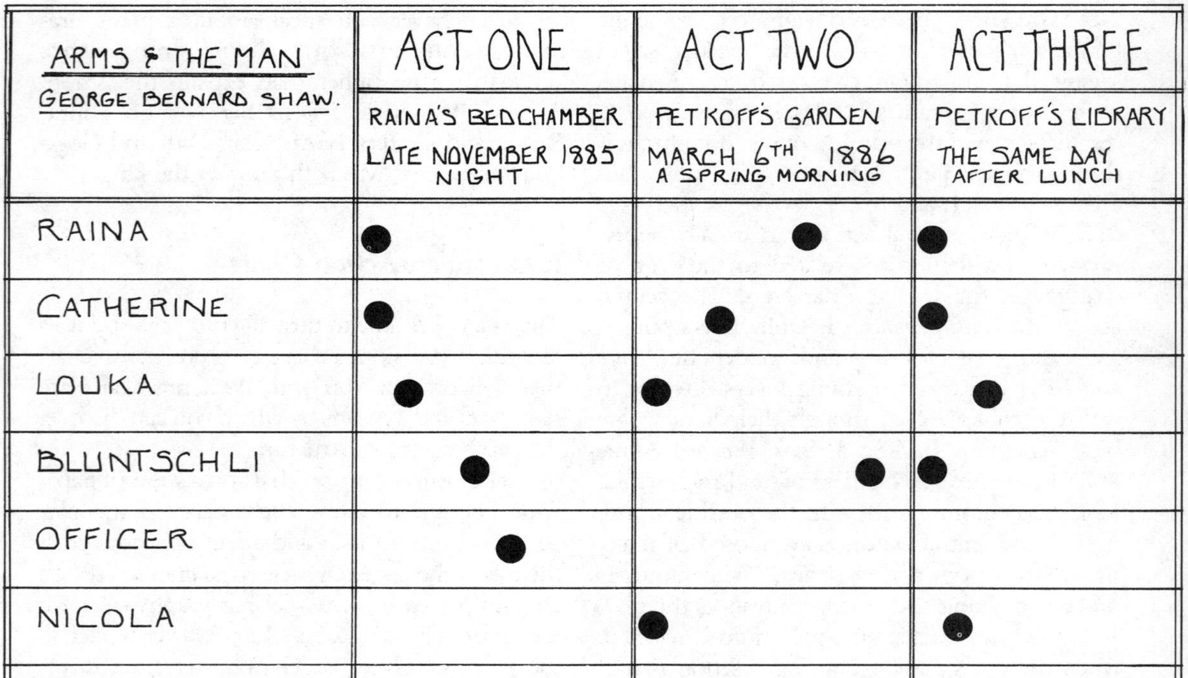

ARMS & THE MAN GEORGE BERNARD SHAW.	ACT ONE RAINA'S BEDCHAMBER LATE NOVEMBER 1885 NIGHT	ACT TWO PETKOFF'S GARDEN MARCH 6TH. 1886 A SPRING MORNING	ACT THREE PETKOFF'S LIBRARY THE SAME DAY AFTER LUNCH
RAINA	●	●	●
CATHERINE	●	●	●
LOUKA	●	●	●
BLUNTSCHLI	●	●	●
OFFICER	●		
NICOLA		●	●
PETKOFF		●	●
SERGIUS		●	●

IX. What Is the Play's Theme?

People always want to know what the theme of the play is and this is probably the most difficult of all things to discover. Few, if any, playwrights begin writing with a theme in mind. They have characters, an incident or two, and usually an idea of what central action they wish to create. But theme isn't usually present in the early stages. A play's theme emerges in the course of the writing and is fully developed only when the work is done. "How do I know what I'm thinking about until I write it?" is actually true for many writers. When the theme does emerge, particularly in a very good play, it becomes the unifying principle of the work, inseparable from every action and every word, an integral wholeness.

Designers perceive theme in a manner much like the playwright discovers it and never until all the action has unfolded and resolution has occurred. Theme results from accumulation of fact, from accretion, and from absorption. The theme of *Romeo and Juliet* , you may say, is the power of love to break down walls of hate. But you will only know this when the play has come to an end.

Theme may or may not inform design. It's difficult to make a play's theme visual since it is largely conceptual, having to do with ideas and intellectual responses. Nevertheless, you will feel that your work is more complete if you complete your analysis with a concise statement of the play's theme.

Conclusion

Analyzing playscripts using the methods described in this chapter can help designers make the leap from what is written by the playwright to its visualization on the stage.

Although it has taken a number of pages, and many words, to discuss these processes, much of the analytical work can be done in a very short time. If you have two weeks for script work prior to your first design conference, you can use it to good advantage. On the other hand, you can accomplish quite a bit in two hours if that's all the time available to you. The quality of your own concentration, which produces visual response and feeling, is what ultimately counts.

The quiet time that a designer spends with a script can be one of the most aesthetically productive parts of the design process. Cherish that time, use it sensitively, and you will be more than ready to move into the more lively world of production.

2
The Production

It is useful to consider designing for the theatre as an accumulation of discoveries which begins when the designer reads the play and ends when the complete production is revealed to the audience—oftentimes the most remarkable discovery of all! Chapter 1 dealt with discovering the play through reading and seeing and with the ways in which visual images can support and sustain the playwright's words without reiterating them, ignoring them, or overwhelming them. These first discoveries are private encounters between the designer and the script.

Chapter 2 moves the designer away from the purely personal encounter into the early phase of practical production. Other people begin to be involved, other ideas, other points of view. This is a particularly exciting phase of the process, but the designer must take care not to lose the private discoveries which were made in the initial script work to the swarm of practical realities that rise up in early design and production conferences.

Prepare to Meet with the Director

The costume designer's first design conference will often be a private meeting with the director. There are many occasions, however, when a producer will be included, and other times when the set designer and possibly the lighting designer will be present.

It is customary for directors in today's theatre to plan a production in more or less the following order:

1. Choose a script to do;
2. Begin thinking about the setting and engage a set designer;
3. Cast at least the key roles;
4. Bring in a costume designer;
5. Bring in a lighting designer.

Even when the costume and set designers begin work at the same time, the director will usually have more specific set ideas than clothing ideas in the early stages of discussion. The costume designer coming into the production discussions after the set design has begun to take shape, must take care not to suppress his or her personal responses to the script, even if they differ from the interpretation being explored. Few productions are designed from first ideas alone, and no theatre designer can afford to be passive. The creative collaboration carries with it the responsibility of sharing.

Therefore, the serious costume designer will appear at the first design conference prepared and willing to discuss the play. Useful aids for this first meeting are a list of specific questions and notes for discussion, an action chart and, perhaps, a rough costume plot. The designer who is eager to collaborate will bring neither conclusions, solutions, formulated statements about the true meaning of the play being discussed, nor costume sketches to this meeting.

No matter how well you know the play, it is difficult to keep all the movements of thirty characters in eighteen scenes in your head while you are discussing it with the director. Figure 2-1 is an action chart for *Twelfth Night* which organizes those eighteen scenes and the thirty-odd characters in a neat, orderly way. It is easy to read and will keep you from having to thumb endlessly through your script to find out exactly who is in Act I, Scene IV. The chart shows you which characters appear in which scenes and what overall movement each character has through the play. You can see at a glance which costumes will play together, a great help when you come to working out color. It also helps you anticipate difficult costume changes and avoid impossible ones.

FIGURE 2-1. An action chart for Shakespeare's *Twelfth Night*.

TWELFTH NIGHT	ACT ONE					ACT TWO						ACT THREE				ACT FOUR			5
	1	2	3	4	5	1	2	3	4	5		1	2	3	4	1	2	3	1
	ORSINO'S PALACE	SEACOAST OF ILLYRIA	OLIVIA'S HOUSE	ORSINO'S PALACE	WITHIN OLIVIA'S HOUSE	LODGING ON SEACOAST	STREET NR. OLIVIA'S HOUSE	WITHIN OLIVIA'S HOUSE	WITHIN ORSINO'S PALACE	OLIVIA'S GARDEN	INTERMISSION	BEFORE OLIVIA'S HOUSE	WITHIN OLIVIA'S HOUSE	A STREET IN ILLYRIA	OLIVIA'S GARDEN	BEFORE OLIVIA'S HOUSE	WITHIN OLIVIA'S HOUSE	OLIVIA'S HOUSE	BEFORE OLIVIA'S HOUSE
ORSINO – DUKE OF ILLYRIA	●			●					●										●
SEBASTIAN – BROTHER TO VIOLA						●								●		●		●	●
ANTONIO – A SEA CAPTN. FRIEND TO SEBASTIAN						●								●	●				●
A SEA CAPTAIN – FRIEND TO VIOLA		●																	
VALENTINE –) GENTLEMEN ATTENDING	●			●															
CURIO –) ON THE DUKE	●			●					●										●
SIR TOBY BELCH – UNCLE TO OLIVIA			●					●		●		●	●		●	●	●		●
SIR ANDREW AGUECHEEK			●					●		●		●	●		●	●			●
MALVOLIO – STEWARD TO OLIVIA					●		●	●		●					●		●		●
FABIAN –) SERVANTS										●			●		●				●
FESTE – A CLOWN) TO OLIVIA					●			●	●			●				●	●		●
OLIVIA – A COUNTESS					●							●			●	●		●	●
VIOLA – SISTER OF SEBASTIAN		●		●	●		●		●			●			●				●
MARIA – OLIVIA'S WOMAN			●		●			●		●		●	●		●		●		
LORDS	●			●					●										
A PRIEST																		●	●
SAILORS		●																●	
OFFICERS																●			●
MUSICIANS	●																		
SERVANT																●			
ATTENDANTS																			●

Perhaps you found the action chart a valuable part of script analysis. Now, as you discuss practical and aesthetic design necessities with the director, it will become an invaluable visual and organizational aid.

The Rough Costume Plot

Some designers make a rough costume plot part of the initial script work while others save this task for later when more specific information is available. The rough plot is a list, drawn from the designer's reading, of exactly what each character might be likely to wear in each scene of the play. The garments aren't described, merely listed: trousers, shirt, belt, socks, shoes, overcoat, and so on. The rough plot, like the character/scene breakdown, can help to give the designer a sense of the play's visual shape and scope. It can become, as the discoveries accumulate and the work on the production moves ahead, the official finished plot for the shop and for the wardrobe staff, noting and describing each piece of clothing worn by each character in the play.

The following costume plots, one rough and one finished, are for Noel Coward's *Private Lives*.

Rough Costume Plot
"Private Lives"

SIBYL		VICTOR	
ACT I	ACT I	ACT I	ACT I
(a)	(b)	(a)	(b)
wig	evening dress	shirt	shirt
dress	purse	tie	collar
slip	gloves	3 pc. suit or separates	tie
garter belt or girdle	shoes	suspenders	vest
stockings	jewelry	cufflinks	dinner jacket
shoes		shoes	trousers
jewelry		socks	suspenders
rings		handkerchief	cufflinks
			collar studs
ACT II	ACT III		shirt studs
hat	*same as Act* II		shoes
suit and blouse *or*	minus hat, gloves, etc.		socks
dress and jacket or coat			
purse		ACT II	ACT III
gloves		hat	*same as Act* II
shoes		shirt	
jewelry		tie	
		suit	
		suspenders	
		cufflinks	
		shoes	
		socks	
		handkerchief	

SIBYL		VICTOR	
ACT I	**ACT I**	**ACT I**	**ACT I**
(a)	(b)	(a)	(b)
wig—blonde	evening dress—tur-	shirt—beige w/white	shirt—boil front even-
dress—dusty pink	quoise printed	stripes and french	ing shirt
printed rayon crepe	chiffon	cuffs	collar—wing
w/ecru collar & cuffs	evening purse—pearl	tie—brown silk polka	tie—black bow
slip—tea rose rayon	beaded	dot bow tie	vest—black brocade
crepe	gloves—cream fabric,	vest—cream w/brown	dinner jacket—black
girdle	over the elbow	windowpane checks	evening trousers—black
long-legged panty	shoes—cream lizard	trousers—cream linen	suspenders—white
girdle	skin sandals	jacket—beige gabardine	cufflinks—gold
stockings—w/seams	earrings—pearl drop	w/back belt	collar studs
shoes—pale beige	necklace—3 rows pearls	suspenders	shirt studs
leather w/strap	bracelet—pearl strands	cufflinks—gold	shoes—black patent
earrings—pearl		shoes—tan brogues	socks—black
wedding ring		socks—beige	
engagement ring		handkerchief—off-white	
		cotton	
ACT II	**ACT III**	**ACT II**	**ACT III**
hat—beige and navy	*same as Act* II	hat—light grey fedora	*same as Act* II
straw	minus jacket, hat,	shirt—light grey striped	
blouse—beige silk w/	gloves etc.	w/french cuffs	
navy polka dots	jacket added during act.	tie—blue/grey/red silk	
skirt and jacket—navy		paisley 4-in-hand	
crepe		suit—blue/grey double	
purse—beige leather		breasted	
clutch		suspenders—grey	
gloves—beige leather		arm garters	
earrings/slip/shoes from		cufflinks—silver	
Act 1 (a)		shoes—black lace-up	
		socks—black from Act	
		1 (b)	
		handkerchief—off-white	
		cotton	

The First Design Conference

Working with Different Directors

It is important to note here that each director, like each designer, has a personal and unique way of working. One may present the designer with a total production scheme, complete with color preferences and accessory choices, at the first meeting. Another won't have a clue how the

35

show might look. Designers favor the director who has strong but general feelings about how the play should be approached and what effect it will ultimately have on an audience, but who encourages the designer to share in the process of creating the total production. Some directors will express their feelings about the play in words; others will allude to the work of a specific artist or to a single painting to convey their response to the play; still others will refer the designer to a piece or type of music.

Whatever the director's manner of approaching and arriving at a production scheme, it is the designer's job to respond to and be inspired and guided by what is conveyed during the first, and subsequent, meetings. It is the director's responsibility to achieve and maintain production coherence, and it is up to the costume designer not only to help plan the production but also to make sure that each garment worn in the play contributes to this coherence.

In the early planning stage it is imperative that the designer understand what the director is saying, seeing, and feeling. If the designer thinks that a painting the director has chosen to convey his or her response to the play is antithetical to the play's spirit, then it is up to the designer to do more than feel confused or decide that the director has no visual sense. Designers are trained to look at paintings in certain ways whereas untrained people will look and respond quite differently. In this situation it is not important to judge the director's taste in art but to discover what the director's response really means in relation to the play. The designer must urge the director to keep on talking until the two reach some degree of understanding. It is not always easy to communicate on visual matters and the designer must use a great deal of tact and persistence to draw the necessary information from certain directors.

Period and Style

From the costume designer's point of view, the most important matters to be considered during the first design conference are those of period and style. Some plays dictate a specific period, while others are less specific and a period and style of production must be considered and decided upon.

FIGURE 2-2. An unusual period choice for Shakespeare's *Taming of the Shrew:* Italy just after WWII. Rose Pickering as Kate, Henry Strozier as Baptista, and Maggie Thatcher as Bianca. Produced by the Milwaukee Repertory Theater. *Costume design by Susan Tsu. Photograph by Mark Avery.*

If the period seems obvious, as in, for example, *Becket* or *A Man For All Seasons*, it can be useful for the designer to take a few clear illustrations of clothing from that period (preferably reproductions of paintings or drawings of the time) to the meeting. Directors vary enormously in their knowledge of period clothing and more than a few appreciate being shown pictures of the particular period garments under discussion. The designer should also be prepared to answer basic questions regarding manners and customs from that era or ways in which the actual garments were worn.

Many of Shakespeare's plays, particularly the comedies, can be placed quite successfully in a wide variety of periods. When a designer is discussing the choice of period with the director, it is important for the designer to find out what overall impression of the play the director wishes the audience to perceive. A formal and restrained *Much Ado About Nothing* might be well supported by choosing late 16th century lines and silhouettes while a romantic approach to the same play could be enhanced by clothing from the 1820's.

The visual style of the production will be related to period choice, but it will also reflect the play's point of view and the director's interpretation. These will, in turn, effect the way in which the designer looks at period research. For example, even though both plays may be set in the 1930's, the visual styles of Noel Coward's *Present Laughter* and Clifford Odet's *Golden Boy* will be very different.

FIGURES 2-3 through 2-10. Sketches and photographs from a production of *Dead Souls* with frankly theatrical costumes and make-up. Directed by John Dillon at the Milwaukee Repertory Theater. *Costume design by Carol Oditz. Photographs of sketches by Frances Aronson. Production photographs by Mark Avery.*

FIGURE 2-4. Judy Dorrel as Mr. & Mrs. Manilov.

FIGURE 2-6. Diane Johnson as the Governor's Wife.

FIGURE 2-8. Peggy Cowles as Sofya Ivanovna.

FIGURE 2-9. *Dead Souls.*

Character and Script

At some point in the first design conference the discussion will turn from the overall production approach toward specific script and character considerations. The designer will have a list of questions organized in an economical way. Many of the questions will fall into the following seven categories:

1. Will characters be eliminated or added? Will actors be cast in more than a single role?

In large-cast plays, small roles are often eliminated, or two small roles amalgamated into one, in order to limit the size of the cast. Such decisions may decrease the number of costumes needed. On the other hand, certain plays, par-

FIGURE 2-10. *Dead Souls.*

ticularly history plays with battles and musicals, require crowds, or choruses, which may vary greatly in numbers. At the first meeting ask for specific numbers but always remember that crowds have a way of growing in rehearsal, particularly in those productions where extra crowd members do not require extra salaries. In such situations be on the lookout for burgeoning crowds. It is important to have in hand, as soon as possible, an accurate list of characters, both speaking and nonspeaking roles.

Character doubling is the use of a single actor to play more than one role. Doubling must be carefully worked into the production design in order to facilitate the necessary clothing changes, sometimes allowing specific garments to be used for more than one character, sometimes providing a wig or face hair to effect a change. The action chart will come in handy for checking the feasibility of doubling.

2. Will the script be cut? Will any changes be made in place or time of day?

Look at all script cuts. A cut that may enhance a scene's dramatic movement may also render a planned costume change impossible. The designer's script should include all text cuts and these should be reflected on the character/scene breakdown chart.

Location and time of day changes may effect the appropriateness of the dress in those scenes and may even add additional outfits to the production.

3. Discuss each reference in the script to specific garments, accessories, and colors.

Ask whether or not the director wishes to adhere to such references. Sometimes the specific garment or accessory will be changed because of the period choice, whereas sometimes the director simply has another preference. Quite often a line referring to a dress color may be dropped or altered because that color doesn't happen to suit the actor playing the role. In such cases the costume will be done in another more becoming color.

4. Does the director plan on using props or accessories not called for in the script?

Canes, parasols, eyeglasses, fans, etc., are often used to help the actor create his or her character. Such accessories should be included in the costume design and, many times, a rehearsal version will be required.

5. Will the actors be called upon to engage in any unusual physical activity that will effect the costumes?

This is particularly important when restricting period garments are required. Most costumes can

be rigged for extraordinary movement but only if the rigging has been worked into the design and construction plans. Choice of fabric may also depend on physical activity. If, for instance, Romeo is to actually climb a rough stone wall on his way to Juliet's balcony, his doublet should probably not be built from a loosely woven, slubbed silk! Ask about sitting, rolling, or crawling on the floor in order to minimize and plan ahead for unusual cleaning.

6. Discuss each character in turn.

It is essential from the first discussion onward that the costume designer knows exactly how the director sees each character in the play. Ask the director to describe physical appearance and to assign general character traits to each. Osric, for instance, may be seen as tall and thin with long curls and a pointed goatee; he is, perhaps, a dandy, full of self-importance but rather stupid. The tall thin appearance and the dandiness can be well supported by the costume design. Polonius, on the other hand, might be perceived as portly, full-bearded, and expensively but conservatively dressed; he is secure in his position in the court, a doting father and a gossip. In this case the actor might require padding underneath his costume and a beard; his position in the court may be suggested by using rich fabrics, employing elegant lines and adding a gold chain of office.

Discuss each character in this manner. Mention age, social status, and occupation. Be as specific as possible about face hair, wigs, and padding since these will directly affect the designs. Note the possibility of any stage business requiring hidden pockets, undressing, or the use of unusal accessories.

7. Who is cast?

If the production has been cast when the first design conference takes place, much of the dis-

FIGURE 2-11. Gilbert Price as Marc Antony in the Milwaukee Repertory Theater production of *Julius Caesar. Costume design by Susan Tsu. Photograph by Mark Avery.*

cussion outlined above will be in terms of specific actors. If it has not been cast, ask the director to describe the sort of actors he or she has in mind for the roles. Whenever possible, it is both interesting and helpful for the designer to attend casting auditions, particularly call-backs. Often the designer can see what the director wants each character to be by the type of actor being auditioned.

When the actors are already cast, the costume designer should make plans with the director to see and measure them before designing the production. If the actors are unavailable and will not appear until rehearsals begin, ask for a photograph, a description, and a few measurements and sizes. Know in advance that the leading lady has a very large bust and is short-waisted and avoid designing a strapless evening dress with a high waist. When the measurement blank reveals that an actor is five feet tall and weighs two hundred pounds, the designer can choose something other than horizontal stripes for his costume.

The costume designer's work is a great deal easier when casting is completed before the designs are due. Unfortunately, this is not always possible, and often the designer has to put pencil to paper long before the actors are chosen. In this situation, the work will be based primarily on character and on the director's description of both character and type of actor desired. Inevitably, once the casting is complete, certain changes will have to be made in the designs in order to accommodate the actors. Expect and plan for such changes.

Although one might assume at this point that the first design conference could easily last for twenty-four hours, the discussion will probably be brisk and much of the pertinent information quickly shared. Some questions will have to be reserved for later meetings, although it is very important for the designer to have as many answers as possible before settling down at the drawing board. The success of the initial design meeting will depend largely on how much script preparation both the director and the designer have done and how specific the designer can be with questions.

Production Realities

Budgeting Time and Money

Next to an exciting and viable production scheme, the two most important pieces of information the costume designer must discover before approaching the drawing table are the budget allocation for materials and the costs and conditions of labor. Sometimes it is possible to get these production details from the director but often this information must come from the producer, the business manager, technical director, or costume shop manager. The costume designer must find out who to see in each situation and, once again, be prepared with specific queries.

Labor and Material Costs

It is virtually impossible to design a set of costumes outside the classroom without knowing what the budget is. Budgets will vary greatly, depending upon the affluence of the producing organization. While there is no doubt that handsome costumes can be designed and built on quite limited budgets, this can only happen if the limitation is known and accounted for in the early design process.

Always consider the total amount of the materials budget in terms of the actual number of costumes required for the production. A one-thousand dollar materials budget has one kind of reality if the production calls for fifteen costumes and quite another if there are to be fifty.

If, after some serious apportioning, the costume designer finds that the rock bottom production demands exceed the budget allotted to costumes, it is up to the designer to point this out immediately. Make up a cost estimate and bring it in for the producer and the director to examine. Never put a set of costumes into the shop if there is insufficient money to construct it.

If more money cannot be found, the designs may have to be greatly simplified or, in extreme circumstances, the production postponed or cancelled.

Costs and conditions of labor vary from one situation to another. If the costumes are to be built in a commercial shop, the designer will present the shop with finished designs and receive an estimated price for their construction. If this amount is more than the budget allotment for labor, the designer may either simplify the designs or go to another shop. Initial bids will often be sought from two or three shops in order to get the best price. It may take some time before the budget and the actual cost are in line and an agreement can be made between the designer and the shop. The arrangement will be for a specific number of garments as designed; any additions or elaborate changes will cost more.

In regional theatres, stock companies, and colleges and universities, costumes will more than likely be constructed in a resident shop staffed by the producing organization. The technicians in these shops will be responsible for building costumes for all the plays produced by the group. In these situations the designer must know the number and experience level of the technicians who will construct the costumes and the length of time that has been scheduled for building.

A wise designer will be sensitive to the skill and experience levels of the people working in the costume shop and will not design costumes far beyond their ability to construct them. This should not be looked on as an onerous restriction for the designer but as one of the many practical considerations that make up the design process. Besides, with the designer's support, even the most inexperienced costume technician enjoys a challenging problem or an experiment with a new process when time permits.

Time and Facilities

Along with assessing the skill of the technicians, the designer must be aware of the total building time and try not to design a set of costumes that cannot be finished by opening night. College and university costume shop crews work a limited number of hours and these work periods must fit into the overall class and study schedule. The shop staff members in most regional and stock theatres are paid a weekly salary for a forty to a forty-eight hour work week, usually with no provision for overtime compensation even though overtime work is the rule rather than the exception. The technicians may receive a few days off at the end of the production period but this, in most cases, does not adequately make up for the many hours of overtime they have devoted to finishing the costumes.

Far too many designers, particularly those who work in many different theatres on a freelance basis, help to exploit the dedication and the good nature of costume technicians by not trying to protect them from excessive overwork in the initial design process. Careful design and thoughtful planning can play a large part in regulating the work load. There is no reason why a designer should not consider the well-being of the technicians along with budget and aesthetics.

If the designs will require more complicated execution than the designer feels the resident shop can handle, or take more time than has been allocated, it is up to the designer to talk with the producer or business manager and request additional personnel. Such requests, made in the early stages of production, can usually be accommodated. Pre-planning is always preferable to last minute scrambling.

A designer working with a resident shop should also know what equipment is available in that shop. If, for instance, there are no fabric dyeing facilities, the designer will either have to shop color carefully or allow for professional dyeing in the materials budget. The presence or absence of millinery equipment, tailor's dummies, a serger, or tools for making jewelry will all effect the design process. In a shop where buttonholes are regularly sent out to be done at a hefty cost, the designer will think twice before asking for practical buttons down the fronts of all the doublets!

Resident shops differ in the ways in which they charge stock supplies to individual shows. Some have separate general supply budgets out of which to purchase thread, tailor's chalk, tracing paper, bones, etc., and such items are not charged directly to the production materials budget. In other shops the materials budget for each production may be charged for each yard of muslin used in draping and every spool of thread purchased for a particular show. Before starting to work, the designer must know exactly what the materials budget is intended to cover.

The resident shop will usually have a costume stock from which the designer may pull at will. The designer should go through the stock in person if at all possible or, if this is not possible, ask a shop staff member to look for specific items from the designer's list. The materials budget will go much farther if basic items such as men's shirts, tights, or petticoats can be pulled rather than purchased or built. There may also be major garments from the appropriate period that can be used with alteration and/or retrimming. However, for the most successful show, the rest of the costumes should be designed with the pulled items in mind. It is not always the best idea to try and fit pulled garments into a set of costumes that is already designed. The availability of stock items should be a very early consideration.

A cooperative relationship between the designer and the shop staff will help create a pleasant work period. Whether the designer is working with a particular shop for the first or the fiftieth time, a careful review of production realities will get the work off to a good start.

Talks with the Other Designers

If the set and lighting designers are not present at the initial design conference between the costume designer and the director, a separate meeting with them should be set up before the design process is too far along. In order for the production to have coherence, it is necessary for all the designers to share a similar understanding of the production scheme. Although the costume designer and the lighting designer should discuss the approach to the show and color ideas as soon as possible, the actual lighting design will not be completed until after the set and costumes are designed.

The conversation between the costume designer and the set designer, however, should cover several specific areas, particularly if the set design is already underway.

1. *Color.* All set colors affect costume fabric choices. As soon as the set designer has made any color decisions, the costume designer should have paint chips, swatches of upholstery fabric, and/or wallpaper samples.
2. *Basic Construction.* The costume designer should always know if there is to be a raked

FIGURE 2-12. Set and costumes that are obviously the result of a fruitful collaboration between designers. Shakespeare's *The Winter's Tale* produced by Arena Stage. *Set design by Tony Straiges. Costume design by Carol Oditz. Photograph by George de Vincent.*

stage and, if so, the degree of the rake. A significant rake can present a difficulty for actors in floor-length garments which, although they may look too short when the actor is coming downstage, may trip the actor moving upstage. The costume designer should also know the height and width of stair treads and the height and width of doorways. High, narrow stair treads may interfere with the actor wearing a long, tight skirt or extremely high heels. Doors must be high enough to accommodate wigs and headpieces and wide enough for panniers and hoops if the production demands them.

3. *Stage Floor Surface.* Many costume budgets have been exceeded because, at the last minute, it was necessary to have dance rubber put on the bottoms of all the actors' shoes so they would not slip and fall. Costume designers should always find out

in advance what the stage floor surface will be like and make plans in accordance with that information.

4. *Furniture.* If the costumes will include wide skirts, make sure the furniture is wide enough to accommodate them and that there is sufficient walking room from one side of the stage to the other. If the furniture is to have a rough textured surface, this may effect fabric choice.

All the designers involved in a production should stay in close touch with one another's work. After the costume sketches are completed and approved by the director, the costume designer should make a set of photocopies with swatches attached for the lighting and set designer. If everyone who is working on the show continues to talk with everyone else, problems will be solved before they have a chance to become too big to handle.

The Production Book

Just before settling in to draw, many designers find it useful to set up a production book which will become the gathering place for all the information pertinent to that partiuclar show. Such a book, well tended, will be an invaluable aid to a busy designer, handy to grab for meetings and for shopping trips. An inexpensive loose-leaf binder will provide an excellent cover for the production book, and filler pages with reinforced holes will minimize the chances of losing sheets. The production book may be just the place for reading and research notes and, if the complexity of the script demands it, a synopsis of scenes.

More specific contents of a production book might be:

1. *Calendar.* Draw a calendar on graph paper

that covers the entire production period. Note production meetings, photo calls, and dress rehearsals, and add in other dates, such as fittings, as they are scheduled.

2. *Addresses and Telephone Numbers.* The stage manager will often compile a list of addresses and telephone numbers of all the people involved in the production which can be placed in the book. Otherwise, the designer should make such a list including cast members, director, producer, other designers and costume shop personnel.

3. *Tax Exemption Number* (if there is one). In some states tax exempt forms must also be presented. The production book is a good place to keep a supply of these forms.

FIGURE 2-13. A designer's calendar.

JANUARY

S	M	T	W	T	F	S
3 COST. SHOP OFF TODAY	**4** PROD. MEETING FOR "YOU NEVER CAN TELL"	**5**	**6** SKETCHES DUE "ARMS & THE MAN"	**7**	**8**	**9**
10	**11** SHOP STARTS "ARMS & MAN"	**12**	**13** SHOW ROUGH SKETCHES "YNCT" TODAY	**14**	**15**	**16**
17 COST. SHOP OFF TODAY	**18** 1ST REH. "ARMS & MAN" TAKE M/MENS	**19** ALL TRIM FOR "ARMS" DUE TODAY	**20** REST OF M/MENS & 1ST FITTINGS "ARMS"	**21** 1ST FITTINGS "ARMS" (MUSLINS)	**22** ALL "ARMS" FABRIC DUE *PROD. MTNG.	**23**
24 COST. SHOP OFF TODAY	**25** ACTORS OFF TODAY	**26**	**27** 2ND FITTINGS "ARMS"	**28** 2ND FITTINGS "ARMS"	**29** PRODUCTION MEETING "ARMS"	**30**

FEBRUARY

S	M	T	W	T	F	S
31 ACTORS OFF TODAY	**1** ACTORS OFF TODAY	**2**	**3** FINAL FITTINGS "ARMS"	**4**	**5** *PHOTO CALL "ARMS" 5:00 / PRODUCTION MEETING "ARMS"	**6** DRESS PARADE "ARMS" 12:00
7 1ST TECH "ARMS" (NO COSTUMES)	**8** SKETCHES DUE "YOU NEVER CAN TELL"	**9** 1ST DRESS "ARMS" 12:00 ½ HR.	**10** 2ND DRESS "ARMS" 12:00 ½ HR.	**11** 3RD DRESS 1ST PREVIEW 7:30 ½ HR.	**12** 2ND PREVIEW 7:30 ½ HR.	**13** "ARMS & THE MAN" OPENS

4. *Materials Budget Breakdown.* A necessary shopping aid!

5. *Cast List.*

6. *Action Chart.*

7. *Costume Plot.*

8. *Wig and Beard List.*

9. *Hat List.*

10. *Rental Lists.* These can be particularly valuable if, as is often the case, garments are rented from several sources. Rentals should be listed in great detail to insure their safe return at the lowest possible rental fee.

11. *Measurement Chart.* This chart is invaluable for shopping. (See Figure 2–6.) It contains all the basic measurements, drawn from the shop's measurement forms, needed for ordinary shopping. In a busy store, it is much easier to consult a single chart in the production book than it is to thumb through a great pile of measurement forms which will, inevitably, end up scattered on the floor.

Costume production book contents will vary from designer to designer. The order in which they are laid out is an entirely personal matter, although it might be wise to consider putting the measurement chart all the way in the back of the book, facing the back cover, for particularly quick reference.

FIGURE 2-14. A measurement chart for shopping.

ACTOR'S NAME	HEIGHT	WEIGHT	BUST/CHEST	WAIST	HIPS 7" 9" DOWN	BRA/INSEAM	OUTSEAM S. WAIST TO FLOOR	PIERCED EARS?	L or R HANDED	ALLERGIES	HOSE/PANTS	GLOVE	BLOUSE/SHIRT	DRESS/SUIT	HAT/HEAD C.	SHOE

Conclusion

Young and inexperienced costume designers may well view the preceding discussion with horror. All this planning does not sound like much fun compared with the excitement of actually sketching costumes. Be assured that the well-informed, well-organized costume designer will, in the long run, enjoy much more freedom to concentrate on the designs and on realizing them than the chaotic designer who, by refusing to do adequate preparation, allows a multitude of practical problems to interfere with the heart of the process. Besides, many of these initial planning steps quickly become second nature and take no time at all to accomplish. And, many of them are fun as well.

3

Costume Research

The first phase of costume research begins as soon as you have read through the script—and sometimes even during the first reading—as you start to imagine the characters in action and to dress them in historical garments pulled from your own memory. If the play is a fanciful one, you will make up appropriate costumes for nymphs or ghosts, fairies or woodchucks, sorting through all the scattered facts and bits of nonsense you have seen and read and filed away for future use.

In the second phase you set out systematically to discover new facts to add to those you already possess. A short but pertinent definition of research describes the process well: "a careful search; a close searching." The emphasis in this chapter is on historical searching but you must keep in mind that costume research also means searching for any and all sorts of design ideas. Don't be surprised if you find yourself looking through pictures of flowers, fish, animals, or insects, or examining fantasy or primitive art. Costume research can take you almost anywhere.

History is Important

The costume designer is irrevocably linked to the past as well as the present, and influenced as much by history as by the events of the contemporary scene.

Motley
*Designing and Making
Stage Costumes*

Ideally every costume designer ought to know social, cultural and political history, art history, and the basic period clothing silhouettes from Mesopotamia to your own home town. You should be able, for example, to give the dates of Queen Elizabeth I's reign in England, to remember a few facts about her character as monarch, and to *see* her silhouette. You should also know which came first, the French Revolution or the American Revolution and how one differed from the other in ideology, action, and dress, and you

FIGURE 3-1. Pencil and gouache sketch of chorus costumes for *Pacifica*. Design by Ann Wallace. Photograph by Frances Aronson.

should be able to name painters whose imaginations were captured by each struggle for freedom.

Such a background, acquired during your years in school and through independent study, is part of the basic preparation you bring to every design project you undertake (along with taste, design sense, drawing and painting skills, and the techniques of clothing construction). This knowledge makes it possible for you to research each play you design in specifics rather than in generalities. If your knowledge of history is sound, your work will have an authority that it cannot achieve otherwise.

What the Audience Sees

A performer's silhouette is the starting premise of any presentation.

BERNARD BECKERMAN
Dynamics of Drama

The first thing an audience sees when an actor is revealed or comes on stage is the outline of the figure against its background. The shape of that outline creates a strong impression of character. It also conveys historical period and social and economic status at a glance. Success with this first impression depends on the designer's ability to create an evocative silhouette in clear, crisp lines, derived from accurate sources and chosen be-cause it conveys the appropriate information about period and character to the audience.

Except on rare occasions, costume design-ers in the theatre are not in the business of reproducing historical costumes in detail on the stage. Theatrical costumes create an *impression* of period. The designer who sees a period accurately knows which elements of the silhouette and which details are most evocative of that period to a contemporary audience's eyes and, therefore, which need to be emphasized in the costumes. Whenever the audience perceives a correct im-pression through character silhouette in the opening moments of a production, that play is off to a good start.

FIGURE 3-3. Andrew B. Marlay's sketch for the costume in Figure 3-2, rendered with watercolor and pencil on watercolor paper. *Photograph by Frances Aronson.*

FIGURE 3-2.
"A performer's silhouette is the starting premise of any presentation." Laurinda Barrett as Mrs. Prest in the McCarter Theatre's production of *The Aspern Papers. Costume design by Andrew B. Marlay. Photograph by Cliff Moore.*

It is not an easy matter to reach the point where you can look at historical garments in paintings, tapestries, sculpture, and drawings and really see them. There is a terrible potential lurking in everyone to look at an Elizabethan dress and, by making subtle and unconscious visual adjustments to what you are seeing, perceive it in proportions that are closer to your own contemporary silhouette. You may also find yourself looking at a piece of research with a preconceived idea of what is there, which prevents you from seeing what is really there. Even designers with excellent research eyes and a good deal of experience suffer lapses in seeing that interfere with their ability to convey a period successfully.

To avoid these lapses, it is necessary for a designer who is doing costume research to look, look, and look again. And, while you are looking, recall all the facts you have about the garment: cut and construction, understructure, type of fabric, method of closing, why and under what circumstances worn. Try to perceive the garment in three dimensions and be sure you know what is hidden from view: the back, where the collar starts, how the belt stays in place, where each sleeve hangs from. Feel the garment's weight and shape and the physical limitations it imposes on the body.

Once you are able to perceive the garment in this degree of detail, it ceases to be merely a flat representation on a page. It acquires depth, volume, and a potential for movement. It becomes three-dimensional in your mind's eye, accurately proportioned and correctly trimmed.

Throughout their lives costume designers continue to sharpen their abilities to see and experience research. They never stop looking at paintings, sculpture, drawings, and photographs. Whenever they have the opportunity, they study actual historical garments, examining seams and the way they hang, methods of stitching and finishing details.

Many of you will become collectors of research materials. You will haunt second hand shops, estate sales, vintage clothing stores, flea markets, and rummage sales for antique clothing, accessories, old magazines, old patterns, illustrations, fashion plates, movie stills, and many other items of primary research interest.

FIGURE 3-4. Laura Crow's costume design for Hypatia in the Academy Festival production of G.B. Shaw's *Misalliance. Photograph by Susan Perkins.*

Seeing by Comparison

When you are involved in a careful search for clothing facts, it's easier to see the costumes of one period accurately if you compare them with costumes of other periods. All clothing evolves from or reacts to that which preceded it, and the best way to view the changing fashion silhouette parade is through its movement from shape to shape. The tails on men's formal coats *were longer* in 1870 *than* they were in 1845. In 1947 fashionable womens' skirts dropped suddenly in length and were, in some cases, *a foot or more longer than* they had been the year before. Comparison is also helpful when you are sorting out geographical clothing differences: An ante-bellum Southern girl usually wore *wider* hoops *than* her contemporary in Boston.

FIGURE 3-5. An afternoon dress from the early 1850's.

Here is a general description of a simple afternoon dress from the early 1850's (see Figure 3-5), using comparison to evoke a sense of the garment.

The bodice of the dress is very tight and must be worn over a corset which flattens the bosom rather than pushing the bosom up under the chin. The waistline is at the natural waist in the back and on the sides but it dips below the waist in front and into a rounded point over the abdomen. The wearer's shoulders appear to be much more sloping than women's shoulders are today because the shoulder portion of the bodice is extended beyond the natural shoulder and onto the upper arm. The armhole is much lower and smaller than anything we are used to seeing in contemporary tailoring. The neckline is at the base of the neck and the bodice fastens down the center back

with small buttons, close together. Because of restriction caused by the low, tight armholes and the placement of the closing at center back, there is no way the wearer of this dress could dress herself.

The sleeves have rows of horizontal ruching and flounces at the wrists. The skirt is in three tiers, each edged with wide lace. The skirt is supported by a small hoop, not as extreme as those that became fashionable late in the decade.

Even though this is an example of a simple dress of the period, it is still much more elaborately decorated than today's dresses; the cutting and construction are more intricate and the undergarments are certainly more complicated. Any woman would feel differently about herself and about her world in the 1850's dress than she would in her modern Anne Klein wraparound.

Reading Well

A sharp eye, trained to look at clothes that have been represented by artists throughout history, is the most important research tool any costume designer can have. Only slightly less important is the ability to read quickly, accurately, and with good retention. You should be able to scan a printed page and pick out important and interesting facts and translate a written description into a mental image.

Effective reading, just like effective seeing, takes practice. It is well worth your effort to strengthen your reading skills through individual study or by taking a short course in reading effectiveness. Designers who read slowly and laboriously will find it difficult to get into the excitement of research and they may well end up with sketchy, incomplete work.

A Research Outline

No matter how extensive your design experience or how much you know about costume history, each and every new production demands a cer-

tain amount of research. Even if you are designing costumes for a play you've done before, a different production will demand its own look. If the play is new to you, particularly if it is set in a period with which you are unfamiliar, you may find yourself with a sheaf of problems to solve and questions to answer before you can sit down to draw.

These questions begin to emerge as you study the script, and they grow in number (and often in complexity) during meetings with the director. Before you consult resource materials, assemble all your notes into a research guide or outline which will help you organize your search and direct your efforts.

Figure 3-6 is a set of notes with which to begin the research for a production of William Gibson's *The Miracle Worker*.

It is at this point that most of you will take pad and pencil in hand and head for the library.

FIGURE 3-6. Research notes for William Gibson's *The Miracle Worker*.

THE MIRACLE WORKER -- RESEARCH GUIDE

- SET IN THE 1880's
- COUNTRY HOME - TUSCUMBIA, ALABAMA
- PERKINS INSTITUTE FOR THE BLIND, BOSTON

  - THE KELLERS ARE GENTLEFOLK; THE HOME
          IS GRACIOUS & COMFORTABLE
  - NEED GENERAL SILHOUETTES & DETAILS FOR:

      1. RURAL SOUTHERN GENTRY - KELLERS
      2. RURAL SOUTHERN BLACKS - VINEY &
                      CHILDREN
      3. RURAL SOUTHERN DOCTOR
      4. URBAN NORTHERN DOCTOR
          (EYE SPECIALIST)
      5. URBAN NORTHERN WOMAN, VERY POOR,
                  ANNIE
      6. BLIND CHILDREN IN CHARITY
          INSTITUTION IN THE NORTH

- WHAT DOES THE SOUTHERN DOCTOR'S STETHOSCOPE LOOK LIKE?
- WHAT SORT OF FACE HAIR FOR CAPT. KELLER?
- FIND PHOTOGRAPHS OF BLACK FARM CHILDREN
- OLDER SILHOUETTE FOR AUNT EV?
- PAY ATTENTION TO CONTRAST BETWEEN CLOTHES
      WORN BY ANNIE & BY KATE. WHAT ARE
      THE SIMILARITIES IN PERIOD AND THE
      DIFFERENCES BETWEEN WELL-TO-DO
      WIFE & STRUGGLING TEACHER?
- VINEY'S DRESS? IS IT A UNIFORM?
- UNDERDRAWERS FOR ANNIE.
- LITTLE GIRL'S CLOTHES - HOMEMADE PROBABLY -
              FOR ANNIE

Libraries

No matter how many costume books a designer owns, a trip to the library is an integral part of almost every costume design process. Designers who have only a few costume books of their own depend almost entirely on libraries for research materials. Whether you use libraries a little or a lot, you should know what you can expect to find there and how to find it in the quickest and most efficient manner possible.

Public Libraries

Nearly all towns and cities in the United States have public libraries. You may expect to find the standard costume history works almost everywhere, although in many places books such as Davenport's *The Book of Costume* and Corson's *Fashions in Hair* will be kept in the reserve book section and not allowed to circulate. Most small public libraries have only the basic and most widely known costume books, plus a few randomly chosen volumes purchased over the years by librarians who might or might not have had any interest at all in costume study. On the other hand, big city library systems, like the New York Public Library and the Enoch Pratt Free Library in Baltimore, maintain comprehensive collections of books on clothing history, construction, fashion, and costume design.

All the resources in a public library are available to people who are taxpayers in that city or town. In addition, there is almost always some provision for people who live in adjacent towns or communities to have full library privileges upon payment of a moderate fee. If you are a visitor, you can always use public library materials on the library premises, although you cannot check them out.

College and University Libraries

Very often the best place to do costume research work is in a college or university library attached to an institution that teaches the theatre arts, especially one that emphasizes theatre design. These libraries always seem to have the widest range of books on their shelves, from standard surveys such as Lucy Barton's *Costumes for the Theatre* to quite specialized volumes like *The Quaker: A Study in Costume* by Amelia Mott Gummere and *Men's Costume 1750-1800* by Zillah Halls. And they usually purchase new books in the field as they appear on the publishers' lists. Sometimes costume books are conveniently housed in a fine arts library building and occasionally there is even a separate theatre library.

College and university libraries are primarily intended for that institution's students and faculty. Most, however, do allow circulation privileges to professional people who are living or visiting in the area and engaged in specific research projects. All you usually have to do to receive these privileges is present yourself to the proper library administration person with identification and an explanation of your work. Sometimes a fee is requested, sometimes not.

Research Libraries

A research library usually has a collection of materials limited to a single field or area of study. The collection, because of its specialization, may be much more extensive than any single subject area you can find in a comprehensive library.

Museums operate research libraries that are particularly good places for costume research work. There is a wealth of clothing information in the research library at the Smithsonian Institution in Washington, D.C., for example, and an excellent library that specializes in research materials related to the history and culture of Native American Indians is operated by the Hey Foundation Museum in New York City.

Access to research libraries is often limited, and the rules governing access vary from place to place. Always phone ahead to find out exactly what the rules are. Research library materials almost never circulate and, if they are heavily used, you may need to make an appointment well in advance of your visit. On those occasions when you need special research materials, a trip to a research library can be well worth the extra planning.

Books and What Else?

In order to take full advantage of your local library, you need to know exactly what materials and services it offers. Large public and university libraries house books, serials (including magazines and newspapers), documents, manuscripts, pamphlets, pictures, clippings, films, and maps. Small libraries have books and a selection of the other things. All libraries can provide you with a brochure listing what they have and what they can do.

Library materials are classified by author, title, and subject, either in the main card catalogue or in individual guides to specific areas. Multiple classifications allow for a great deal of flexibility in what information you must know in order to find what you need.

A special service of many big city libraries is the ready reference division, a group of specially trained librarians who can give you certain kinds of information by phone. Who wrote *The Moon is Blue?* What year did Henry VIII officially create the Church of England? What is the correct mailing address and telephone number for Western Costume Company in Hollywood, California?

The Card Catalogue

The card catalogue is usually kept in banks of small filing drawers located near the main library entrance. The drawers contain individual reference cards, cross-indexed under author, title, and subject (or subjects) for all books, manuscripts, pamphlets, theses, and dissertations in the library.

The author card for each book is its main entry and gives the most complete information. Author's names are filed alphabetically with the last name first: Barton, Lucy. Title cards are filed alphabetically using the first word of the title but disregarding A, An, or The. If the book covers several subjects, there will be a subject card for each, filed, of course, alphabetically: *Costume—Roman, 1st C. A.D.* and *Roman—Costume, 1st C. A.D.*

The two most popular library classification systems are the Dewey Decimal System and the Library of Congress System. You will probably encounter the Dewey Decimal System in public libraries and the Library of Congress System in college and university libraries. (Research libraries may use the Library of Congress System or a private system of their own devising.)

Classification systems allow librarians to group books of like subject matter together and to assign each one a specific place within the system which determines where it will be shelved.

Each book has its own set of call numbers, also called identification numbers. Call numbers are placed in the upper left hand corner of the catalogue card and on the outside (usually on the spine) of the book. Call numbers are composed of two symbols. The top symbol is called the *class mark* and it identifies the specific classification group into which the book's subject matter places it. Below the class mark is the *author mark*, which usually includes the author's initial, and indicates where the book belongs within its classification group.

Here is an example of a Library of Congress System set of call numbers, with each portion explained:

A Handbook of Costume
   by Janet Arnold
   GT
   510
   .A75

class mark: GT
          510

   GT—the portion of the class mark that is the standard classification for all books in this subject area within the Library of Congress System

   510—refers to the general shelf area where this book is placed in this particular library

author mark: .A75

   A—Miss Arnold's initial

   75—indicates the exact place where this book is placed within its subject classification section in this particular library

Here are catalogue cards for Michael and Ariane Batterberry's *Mirror, Mirror; A Social History of Fashion*. One is a Dewey Decimal card from the Dallas Public Library and the other is a Library of Congress card from the Southern Methodist University Library. Notice how much information is available to you on the Library of Congress author card.

The "q" at the top of the identification number tells you the book is oversized (a quarto) and that it will be shelved in a portion of the stacks reserved for large books. From the notation at the bottom of the identification number you discover that the book is part of the library's Marcus Collection. Items 1 and 2 (Costume—History and Fashion—History.) are the Library of Congress subject headings under which this book will be catalogued. The acquisition date is at the bottom of the card and the book's Library of Congress number is in the bottom right hand corner.

```
q
GT 511        Batterberry, Michael
  .B37          Mirror, mirror: a social history of
MARCUS        fashion / Michael & Ariane
COLL.         Batterberry.  1st ed.  New York: Holt,
              Rinehart and Winston, c1977.

                400 p. : ill. ; 32 cm.
                "A Chanticleer Press edition."
                Bibliography: p. 392-393.
                Includes index.

                  1.  Costume--History.  2.  Fashion--
              History.  I.  Batterberry, Ariane
              Ruskin, joint author   II.  Title

TxDaM         26 SEP  78                 77-71372
```

FIGURE 3-7.
Library of Congress
System Catalogue Card.

```
              Costume - History

391
B3222         Batterberry, Michael
                Mirror, Mirror; a social history of fashion
              by  Michael and Ariane Batterberry.  1st ed.
              New York, Holt, Rinehart and Winston, c1977.
                400 p.  illus. (some col.)

                Bibliography: pp. 392-3.
                Includes index.
```

FIGURE 3-8.
Dewey Decimal
System Catalogue Card.

Open and Closed Stacks

After you have consulted the card catalogue and found the call numbers for the books you want, the job of finding them on the shelves may be up to you or it may be up to a library employee.

If the library has *open stacks,* you proceed into the shelving area to do your own looking. Most libraries have location charts to help guide you to the proper section. Shelf units are clearly marked and, of course, each book has its call number clearly visible. Open stack libraries are a great boon to costume designers because you can browse through everything in that section and sometimes find useful and interesting books you overlooked in the card catalogue.

In a *closed stack* library, however, you must give the call numbers for the books you want to a library employee whose job it is to get them for you from the shelves. This system is fine if you know exactly what you want but it does not offer you the opportunity to browse, except, of course, through the catalogue cards. Because some closed stack libraries do allow serious researchers into their stacks under certain, specified conditions, you should always find out if your work makes you eligible for a stack pass.

If you must wait while books are being found and brought to you, remember that it usually takes ten or fifteen minutes for them to make the trip. Bring along a sketchpad or something to read so the waiting won't grow tedious.

Finding Books Not in the Library

Sometimes you can't find what you need in your library. Don't despair. Libraries also have excellent resources for finding out about books they don't have on their shelves. Once you know the author, title, and publisher of the book that will answer your questions, you may be able to buy it, borrow it from a friend or colleague, or even from another library. The volumes that help you locate books on specific subjects are kept in the reference section and the following standard resources are available almost everywhere:

1. *Book Review Digest* began publication in 1905. Monthly. An index to reviews of current fiction and nonfiction books published in the U.S. To be included, a nonfiction book must have had two or more reviews in a selected list of journals.

2. *Publisher's Weekly* is a listing of books as they are published in the U.S.

3. *Books in Print* appears in three versions: *Authors, Titles, Subjects.* All books in print in the U.S. are listed. (*Books in Print* for England and Canada are also usually available.)

The following reference works can be particularly helpful for looking up older books and ones no longer in print.

4. *The Cumulative Book Index*—books published in the English language from 1957 until the present.

5. *The United States Catalogue*—books published in the U.S., including many published in England and imported by American and Canadian firms—from 1898-1928.

6. *Cumulations of the Cumulative Book Index* (issued as supplements to the United States Catalogue)—books published in the U.S. from 1928-1956.

7. *American Catalogue of Books*—books published between 1876-1910, mostly American, many English.

8. For books published before 1875, look at the assorted book catalogues listed in the preface of *The United States Catalogue.*

Interlibrary Loan

If you cannot buy the book you need or borrow it from a colleague, you may want to embark on an interlibrary loan. Be warned at the outset that interlibrary loan is not a swift process; it may be anywhere from ten days to a month before you hold the book in your hands. However, if you know well in advance that you are going to need a specific work, the interlibrary loan network might be the answer. For example, as you begin to design the costumes for a production of Jack Heifner's *Vanities,* you might find it very helpful to get a copy of the 1968 Southern Methodist University Annual through interlibrary loan and see what those co-eds really wore.

Interlibrary loans are facilitated if you can give your own librarian as much information as possible about the book you need. Be sure you

FIGURE 3-9. Eda Zahl, Shellie Chancellor, and Elaine Hausman as the three Texas cheerleaders from Jack Heifner's *Vanities* at the Milwaukee Repertory Theater. *Costume design by Ellen Kozak. Photograph courtesy of the Milwaukee Repertory Theater.*

have a complete citation: title, edition, author, publisher, and date of publication. You will save even more time if you already know which library has the book; you may be able to find out this information by calling your state library (usually located in the state capitol) catalogue or the catalogue at the central headquarters of the state university library system. If, however, the book is quite rare and not listed in either of these central catalogues, you will have to rely on your librarian's special skills to find the book for you, and the wait will be longer.

Here are some things you should know about interlibrary loans:

1. Loans are made from one library to another and *not* to an individual. Therefore you must be eligible to use the library through which you make the request. Most college and university libraries will only undertake interlibrary loans for their own faculty members and graduate students.

2. Sometimes the library loaning the book will stipulate that the book not leave the library to which it is being loaned, in which case you will have to do your work in the library.

3. Lending is restricted to items not easily procurable elsewhere, is limited to one or two items, and excludes rare books or potentially perishable materials.

4. The period of the loan is usually ten days to two weeks, and the borrowing individual (not the borrowing library!) is liable for all shipping charges to and from.

A more recent alternative to interlibrary loan is photocopying. After you have located the book you need at a distant library, you can often have that library photocopy the portions necessary for your work. Most libraries offer photocopying services, and the cost may well be less than the shipping charges you would incur in interlibrary loan. Your own reference librarian can make photocopying arrangements for you.

Periodicals

Periodicals are particularly valuable resources for costume designers because so many are devoted to fashion, lifestyle, and the daily activities of ordinary people. Within this century, *Look* and *Life*, with their predominantly picture format, are endlessly useful. Other periodicals that designers turn to again and again are: *Vogue, Town and Country, The Tatler, Punch, Harper's Bazaar,* and *The National Geographic.*

The points of view expressed in periodicals are contemporary, more up-to-date, and less contemplative than those in books. They are of particular interest to costume designers whose search is for the peculiar essence of a period rather than for a generalization. A photograph in a 1942 issue of *Life* shows you precisely what one group of women wore to work in a defense plant. Such a picture can be far more informative to your work than a general description of such clothing in a costume history book.

In most libraries, current issues of periodicals are shelved in the reading room while back issues, and magazines no longer publishing, are bound and kept in the stacks. Because they are not easy to replace, periodicals almost never circulate.

The names of the periodicals a library has may be listed in the main card catalogue but a listing of the individual articles which appear in them cannot be found there. There are a number of periodical indexes, each listing the articles in a certain group of magazines. Here are some of the guides that might be of specific interest to you:

1. *Art Index*—Quarterly with annual and biennial cumulations. Began in 1930; indexes over 100 magazines and museum publications in English and foreign languages including *American Fabrics and Fashions, Design Quarterly, Journal of the Warburg and Cortauld Institutes* and *The Textile Museum Quarterly.*

2. *Readers' Guide to Periodical Literature*—monthly. Began in 1900; indexes a wide selection of popular periodicals from *Life* and *Time* to *Opera.*

3. *19th Century Readers' Guide to Periodical Literature*—fifty-one periodicals indexed from 1890-1899.

4. *Humanities Index*—quarterly. From 1974 to present. (From 1907-1974 included in *Social Sciences & Humanities Index.*) Indexes English language periodicals that specialize in: archaeology, classical studies, folklore, history, language and literature, literary and political criticism, performing arts, philosophy, religion and theology.

All periodical guides are cross-indexed under author, title, and subject; the author citation is the most informative listing.

Newspapers, Clippings, and Pictures

There are some occasions when you will want to go to old newspapers to do a bit of research. Maybe you need some information about a playwright who was written up in the N.Y. *Times* a few years ago or want to read the reviews of earlier productions of the play you're designing. Perhaps you're working on a play based on historical events within the past century and are anxious to read first hand, contemporary accounts. Fortunately, many libraries can make old newspapers available to you.

Because newspapers are bulky and printed on highly perishable paper, libraries usually store them on microfilm. When you want to read a specific issue of a newspaper, you have to request the appropriate microfilm strip and read it on the screen of a microfilm machine. Thanks to microfilm, thousands of newsprint pages can be preserved and stored in the same space formerly required by only a few hundred dried and crackling bundles of newsprint.

The only really comprehensive newspaper index is the *New York Times Index,* begun in 1851 and published semi-monthly. The *Times* index is arranged in dictionary form with many cross-references to names and related topics. Events under each main heading are listed chronologically. Reviews are conveniently listed under "Theatre Reviews."

Some libraries maintain clipping and picture files with the materials sorted and stored in envelopes or folders according to subject. Needless to say, this service can be invaluable to costume designers. The Picture Collection of the New York Public Library System on Fifth Avenue is undoubtedly one of the best. You can find pictures and prints on subjects as diverse as Welsh coal miners, debutante parties in the 1950's, and French Army uniforms in the Second World War, and, if you are a New York City resident, you can check out a number of pictures from a subject file and study them in the comfort of your own work room.

Other libraries across the country have clipping and picture files, more or less extensive depending upon the interest they have in doing the work necessary to maintain them, but it's doubtful you will find one anywhere that holds a candle to the Picture Collection at the New York Public.

Museums

It is sad indeed that visits to museums play such a small role in actual, day-to-day costume research. The schedules under which costume designers normally work make it impossible for them to find the time to travel all the way across town, or into the city, to examine a few paintings, a piece or two of sculpture, or some original garments. It's much easier, and certainly quicker, to study pictures of these items in books and to rely on the expertise of art and clothing historians who have prepared the explanatory texts.

Yet there is no comparison between the impact of a medieval tapestry hanging on the wall of the Metropolitan Museum in New York and even the finest photograph of it. One is alive with color and texture, rich in detail; the other is flat, usually shiny and by nature diagrammatic. No doubt the photograph will give you enough information to design an accurate period costume, but a look at the real thing may inspire you to add subtle touches that will enrich your design immeasurably.

And, of course, there is no way you can really understand how a late nineteenth-century corset manipulates and shapes the body until you have examined one with your own eyes and hands. Even Norah Waugh's excellent *Corsets and Crinolines* cannot give you all the details you can discover in hands-on study.

Learn to make the time to visit museums a necessary part of your working life, sometimes to research a specific costume piece (corsets, armor plate, beadwork, uniforms), and sometimes for the simple enrichment of your own sensibilities. Go to art museums and to museums of natural history and don't ignore small town historical museums and specialized collections maintained by industries and fraternal organizations.

Where to Look

Before you set off on holiday travel, take a look at *The Official Museum Directory* in your library's reference room. This wonderful book lists museums in the United States by states and by cities, gives you addresses, phone numbers, hours, admission charges, and descriptions of what you will find on display. If, for example, your camping trip takes you through the small town of Shelby, Montana, the *Directory* can tell you about the Marias Museum of History and Art which has displays of frontier women's clothing, cowboy dress, old sewing machines, and barber shop equipment.

Look also at Irene Pennington Huenefeld's *International Directory of Historical Clothing*. This helpful book can supply you with the information that The Charlestown Museum in Charleston, South Carolina has a collection of old jockey jackets, that the Museum of History and Industry in Seattle has a display of nurses uniforms from many periods, and that the Nutley Historical Society Museum in Nutley, New Jersey has Red Cross uniforms.

Should your vacation take you to England, be sure to read Chapter 7 in Janet Arnold's *A Handbook of Costume* which describes eighty-nine costume collections in England, Scotland, and Wales. Along with the displays you can expect to find, you will also learn how to make arrangements to see stored items and go equipped with addresses and telephone numbers.

The effect of seeing the real thing is long-lasting. Once you have experienced many original works of art, examined antique dresses and jackets and a variety of accessories, and seen with your own eyes just how big a medieval broadsword really is, the book illustrations you normally turn to for research will have much more life and meaning.

Record and Document Research Information

Every designer ends up with some unique and personal method of recording and organizing sketches and notes. Whatever way you devise, you should develop a storage system that allows you to find the information in the future.

You may choose to record your work on cards. Cards can be conveniently filed, both for current and for future use, in commercially produced filing boxes (plastic, metal, or heavy cardboard), or in child-size shoe boxes. Or you may put your notes and sketches in looseleaf notebooks or in individual folders and store them in shelves or in filing cabinets. Whatever your system is, it is worth the time it takes to organize and label your research.

Include Sources

It is particularly important that you write down your sources. There is nothing more frustrating

than knowing that a book you once consulted for general information on military uniforms contained a detailed description of the way helmet cords were supposed to be worn by generals in the United States Army in 1874 but, because you did not make a note or jot down a citation, you cannot find the information again.

And, as long as you are training yourself to make bibliographic citations, get in the habit of jotting down the facts in an accepted format. This way you will be sure to have all the information you need and you will also have the makings of a valuable costume bibliography that you may someday want to share with others in your profession. Here are some examples:

Bernstein, Aline. *Masterpieces of Women's Costume of the 18th and 19th Centuries*. New York: Crown Publishers, 1959.

Boehn, Max von. *Modes & Manners*. 4 vols in 2. Translated by Joan Joshua. 1932. Reprint. New York: Benjamin Blom, 1971.

Gullbert, Elsa & Paul Astrom. *The Thread of Ariadne: A Study of Ancient Greek Dress*. Studies in Mediterranean Archaeology. Goteborg, 1970.

Garren, Lois Zierk. *A Study in the Process of Aging Theatrical Costumes*. Master's Thesis. University of Virginia, 1978.

Learn to take good notes and, unless you have total recall of research facts, don't rely on your memory. Trace or make quick drawings (paying careful attention to proportion!) of clothing illustrations or, if you prefer, photocopy the appropriate pages. When you trace or draw, make sure to jot down any written facts that are there to help identify and explain the illustration. Make sure to include correct citations and page numbers.

General Historical Background

Your analysis of the script you are designing will give you most of the historical facts you need: dates, locations, climate, political leadership, major political events. An interesting book that can help you to see all these facts in connection with each other is *The Timetables of History: A Horizontal Linkage of People & Events* by Bernard Grun (New York: Simon and Schuster, 1979). In what amounts to a huge, book-length chart, this work presents the concurrent history of man in seven columns:

1. History and Politics
2. Literature and Theatre
3. Religion, Philosophy, and Learning
4. Visual Arts
5. Music
6. Science, Technology and Growth
7. Daily Life.

Locate the year of your play on the left hand side of the page and as you move across you will discover the kings, wars, writers, books, painters, paintings, composers, compositions, inventors, and others who simultaneously affected the course of history.

Before you can get to know your historical characters well enough to dress them, however, you will have to discover your own personal feeling for the time, its mood, rhythm, and peculiar style. You may be able to begin with encyclopedias and historical overviews but then you must turn to social history, popular history and biography, diaries, collections of letters, and even to novels. The following works contain portions that are of particular interest to costume designers. They have been chosen at random in order to give you an idea of the kinds of choices that exist:

Pepys, Samuel. *The Diary of Samuel Pepys*. Covers the years from 1660-1669.

Tuchman, Barbara S. *A Distant Mirror: The Calamitous 14th Century*. New York: Knopf, 1978.

Evelyn, John. *The Diary of John Evelyn*. 2 vols. Editor, William Bray. New York & London: M. Walter Dunne, 1901.

Purefoy, E. & H. *Purefoy Letters 1735-1753*. Letters written by Elizabeth and Henry Purefoy. 2 vols. Editor, G. Eland. London: Widgwick & Jackson, 1931.

Uzanne, Octave. *Fashion in Paris: The Various Phases of Feminine Taste and Aesthetics From the Revolution to the End of the XIXth Century*. Translator, Lady Mary Loyd. London: William Heinemann, 1901.

You can experience different views of life in Victorian England by reading such delightful novels as Jane Austen's *Emma* and *Northanger Abbey,* Elizabeth Gaskell's *North and South,* any number of works by Charles Dickens, and John Fowles' *The French Lieutenant's Woman.*

Primary Sources

For a close look at exactly what folks were wearing at a given time, examine primary resource materials first. Some of your primary source hunting will take you to museums and galleries. Most of the time, however, you will look at pictures of primary sources in books and in magazines. Never rely solely on costume history books in which a single illustrator has redrawn all the clothing. These books are excellent for silhouette recall and early impressions but they are not sufficient for specific production research.

What follows is an outline of basic primary sources for clothing, both to look at and to read.

Prehistoric Man
Cave paintings.
Figurines.
Surmise from study of archeological digs, tools, dwelling places, etc.
Surmise from the study of contemporary primitive societies.

Ancient Civilizations
Vase paintings.
Statuary.
Tomb artifacts.
Ancient texts: records and lists, law codes, letters.
Literature, mostly myths & legends, including the Bible.
Epics and drama, philosophy, and scientific writings after the fifth century, B.C., in the Greek world.
Wall paintings (very limited in number)

The Dark and Middle Ages in the West
Church statuary.
Religious paintings.
Manuscript illumination.
Tapestries.
Laws (especially sumptuary laws).

Heraldic emblems.
Literature.

Renaissance through Mid-Nineteenth Century
Paintings—the mediocre painter is often better for detail than the famous painter, perhaps because he has less imagination and tends more often to paint exactly what he sees, wrinkles and all.
Sculpture.
Drawings and etchings.
Dolls, after the late sixteenth century. Watch the proportions as they are not always accurate for people.
Extant clothing—Use with care. Extant garments are not usually the most typical garments of their age. Always ask why they still exist: Out of sentiment, because they were worn at a special occasion like a wedding or a funeral? Because they were never successful, didn't fit, or weren't becoming? Because they were too complicated to alter or remake? You can be sure that the favorite and most common garments from another age, worn daily, wore out ages ago.
Diaries.
Letters.
Fiction.
Travelogues.
Wills.
Household inventories.

After Mid-Nineteenth Century, Add
Photographs—not truly representative of ordinary dress until family box cameras become available and casual snapshots appear.
Fashion magazines.

In the Twentieth Century, Add
Newspaper and popular magazine photographs. Television and motion pictures.

Reliable Costume History Books

The more costume research you do, the more discrepancies you will discover. Sometimes it seems as though there are as many different ideas and interpretations as there are costume historians. Don't let yourself be confused or discouraged by conflicting names, dates, or details. Keep on looking and reading and eventually you will decide who to rely on and what to believe.

Here are a few costume history reference books which are considered particularly reliable. The list is certainly not inclusive.

Arnold, Janet. *A Handbook of Costume*. London: MacMillan, 1973.

Boucher, Francois. *20,000 Years of Fashion*. New York: H.N. Abrams, 1967.

Davenport, Milia. *The Book of Costume*. New York: Crown Publishers, 1948.

Cunnington, C. Willett, Phillis Cunnington & Charles Beard. *A Dictionary of English Costume*. London: Adam and Charles Black, 1960.

Waugh, Norah. *The Cut of Men's Clothes, 1600-1900*. New York: Theatre Arts Books, 1964.

Waugh, Norah. *The Cut of Women's Clothes, 1600-1930*. London: Faber & Faber, 1968.

Waugh, Norah. *Corsets & Crinolines*. New York: Theatre Arts Books, 1954.

Also, the *Handbook of English Costume* series by C. Willett and Phillis E. Cunnington with volumes for the sixteenth, seventeenth, eighteenth, nineteenth, and twentieth centuries.

FIGURE 3-10. Designs by Michael J. Cesario for the Alley Theatre's production of *The Importance of Being Earnest* with inspiration from the work of Charles Dana Gibson. Figures rendered with pencil, watercolor, ballpoint pen, and felt pen on charcoal paper; cut out and mounted on board. *Photograph by Frances Aronson.*

FIGURES 3-11 and 3-12. Two scenes from the Hartford Stage Company's production of Shakespeare's *Antony and Cleopatra. Set and costume design by John Conklin, inspired by the paintings of Tiepolo. Photographs courtesy of the Hartford Stage Company.*

Costume Research is Everywhere

Libraries and museums are not the only places you will go to research clothing for plays. Contemporary costume research may take you out into the streets to look for sources, to specific neighborhoods, parks, or shops. Costume designers have been known to spend an afternoon drinking hot chocolate in a ski lodge in order to see what people wear on and off the slopes or to visit a hospital to look at the latest nurses' uniforms.

Make it a habit always to see what the people around you are wearing whether you are at a family picnic or in the supermarket. Much of what you see in real life is far too bizarre and unbelievable for the stage but you will also collect wonderful ideas for future use.

Researching very specific costume pieces can lead you on merry chases. Religious vestments—and the correct ways of wearing them—are the subjects of many costume searches. If all the books you can find on the subject fail you—and they often will with ecclesiastical dress—call a church of the correct denomination, a theology school, or denominational headquarters to ask for help. You will usually get it.

Contact the Police Department for facts about police uniforms and the Fire Department for information about firemen's uniforms. Both agencies usually have photographs and descriptions of past as well as present uniforms. Occasionally you may even run into a fireman or a policeman who has an old uniform you can borrow.

Other places where you might be able to solve particular costume problems are foreign embassies, consulates, the headquarters of a fraternal organization, or a fox hunting club. For details about old military uniforms get in touch with the Society of Military Historians and Collectors and for current uniform regulations go to the appropriate military recruiting office.

The classified pages of your telephone book contain dozens of links between you and the answers to your most baffling research questions. Make full use of this resource.

The only things that can obstruct your ability to solve all your costume research problems are lapses in energy and imagination. If you cultivate· persistance, strong legs for walking, a keen eye for seeing, and a stout finger for dialing, you'll come up with an answer every time.

Painters for Research

A list of painters whose work is particularly useful for costume research begins on page 228. It is not an exhaustive list, but one that can help get you off to a good start.

4
Preliminary Sketching And Color Layout

By now you are well acquainted with the script. You have talked with the director and know how he feels about the play. You have settled on the exact historical period in which the play will be done. You have probably chatted with the scene designer and, if you are lucky, you have a cast list. You have a pile of research notes and a pad of research drawings. Now you are ready for the most exciting part of your work. It's time to go to the drawing board and sketch costumes.

Preliminary Sketching

Preliminary sketching, or idea sketching, serves the costume designer in two ways. First, the sketches will be your initial means of visual communication with the director. From them the director will be able to see what you want the costumes to look like. Second, but even more important to you, it is through the preliminary sketching process that most designers discover for themselves what the costumes are going to look like.

Only rarely do costume designers conjure up complete, detailed costumes in the mind and then represent them on paper. The mind is more apt to visualize fragments, bits and pieces, that illuminate character perceptions. Or it may create large inclusive images that reflect the play's mood or overall rhythm. You may have a notion that the sleeves should be long and flowing; you may see small pearl buttons down the center front; you may know that the skirt must trail on the ground. Then, when you have your pencil on the drawing paper, the individual images and notions come together into a design.

There is a great deal to discover about a script before you sit down to draw, but you should never put off sketching until you have designed everything in your head. That wait may well be in vain. The process of sketching *is* the process of designing. A sketch is not an illustration of a design, it *is* a design.

69

Drawing

Paintings are but research and experiment. I never do a painting as a work of art. All of them are searches. I search constantly... .

PICASSO
to Alexander Liberman

Designers who draw easily and quickly and without any gnashing of teeth seem to those for whom drawing is laborious and slow to be particularly blessed. It is probably safe to say, however, that most costume designers, no matter how well they draw, would like to draw better than they do, not just to have their sketches look better but to facilitate the design process itself. Everyone becomes frustrated with a head full of exc iting ideas and images and hands that are not facile enough to combine and communicate them on paper.

This is not to suggest, however, that a costume sketch, either in its preliminary or its finished state, is the end product of the designer's work. (Whether or not the sketch is a work of art is absolutely beside the point.) A good costume sketch is a road map leading to the costume that will eventually be cut and stitched and worn by an actor on the stage. The costume will be judged to be successful or unsuccessful, not the sketch.

Yet, the road map is important, particularly if it suggests the quality of the landscape as well as describing the route to be taken. A satisfactory rough sketch usually indicates that the designer is well prepared both with facts and with evocative design images. Good preliminary sketching will, more often than not, lead the way to clear, direct final sketches and successful costumes.

The ability to draw with some modest degree of skill is essential for all costume designers. Fortunately, basic drawing skills are not gifts from the gods; almost everyone can learn to draw well enough to communicate visual ideas. Betty Edwards, in *Drawing on the Right Side of the Brain*, says:

...drawing is a skill that can be learned by every normal person with average eyesight and average eye-hand coordination—with sufficient ability, for example, to thread a needle or catch a baseball. Contrary to popular opinion, manual skill is not a primary factor in drawing. If your handwriting is readable, or if you can print legibly, you have ample dexterity to draw well.

Drawing People

Though the ability to draw people did not come easily to me, with constant and continual observation it did come.

PAUL HOGARTH
Drawing People

Everybody believes that drawing people is more difficult than drawing anything else, be it houses, horses, boats, books, cats, or canaries. Whether or not this belief is technically true is of no real importance since the conviction that it is true saddles most people, costume designers included, with a huge mental block when it comes to sketching human figures. Since virtually all clothing requires a body to hold it up and out and since costume designers must face the prospect of drawing bodies every time they pick up a pencil, this is one block that should be worked through as quickly as possible.

People who have successfully learned to draw know that the eye is more important to the process than the hand. What you see is what you draw. In the quote at the beginning of this section, Paul Hogarth attributes his success with drawing people to "continual observation" and not to continual drawing, although it is certain that he sketched what he observed. Training your eyes to see accurately, in correct relationships and proportions, is at the heart of learning to draw.

You can practice seeing on your own. Your brain is already alerted to keep your eyes on the lookout for interesting garments and combinations of garments as you wander the aisles of your supermarket. Decide to observe human figures as well. Look at bodies as groups of relative parts which relate to each other in fairly predictable ways. For instance, about half way down the length of most bodies, the single column divides into two legs. Most elbows, when the arms are hanging straight down, are near the waistline.The corner of the eye and the join of the ear to the head are about on a line with each other (which is what makes it possible for us to wear corrective curved lenses with a minimum of distortion). Shoulders are usually wider than hips.

When you are alone, ask yourself if you can close your eyes and see how long most arms are in relationship to upper legs, how much head most people have above and below the eyes, and what are the relative lengths of the five fingers. If you discover you cannot see these human proportion details in your mind's eye, go look at people or at yourself in the mirror.

Everyone who is actively involved in learning to draw the human figure should work to become acutely aware of his or her own body and its proportions. This is not the time to view one's own body critically—My hips are *too* big!—but analytically instead—Look how my hip joint moves both up and out when I shift my weight to that leg. Your goal is not to *define* your body, as you might do by memorizing the bones and muscles and the physiology of motion in an anatomy class, but to *see* it fully and completely, so fully and completely that you can reproduce what you have seen in a mental image and onto a sheet of drawing paper.

Some designers are so in tune with the shape and proportions of their own bodies that they tend to draw their own figures over and over again as models for their costumes. It is a good idea to guard against this propensity because altering garment proportions for individual actors is an important part of the costume design process. Get in the habit of *seeing* an actor's body

quickly and proportionately. Try to indicate outstanding differences from what we consider to be the norm (extremely long legs, short waist, no neck, narrow sloping shoulders) even in the earliest sketches. Eventually the costume will have to take all physical attributes into account, and it is well not to wait until you get to the fitting room to begin to tackle proportion problems. If time permits, some designers like to visit a few early rehearsals and make quick sketches of the actors as they work.

If your emphasis is on training the eye to see more completely, all drawing practice brings improvement. Most costume designers draw regularly in the day to day performance of their work. Many, in addition, draw on their own for pleasure, and others enjoy the stimulation of attending figure drawing classes. A surprising number of designers in New York take advantage of the modestly priced drawing classes at the Art Students' League.

The better you see bodies, the better you will see clothes and the more apt you will be to create costumes that fall or curve correctly and enhance the peculiar qualities of the human figure at rest or in motion.

Stock Figures

There are designers for whom drawing the human figure is so stressful that it robs them of the freedom to concentrate on costumes at all. These designers usually *see* the figure quite adequately and can use what they see to inform their designs, but they cannot rid themselves of the block that prevents them from drawing bodies with ease.

Designers who cannot face sketching a new figure under each costume often use stock figures which they may have drawn previously or copied from other sources. It's fairly easy to change the basic positions of stock figures and you can, to some degree, alter proportions to reflect individual actors. With the aid of tracing papers, graphite or colored transfer paper, or a tracing table, you can reproduce the stock figure on your drawing paper and get on with sketching the costume.

Designers who use stock figures often keep a collection of figures in interesting poses which they have clipped from magazines and newspapers. Different periods require different poses, and some costumes rely on particular poses in order to be seen to the best advantage. A bustle dress, for example, demands a profile or three-quarter view so the bustle portion is visible. You can save time by having a good selection of possibilities available.

Figures 4–1 and 4–2 are normally proportioned male and female figures in poses that are useful for displaying some kinds of clothing. Similar figures are readily available in fashion design and figure drawing books.

FIGURE 4-1. Sketch of a male figure.

FIGURE 4-2. Sketch of a female figure.

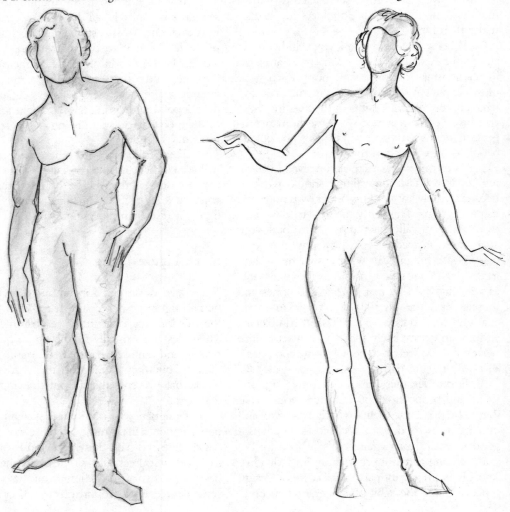

Successful Preliminary Sketching

In order to communicate visual design ideas to a director, the preliminary sketch must show period line, accurate proportion, and appropriate detail.

FIGURE 4-3. Rough sketch on tracing paper by Andrew B. Marlay for the Pennsylvania Stage Company production of *Count Dracula. Photograph by Frances Aronson.*

LINE

A good rough sketch catches the correct period and character line with firmness and authority. The costume should not translate to the director as "sorta high-waisted" or "kinda drop-shouldered." A successful sketch makes its statement as simply and as directly as possible: This is the waistline. The puffed sleeves are that high. There is where the jacket hem is.

PROPORTION

In a discussion of costume it is almost impossible to consider line and proportion separately. The line of a garment is usually inextricably related to its proportion. The Empire line, for instance, is created by the relationship between bodice and skirt; a very short bodice, ending high above the natural waist, and a long, slim skirt. If you change this particular proportion between bodice and skirt, you change the period line. A good rough sketch indicates proportion without ambiguity, sleeves in relation to body, lapels in relation to shoulder width, etc.

Along with correct proportion within the garment, the rough sketch should also reflect correct body proportions, both for the actor (if the actor is known) and for the character (no willowy Falstaffs, please!).

DETAIL

Both period and character will demand some surface detail on most costumes: striped or printed fabric, slashing, puffing, ruching, gathering, pleating, beads, bracelets, pins, hats, handbags, or swords. The rough sketch is not the place for specific details of this nature since the work is still in a preliminary stage and may change—but it is the place to suggest the necessity for detail. This area will be a brocade of some sort; there will be some kind of decoration at the neck; she will need a big hat, perhaps with feathers. Suggest these details as simply and as clearly as possible. If they are worked into the design from the beginning, there will be no chance that they will look "tacked-on" later.

If your sketch gives this information, you can be reasonably sure you know the play, the period, and the characters and can communicate your ideas to the director.

FIGURES 4-4 and 4-5. Rough sketch and finished sketch for Elizabeth in *Pink Thunderbird*, designed by Michael J. Cesario for the McCarter Theatre. The rough sketch (above left) was done with colored pencil on bond paper. The finished sketch (right) was rendered with colored pencils and watercolor on illustration board. *Photographs by Frances Aronson.*

FIGURES 4-6 and 4-7. Rough and finished sketches for *Lion in Winter* by Arnold S. Levine. The rough sketch (below left) done on bond paper with pencil. The finished sketch (right) is watercolor wash and felt-tip marker details on illustration board. *Photographs by Frances Aronson.*

Pencil and Paper

While you are in this stage your sketches should be expendable. It should not cause you pain to crumple one up and toss it in a wastebasket, or erase it, if the images and the ideas are not working. It is seldom productive to labor unduly over a preliminary sketch. In order to encourage yourself to work freely and toss without regret, use simple, inexpensive materials for the early work.

An ordinary drawing pencil is the most versatile and expressive drawing tool available to you; it is almost always the preferred medium for preliminary sketches. Pencil lines are easy to erase and there is something about the character of pencil sketches that makes them seem far less permanent and intimidating than, say, ink sketches.

The most common papers for preliminary sketches are newsprint, butcher paper, layout or inexpensive drawing or tracing paper. All of these, except drawing paper, are available on rolls as well as in pads. None is particularly costly; newsprint is the cheapest and tracing paper is the most expensive. (Tracing vellum is quite expensive and not the best choice for rough sketches.) Layout paper is especially versatile since it is available in a wide variety of weights and surfaces, is very white, very stout and, in most weights, can be used for tracing as well as for direct drawing.

To avoid the necessity of transferring or redrawing a sketch later, some designers do their preliminaries in a light pencil line directly on the finished sketch surface, usually watercolor paper or illustration board. Lines can be erased and changes made as the work progresses. Designers who work this way generally have a good deal of confidence in their way of working and often have some prior experience with the director.

FIGURE 4-8. Inexpensive paper for preliminary sketching. *Photograph by Colleen Muscha.*

The Whole and Its Parts

*...the appearance of any element depends on its place
and function in the pattern of the whole.*

RUDOLPH ARNHEIM
Art and Visual Perception

At no point in the costume design process can a
designer afford to concentrate solely on a single
element to the exclusion of the others. Each part
of a costume must relate to the whole ensemble,
and each costume must relate to all the others on
the stage. Scenery, lighting, the color of the
actor's complexion, and the size and configuration of the stage all make specific demands on
costume design. The most basic problem a costume designer faces is how to do everything at
once.

Very often when you sit down to begin
preliminary sketching, it is difficult to assimilate
all the discoveries and demands your script work,
conferences, and research have showered upon
you. A mountain of detail stands between you
and your drawing paper, and it is difficult to
imagine how everything you know can be translated into shirts and pants, dresses and hats.

This is the time to take a good deep breath,
turn on some appropriate music, refill your coffee
cup or glass of lemonade, and reflect on your
earliest responses to the play, including initial
production ideas. Recall your emotional response
as well as your intellectual response. Allow the
mountain of details to subside into your sense of
the whole. Don't worry about forgetting specifics because you won't. Simply allow all the details
to become part of the whole play. Breathe some
more and then begin to sketch.

THUMBNAIL SKETCHES

Some designers find it easier to maintain a sense
of the whole play by executing their preliminary
sketches in small scale, several to a page. These
are often called thumbnail sketches. Thumbnails
may be four to six inch figures and they are
usually grouped as they relate to each other in the
play, making it easy to see at a glance how the
costume shapes will interact.

FIGURE 4-9. Thumbnail
sketches for Shakespeare's
Merchant of Venice done by
Rosemary Ingham. Colored
pencils and drawing pen on
layout paper. *Photograph by
Frances Aronson.*

Laying out several thumbnail sketches on a single sheet of paper will also make it possible for you to work on several costumes at once, first roughing in silhouettes, then adding details. Large cuffs on one gentleman's doublet may effect some bit of decoration on the lady. A striped fabric here may demand a solid surface there.

If your preliminary work is done in the same scale as the finished sketches, make it a practice to arrange the sketches around your work space so you can keep a sense of the whole as you draw. A large pin-up board adjacent to your drawing table is very convenient.

Experiment with different approaches to preliminary sketching but always make sure that you are not designing individual costumes in isolation from all the others.

The Element of Color

In a working situation, choosing costume color does not necessarily follow sketching. In all likelihood the creation of color and of shapes will move along at the same time and, in some instances, color will be chosen well before the sketching begins. It is only the demands of written organization that cause a discussion of color to follow a discussion of sketching, not a suggestion that the work be done in this order.

Many costume designers lay out a basic palette that reflects their response to the play as a whole before choosing which of the colors will be worn by which character. Others may pick out appropriate colors for leading characters and assemble a general palette for the secondary group, or groups.

A color layout, separate from costume sketches, shown to the director in the early stages of the work, can provoke especially good conversation about the play. It is always exciting to see how sensitively a play can be illuminated by color alone, how clearly forces can be opposed, lovers united, and resolutions sustained.

Although there is not space in this book for a lengthy discussion of color, the following few pages will review some basic color concepts and offer a few hints for good color use. Always remember, however, that your own personal feeling for color harmony should be your guiding principle. If you follow some of the rules you may escape choosing really awful colors but selecting distinguished color is entirely up to your own sensibilities and cannot be achieved through any prescription whatsoever.

Color and Color Perception

Color is an effect caused by the reflection of certain rays of light.

JOHN L. KING
The Art of Using Color

A detailed explanation of what color is and how it is perceived involves the sciences of physics, chemistry, and psychology and is far beyond the scope of this work. Yet it is important to convey some sense of the subject's complexity in order to suggest how potentially powerful color is. When the human eye looks at a brilliant yellow jonquil, the process by which the color is experienced involves several neurophysiological processes. Many parts of the body are affected. Minute but measurable changes occur in heart rate, respiration, and skin temperature, changes that must, it seems on reflection, contribute significantly to the simple pleasure experienced by the conscious mind when it sees a pretty yellow flower. Color indisputably involves us from head to toe.

And yet the jonquil is not even yellow. The yellow that you perceive the jonquil to be is merely a property of the light which shines on the blossom. You see yellow because of the way in which light hits the object's surface and because of the particular ability of your brain to perceive the event.

What you call light is produced by a tiny part of the electromagnetic field called the visible spectrum. Color is a natural part of the visible spectrum—a fact that Sir Isaac Newton demonstrated around 1666—and is created when light is broken down into electromagnetic vibrations, or waves, of different lengths. These wavelengths, when refracted or bent by the glass in a prism, arrange themselves into a series of colors determined by length: indigo, blue, green, yellow, orange, and red. The longest wavelength creates red, the shortest indigo. If these color wavelengths are recombined—which Newton also demonstrated—they become white light again.

The color effect occurs when light encounters a surface. The molecules that make up the surface absorb some of the wavelengths from the light and reflect others. The color you perceive is reflected wavelengths. If the surface absorbs all of the wavelengths, it is perceived as black.

Color Response

Like the notes of the basic scale when expanded into a symphony, color has seemingly unlimited variation and enormous capacity to manipulate our emotions. It is therefore one of the most powerful tools of the designer.

> MARJORIE ELLIOTT BEVLIN
> *Design Through Discovery*

If color is a natural part of all light, and human perception of color affects a significant portion of your physiological being, it is not surprising that people respond more intensely to color than they do to any other design element. Language often gives us away. Visitors to modern art galleries speak of having been "assaulted by color." Most people have colors they "love" and colors they "hate" and would agree that all human moods are to some degree affected by surrounding color.

People respond to color in many complex and interdependent ways. The society in which you live conditions you to some color responses; laws, customs, or traditions handed down from the past provide others. Associations with a specific group of people provide you with color responses you share with members of that group, and purely personal associations will inform your individual feelings about color. There is even recent investigation that suggests some color response may be purely physiological, acting directly on the nervous system without any cognition whatsoever.

Some of the following color examples fit into a single response category while others seem to overlap and involve two or more responses. In all of them you can sense the powerful role color plays in human life.

TRAFFIC LIGHT RESPONSE

As children you learn to walk across the street when you see a green light and stop when you see a red light. It is the law. In a short time the conscious concept of law is forgotten, and you and your neighbors respond directly to color as you walk on green and stop on red.

ROYALTY RESPONSE

Purple is the color of kings, and it is a rare child that doesn't give the coloring book king a royal purple robe. Once upon a time the color purple, which was then derived from a shellfish known as Murex and was very costly, was, by law, forbidden to anyone but the emperor. You don't necessarily have to know the fact in order to possess the association.

LOVE RESPONSE

Your favorite grandmother often let you make cookies with her and, to protect your dress, would wrap you in a peach-colored bib apron. Those were the happiest times. Now, grown up, whenever you are shopping for clothes, your eyes automatically fall on peach-colored garments, your favorite color.

RED AND BLUE RESPONSES

Without having any notion why, you participate to some degree in the general tendency of this culture to associate the color red with danger, blood, fire, energy, and passion; the color blue is associated with virginity, hope, and truth. Polls state that the favorite color of the vast majority of Americans of both sexes and all ages is blue. In a related response, it has been demonstrated that a person driving an automobile in traffic will feel a much stronger urge to pass a red car than a blue car, whatever make, model, or size the car might be.

OTHER RESPONSES

People's appetites are increased in rooms where there is a great deal of orange. Agitated prisoners or hyperactive mental patients calm down in rooms where the color green predominates. Totally blind children can identify rooms that are identical in size and shape and differentiated only by one having red walls, one blue walls, and one yellow walls.

Color Response in Design

Costume designers employ general color response in order to communicate obvious information: the villain wears a black hat, the hero dons a white hat, the turncoat has a green vest on, and the adulterous woman wears a red dress. And if you are looking for more subtle communication, which is usually the case, you can apply the same color dynamic by introducing touches of the appropriate associative color: a bit of blue on a virtuous maiden's blouse or a warm brown shawl on lovable Aunt Emily. In most instances you will discover that you have chosen the psychologically correct color without conscious thought, simply because your own responses are in tune with those of your society.

It is very important, as you work with color in design, to study and explore your personal responses to hues and harmonies. Discover what excites you and use these combinations to build a personal aesthetic.

Never stop looking for new color experiences to feed your sensibilities. Collect prints and advertising layouts and photographs whose color has a strong effect on you. Visit museums just to look at color. Enjoy your ability to be surprised by new ways of using color and encourage your sensibilities to be challenged and stretched by what you see. The more sensitive you are to color, the better able you will be to affect an audience with your use of it.

Color Properties

Sometimes it seems as though there are too many colors in the world. If you look around you right now, in any direction, you will see dozens of discernible colors. The vast array of colors you meet each time you enter a fabric store may seem overwhelming. If you purchase a Pantone Color Specifier (a selection of tear-out color chips from Pantone printing inks—an excellent aid for designers) you will be faced by no less than five hundred choices, plus shades and tints. Indeed, it has been estimated that the human eye can perceive one hundred and fifty different colors and two hundred gradations of value within each of them—thirty thousand shades and tints! How, in the midst of such a variously colored world, can a designer choose a palette and compose color in such a way that it is anything but a jumble?

One answer is to begin simply. Understand the basic properties of color. Study a system of primary colors and learn how to mix them. Explore the ways in which colors alter each other in combinations. Adopt a set of terms through which you can describe color relationships to your satisfaction. Then practice using common color schemes until you feel secure enough to strike out on your own.

Color Wheel

When the band of colors that makes up the color spectrum in light is joined end to end, the result is a circle in which one color seems to flow into the next. It was this observation that led to the development of the color wheel to explore these relationships. A number of different color wheels have been devised; perhaps the simplest and most widely used resulted from the work of Herbert E. Ives. It is especially relevant to pigments.

The primary colors in Ives' color wheel are red, blue, and yellow. The theory is that these colors cannot be mixed and that all other colors can be mixed from them. This is true enough in practice to be a useful working theory.

A mixture of two *primaries* will produce a *secondary* color:

1. red + yellow = orange
3. yellow + blue = green
3. red + blue = violet

Mixtures of two *secondaries* produce *tertiary* colors:

1. red + orange = red/orange
2. yellow + green = yellow/green
3. blue + violet = blue/violet
4. yellow + orange = yellow/orange
5. blue + green = blue/green
6. red + violet = red/violet

Developing a color wheel gives you basic assistance in mixing color. More importantly, it provides you with a key to some of the effects colors achieve in combinations.

Colors that lie directly opposite each other on the color wheel are called *complementary* colors. Red and green are complementary; so are yellow and violet, orange and blue. Complementary colors are as different from each other as it is possible to be. They tend, when placed side by side, to intensify each other and are, as a result, quite inharmonious.

One of the most useful ways of toning down a color, however, is by mixing in a bit of that color's complement. An equal mixture of two complements will produce a *neutral* which does not have the characteristics of either.

One of the most mysterious pieces of behavior exhibited by complementaries is the phenomenon of *afterimage*. If you stare at a color intensely for half a minute or so, then look away, you will see an afterimage that is some version of the color's complement. Another attribute of afterimage is that when you place a color on a light neutral background, the neutral will acquire a tinge of the color's complement.

Although basically inharmonious in their pure states, complementary colors exhibit an affinity for each other which cannot be overlooked. Bland soups can often be improved with a touch of salt; bland color layouts sometimes want a dash of complement.

The relationship referred to as *split complements* involves a color and the two colors on either side of its true complement. This would combine, for example, orange with blue/violet and blue/green. Split complements tend to intensify each other and are not, by nature, harmonious.

You can also use the color wheel to explore harmonious color. The simplest route to color harmony in design is *monochromatic* color, the use of a single color with light and dark variations.

FIGURE 4-10. This scheme for creating a palette from pigment primaries was developed by artist and designer Richard Casler.

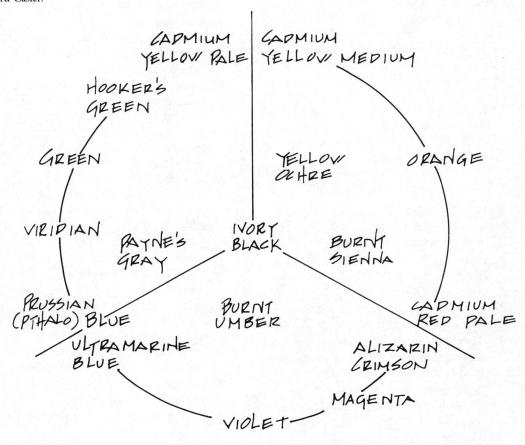

A flexible and varied palette can be developed based on the three pigment primaries, red, blue and yellow. Because the intervals between the three are so great, direct mixing to create the secondary orange, violet, and green shades tends to become muddy. By splitting the primaries, most shades can be clearly and intensely achieved. The three split pairs are as follows:

Cadmium yellow pale
Cadmium yellow medium
Cadmium red pale
Alizarin crimson
Ultramarine blue
Pthalo (Prussian) blue.

The preceding selection will enable the designer to develop a fairly complete high-intensity spectrum of colors. The addition of several low-key earth tones is helpful in simplifying the reduction of intensities:

Yellow ochre
Burnt sienna
Burnt umber
Payne's gray
Ivory black

Also, with today's high-intensity chemical pigments, clear greens (Hooker's green and Viridian) and magentas may need to be added.

The chart shows the interrelationship for mixing these colors on the color wheel.

Analogous harmony joins colors that are next to each other on the color wheel, such as red/violet, violet and blue/violet.

Triad harmony combines any three colors that lie equidistant from each other on the color wheel. The three primaries form a triad and so do the three secondaries. There are two potential tertiary color triads. Triad harmonies are particularly exciting; they often call up memories of children's art and comic book illustration. When triad colors are mixed with each other, however, they form grayish or brownish hues of exceptional muddiness.

Here are a few generalizations concerning the effects colors can have on each other:

1. Dark hues appear weaker on a noncomplementary dark ground and stronger on a complementary dark ground.

2. Light colors appear weaker on a noncomplementary light ground and stronger on a complementary light ground.

3. A bright color against a dull color of the same hue will further deaden the dull color.

4. When a bright color is used against a dull color the contrast will be strongest when the dull color is complementary.

5. Light colors on non complementary light grounds are greatly strengthened if bounded by narrow bands of black or complementary colors.

6. Dark colors on noncomplementary dark grounds can be strengthened if similarly bounded by white or light colors.

Try out the following color schemes for practice. Also, make it a habit to see the color schemes in your favorite paintings, illustrations, and designs.

1. *One color* (single value and intensity), with white, gray, or black.

2. *Monochromatic* is a single hue in all desired tints and shades (with and without white, gray, or black).

3. *Modified monochromatic* is the addition of small touches of bright color in an otherwise monochromatic scheme.

4. *Analogous* colors are related to each other with a common factor. Example: orange, yellow, yellow/green; all contain the common color, yellow.

5. *Analogous with dominant hue* achieve dominance through (a) size of area, (b) its dark value against lighter ground, and (c) its light value against darker ground. The presence of the dominant hue will relieve monotony.

6. *Analogous with complementary accents* consists of the introduction of small but sometimes very intense bits of complementary color which can give surprising life to the whole.

7. *Complementary scheme* is any pleasing scheme which conspicuously introduces opposite colors. Control contrasts to avoid chaos. (*Note:* You will almost never base a color scheme on complementary colors in equal amounts if the colors are full strength. Balance the scheme with unequal amounts and/or unequal intensities.)

8. *Near or split complements* combine a color with the colors on either side of the complement. These combinations usually seem more harmonious.

9. *Triads* are color combinations that form equilateral triangles on the wheel. Triad colors will fight with each other for prominence. Choose one to dominate and veil or neutralize the others with the dominant color.

Color Vocabulary

A satisfactory color vocabulary can be a great help to you as you approach a palette. In order to be able to discuss colors, you must be able to describe their attributes. The following terms are quite commonly used although no set is universal.

Hue is the name of the color. It is synonymous with color. Red is the hue of an apple. Mixing one color with another will result in another hue.

Values are the gradations between the lightest and the darkest varieties of a color. Some refer to this attribute of color as brilliance. Values that are darker than the pure color are called *shades*; values lighter than the pure color are called *tints*.

Intensity refers to the vividness or distinctness of a hue. Some would define this as strong color versus weak color. Other words synonymous with intensity are saturation or chroma. Colors can be rendered less intense by graying them. You can change intensity without changing hue.

Warm and Cool Colors

One of the most exciting of all color properties is psychological temperature. Certain colors—red, yellow, orange—convey a sense of warmth, while others—green and blue—seem cool. There are obvious associations that help to explain this phenomenon. The warm colors are reminiscent of fire and sunlight, the cool ones of water and foliage.

In addition, every color also has warm versions and cool versions. Mixing warm and cool colors together can alter their psychological temperatures. Color combinations also affect the warmth or coolness of individual hues; you can warm up a cool color simply by placing it in a warm environment.

A good color sense is largely a product of intuition, association, and constant study.

LYNN PECKTAL
Designing and Painting for the Theatre

Color and Form

The size and shape of a human silhouette against a background can be remarkably affected by color. For instance, a light figure on a dark ground appears larger than a dark figure of the same size on a light ground. Everyone knows that you can minimize the bulk of a stout figure by dressing it in dark colors. That bulk can be minimized even more if the background is light.

Warm and cool colors in combination can also seem to alter form. Warm hues, for example, appear to advance and expand while cool hues contract and recede. If you put a red/orange circle on a blue/green background, the circle will seem to pop forward, appearing to be in front of the background rather than part of it. The opposite is also true. When a blue/green spot is placed on a red/orange ground, the background seems to come forward and the spot becomes a hole.

The effects of warm and cool colors on form probably have a physiological base. The lens in your eye has to thin out to perceive cool colors and thicken to perceive warm colors. When forced to focus and refocus on extremes of warm and cool color, the lens is in a constant shifting state which does not allow the forms to remain integrated.

Finally, both cool colors and tints seem lighter in weight and less substantial than their counterparts. Warm colors and shades appear heavier and more dense.

Color Display

Rough sketches, even if they are executed in color, are usually accompanied by some kind of color display. As soon as you begin to compose your color layout, decide what materials you want to use for it. No one material is any more correct than another, although one may be better suited to a particular project. Bright, bold costumes for a children's play might be most successfully represented with paint chips. For a set of costumes that employs a narrow range of monochromatic values for its effect, paint may be the only medium through which you can demonstrate your intent. A large show with costumes that will have many prints and subtle color relationships is best represented by fabric swatches.

USING FABRIC SWATCHES

The most common color layouts for costumes are executed in fabric swatches for some very good reasons: There seems to be an almost endless variety of possible colors. Fabric swatches are easy to come by and cost little or nothing. Fabric suggests clothing more directly than colored papers or paint chips, and fabric includes texture, which is so intimately related to color effects in design.

The presence of fabric texture and weight in swatches may be troublesome to you if you are selecting fabric pieces entirely for color and do not mean textural associations to be made. Some people find it very difficult to separate their response to texture from their response to color. A square of pale pink satin may convey exactly the correct color for a chiffon scarf. Your director may be turned off by the satin and thus reject the pink. "No," the director may say, "that's not right," without knowing where the negative response comes from.

If you are using fabric swatches to communicate only color, be very specific about your intentions. It is far better, if at all possible, to select swatches that reflect both your color and textural choices.

ATTACHING COLOR SAMPLES

There are many ways of attaching color samples for display. If you are doing a single layout, arrange the samples on a stout piece of paper or board, and glue or staple them in place. (For the paper or board on which the samples are displayed, some designers choose a color which is as near as possible to the overall set color.) Staples are the most secure; rubber cement, household cement, or spray adhesives are quite reliable. Ordinary white glue is less permanent and may give way if the layout is excessively handled.

Designers who do individual color layouts for each character rather than an overall display often staple (or glue) their color samples to 3 × 5 or 4 × 6 cards, which can be arranged and rearranged to show changing relationships and different scenes. They may be placed on the rough sketches. Later on, if the swatches are fabric pieces from the actual cloth of the costumes, the swatch cards can be attached directly to the completed sketches.

Color samples may go right on the rough sketches. Again, staples are best but glue, or even paper clips, will do. Refrain from attaching fabric swatches to sketches with straight pins since someone is bound to get stuck as sketches go from hand to hand.

Sometimes the perfect color layout presents itself in another representation, such as a painting, a tapestry, or a patterned carpet. If you can't improve on it, use it.

A Swatching Trip

Even though you may be using watercolors or paint chips to work out a color scheme for your costumes, you should take at least one trip through the shops to swatch fabric during the early stages of your work. Looking at actual fabrics may help you work out color. Also, unless you are able to have fabrics woven and dyed to your specifications—an unheard of extravagance in most theatres—you will be dependent upon the fabrics that are in the stores, so you should see what is available and collect representative samples.

There are no fixed rules of etiquette for

FIGURE 4-11. Supplies for a swatching trip. *Photograph by Colleen Muscha.*

requesting fabric swatches. Some shopkeepers welcome designers and dispense samples readily, others are very grumpy about giving away bits of cloth, and a few will not part with a thread unless you pay for it. In general, it is easier to swatch in cities where designers regularly shop for costume fabrics: New York, Los Angeles, Chicago, Washington, Milwaukee, Seattle, and so on. The shops in places where there is not much theatrical activity may not be so understanding about the way designers work. You should be careful to explain what you are doing and why, and you should tell the shopkeeper that you intend to eventually purchase cloth selected from the swatches you are considering. As with most human encounters, the more open and friendly you are, the more cooperation you are likely to receive.

Equip yourself fully for a swatching trip. Take masking tape, scissors (some stores will actually let you cut your own swatches!), a ballpoint pen, and a supply of envelopes.

Stick a piece of masking tape on the back of each swatch. Write the price and width of the fabric on it and also the name of the store where you got it. File the swatches in the envelopes by colors or by characters or by any other method that organizes your project.

Keep in mind the approximate yardage you will need; don't take a swatch of a cloth if there is only a yard on the bolt and the garment will require twenty. Ask, of course, if there is more of the fabric stored away or if it can be ordered. Be aware that it often takes a long time to get fabric on order; many designers have had to make a poor second choice because delivery took longer than was expected.

If you see a bolt of fabric that you are quite certain you will want to purchase but cannot on that day, ask the store manager to hold it for you. Many will do so gladly, although they will usually give you a time limit for picking it up.

Be sensible about prices even when your designs are not complete. You already know your budget. If it is not large enough for a great many expensive fabrics, don't swatch a great many expensive fabrics; you will only be frustrated later on. At the same time, never hesitate to ask the shop if they will consider selling the fabric to you at a discount, particularly if you are shopping for a nonprofit theatre. Some shops are willing to discount prices, especially if you purchase a significant number of yards.

Many fabric stores have backrooms or basements stuffed with old or unusual fabrics that may not have much sales appeal to the general

85

public but are infinitely appealing to costume designers. Always ask if such a storage area exists.

Keep all swatches you don't use on one project and add them to your swatch collection for future color work. Take care, however, not to become devoted to a particular swatch from your collection during the planning stages of your designs, only to discover it is one you collected five years ago and the fabric from which it was cut has long since disappeared from the store's shelves.

Incorporating Stock and Rental Costumes

If the production you are designing must include garments pulled from the theatre's stock or rented from a commercial costume rental company, it is important to have some notion of what is available to you as you work on rough sketches and compose color. Visit the stock area if it is at all possible and look carefully at all appropriate coats, vests, dresses, shoes, etc., sketching shapes and noting colors. If you are not able to go to the rental company and participate in the selection process, ask for specific descriptions, including color, of what they have.

Include pulled and rented items in your rough sketches and their colors in your color display. Integrating costumes to be built with existing costumes in these early stages of the design work can save you the unpleasant experience of having a group of unconsidered, hastily assembled servant's costumes suddenly arrive to completely destroy the harmony of your work.

Showing Rough Sketches to the Director

The day on which you are scheduled to show rough sketches to the director was probably set during a preceding conference. In some produc-

ing organizations all meetings and deadlines are pre-scheduled. At any rate, you will know about the meeting in advance, so be ready for it. One of the most counter-productive things a designer can do to the collaborative process is to turn up at a design meeting unprepared. If some emergency prevents you from completing the preliminary work by the appointed day, call and postpone the meeting, but do not, under any circumstances, come empty-handed.

Lay out the sketches in whatever manner the project demands, by scenes, by factions, or all together. Don't talk right away. Give the director a chance to look. Remember, you have been looking at the sketches for days and have probably committed them all to memory; the director has probably not seen them at all. It takes time to see.

Don't expect universal praise for every costume sketch. Even if your prior collaboration on the production has been most satisfactory, it is highly unlikely that you and the director will agree on everything. Expect some changes to be made and assume that the changes will be improvements. This is not the time to be even faintly defensive about your work.

After the period of general looking, begin to explain each sketch in turn. Comment, if you can, on the cut, the fabric, the way it might move. If color is not included in the sketch, relate the sketch to the color display. Mention trim and accessories, hairstyles and facial hair. Try to make sure that the director is seeing everything you have indicated. Discuss the costumes in the sequence in which they will appear on stage, noting all repeats and all changes, as well as any problems that might arise because of actors' doubling.

Then listen. Listen carefully to the director's response to what you have presented. Make sure you understand what is being said: which things the director finds appropriate and which things he thinks unclear. Make suggestions and take suggestions. However, if you are asked to make major changes in your work, don't decide on them until you have had time to reflect on everything that has been said. On the spot, cut-and-paste costume design is seldom successful. Go home, get back to work, and return another day with new and better sketches.

More often than not, if your preparation and the original collaboration have been sound, the director will approve the original work with few changes and additions, and you will soon be back at your drawing table ready to prepare the final sketches for the shop.

5
Final Sketches

All of the costume designer's research, exploration, and preliminary drawing come together in the final sketches. There are very few rectangles of paper or board anywhere else in the world that must communicate as much information, aesthetic as well as practical, as a costume sketch. A complete costume sketch conveys, among other things, line, shape, proportion and color, history, script, and character analysis. It indicates, as clearly as possible, what the actor will wear and what the audience will see. The shop technicians look at the sketch to guide draping and pattern drafting, trim arrangement, fabric dyeing, and the creation of hats and other accessories. Finally, the sketch becomes a part of the designer's work portfolio and may be examined by producers and directors as part of a job interview.

In light of all these demands it may seem ridiculous to say that simplicity is one of the chief attributes of a fine costume sketch. Yet this is true. The simple, direct sketch that manages to "organize a wealth of meaning" and say a great deal with a minimum of fuss is always the most effective. A flashy, overworked sketch, like wordy, overblown rhetoric, too often obscures the facts and confuses the issues. It is a mistake to equate good costume sketching with technical virtuosity and multi-media displays.

On the other hand, whereas simplicity is desirable in a costume sketch, a simplistic sketch that represents the costume with only a half dozen sensuous lines may be an exciting drawing yet fail as a final costume sketch. This is because it does not give significant information to the shop and to those members of the production group who only want to know what the costume will really look like.

Somewhere in between overdone and underdone lies the thoroughly professional, clear, direct, and beautiful sketch which is the goal of every serious designer. This chapter focuses on the more practical matters you will deal with every day while moving toward this goal: working habits and working materials.

FIGURE 5-1. Lowell Detweiler's costume design for *Les Patineurs*. Acrylics and colored pencil on charcoal paper. *Photograph by Frances Aronson.*

FIGURE 5-2. Mexican woman in *Streetcar Named Desire. Costume design by Susan Tsu. Photograph by Frances Aronson.*

FIGURE 5-3. Andrew B. Marlay's costume design for Margaret Lord from *Philadelphia Story*. Pencil, watercolor, and acrylics on canvas paper; background is magic marker spray. *Photograph by Frances Aronson.*

89

Place and Time

The Work Space

Most designers are greatly affected by the atmosphere of the place where they work, its volume, its floor plan, its light source, the color of its walls, and the position of the waste paper basket. Frivolous as these concerns may seem to some, they are worth a few words if only to comfort those of you who might feel guilty because you cannot put effective paint to paper in surroundings you find unpleasant. Such failings do not indicate a lack of character.

William Faulkner, the great Southern writer, once said that if a writer was to do good work, he must find himself a "warm room." Faulkner was using these words metaphorically; one writer's warm room will be quite different from another's in the same way that the physical arrangement and decoration of one designer's work space will not resemble another's. It is true,

however, that a certain degree of individualized psychological and physical comfort must be present for most writers to write and for most designers to design.

If your work space is not as conducive to your work as you would like it to be, take a little time to see how you can improve it. Is the light satisfactory? Is your chair or stool the correct height for your drawing surface? Are your supplies conveniently arranged or must you be constantly getting up and down while you try to work?

Work spaces need not be elaborate or contain expensive furniture and equipment to be efficient and pleasant. A drawing surface, light, and a place to sit are the only necessities. Meet those needs first. Spend your money where it counts, on a chair that is kind to your own skeletal configuration, a sturdy drawing table, a moveable light source.

FIGURE 5-4. A pleasant work area. *Photograph by Colleen Muscha.*

YOUR DRAWING TABLE

Make sure your drawing surface is stable. Nothing irritates people more than trying to draw on a surface that rocks back and forth.

Drawing tables come in a wide variety of brands and styles; they range from extravagant models that raise, lower, and tilt at the touch of a button to more pedestrian varieties that change position through the use of hand-operated thumb screws. The size of the board itself may range from approximately 23″ × 31″ to 31″ × 42″. When you choose a drawing table, think carefully about your own needs, the available space, and your pocketbook. Shop around and be sure to investigate the possibilities of purchasing your drawing table second hand.

Some designers prefer to work on a flat table or desk with, perhaps, a portable drawing board. You can prop the board up with books, a brick, or with a set of metal brackets sold for that purpose. You can also buy a portable drawing board with legs that fold down to effect the tilt.

Whatever drawing surface you choose, make sure the area on which you draw is smooth and clean. Some designers cover their boards with a sheet of white cardboard which can be removed and replaced as necessary. An excellent material for your drawing surface is Vinyl-Flex

drawing board cover. It is sold by the yard, cuts easily with scissors or a knife, and can be fastened down with Dubl-Stik tape. One side is pale green, the other ivory, both good colors to relieve eyestrain. Vinyl-Flex is washable and resistant to nicks and cuts.

SEATING CHOICE

Choose a chair or stool that is the correct height for your work surface. Too many hours spent in a hunched-over position will result in chronic backache. You may want a back rest or support, but it is best that this be adjustable; a back rest that presses into the wrong part of your spine is worse than none at all. Don't ever purchase a work chair or stool without actually sitting on it.

FIGURE 5-6. A small drawing table with good light and a comfortable chair with good back support. *Photograph by Colleen Muscha.*

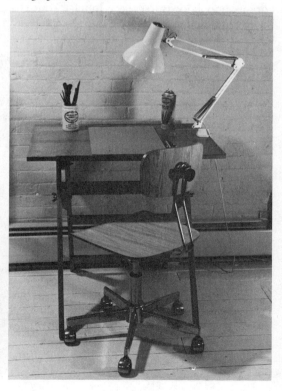

FIGURE 5-5. A tilted drawing table. *Photograph by Colleen Muscha.*

LIGHTING CHOICE

You must also have a good lamp. Ideally it should be adjustable. The Luxo Crownlite Lamp, #CS–4M, using a 60-watt incandescent light bulb is widely used because it is quite inexpensive and adaptable to many spaces. Adjust your lamp so there is no glare on your work. Glare is a heavy contributor to the weeping, burning eye syndrome known as eyestrain.

BE CREATIVE

Rely on imagination to help make your work area pleasant. If the faded-flower wallpaper causes discomfort, paint over it or cover it with fabric, a sheet, or even brown paper. Pin up hats on the wall if you like them, surround yourself with plants if they make you feel good or with baskets of cloth if you find that exciting. Pay attention to your needs; a work space need not follow any rules of interior decor, and you should not care how it looks to others. Indulge yourself. There are times when the best thing you can do for yourself and for your work is to purchase a beautiful stoneware pitcher that has captured your fancy and put it on your drawing table to hold brushes.

Work Hours

A costume designer's work hours are regulated only in the broadest possible sense by the production deadlines. Each day is yours to schedule; no one asks you to punch a timeclock or to report on your accomplishments at the end of each work day. You are quite free to work in fits and starts, procrastinating and postponing for several weeks and then attempting to complete all 67 final sketches in the 24 hours before the costumes must go into the shop. Some designers do this.

However, you are also free to program your work in regular, daily blocks, adjusting and readjusting your schedule to meet the changing needs of the project. Even when the amount of work seems overwhelming, you can always organize it in a way that will not leave you a basket case during dress rehearsals, the very point in the production process when you need to have your wits as sharp as possible.

Observe your work habits and figure out when you do your best work. Many times the pressure of the work will demand that you draw and paint through the night but, if you have a choice in the matter, plan your day so you are painting when you paint best. It is much easier to work with colors during the daytime hours when natural light is available. Artificial light, no matter how good the quality is, produces more strain on your eyes than natural light. Most people work more efficiently when they get an early morning start, well before telephones and the assorted cares of the day intervene.

Sketch Size

Before you go off to the art store to buy materials for final sketches, be sure you have decided what size figures you will use because this determines the amount of paper or board you will need.

It is probably a good idea to make all the figures the same size. It's easier to work out design details when your figure proportions are consistent, and the technicians, actors, and directors will certainly find the sketches easier to read. A general exception to this might be a very large costume show with many supporting or chorus characters. Designers often sketch these characters in groups with figures a third to a half of the main character sketch size.

The actual size of the figures is up to you. Some designers hit on a personally optimum size figure for all their work, others vary the size with the project. In any case, the figure should be large enough to convey the necessary information and small enough to be portable. Don't forget that you must carry the whole lot with you to meetings and to read-throughs and to the shop,

and if the sketches are too big you will have problems doing so.

Whatever the figure size, be sure that each sheet of paper or board, frame or mount, is uniform in size. There is nothing more cumbersome than trying to transport or show a lot of different sized costume sketches. If, as is often the case, they must go through the mail, it is very difficult to pack them if the outside dimensions vary.

Media

Costume designers work in many different media. Some of these are discussed individually beginning on page 94. Decide ahead of time what you want to use and what you need to purchase. If you always work in the same medium, check your supplies and make a note of additional or replacement colors you need. Many designers, however, like to try different paints and inks and methods, exploring new means to effective sketches. If you are purchasing supplies that you have had limited experience with, be sure to find out exactly what you will need to work with that medium, what papers, what additives, and what applicators. A good, up-to-date handbook of artists' materials, such as *Commercial Artist's Handbook* (New York: Watson-Guptill, 1973) will be a help to you.

Buy Everything at Once

Don't allow yourself to get caught at 2 AM, in a fever of inspiration, without an item you need to work with: paper, white gouache, brown ink.

FIGURE 5-7. Susan Tsu's sketch for Artimedora in *Julius Caesar* (Milwaukee Repertory Theater). Baked white glue and acrylics on a surface of heavy colored paper and plaster bandages. *Photograph by Frances Aronson.*

Before you begin any project, make a careful list of all you will need to complete it and purchase those things before you begin. If, in the course of the work, you run short of something, replace it immediately, between 9AM and 6 PM, before the shops close. Even your closest designer friends won't be happy about loaning you a bottle of ink at 4 AM and, furthermore, no one else is apt to have exactly the color or brand you hunger for.

Art Supplies and Materials

You are about to venture into your favorite—or the most conveniently located—art supply store. Whether the store is large or small, you need to know a bit about the products sold there in order to shop effectively. The multiplicity of brands and of types in every area can be bewildering. New products or "improved" products appear on display all the time.

The following sections in this chapter are concerned with artists' paraphernalia. The information contained here is certainly not exhaustive; it is intended only to hit the high spots and help you chart a course through the media maze.

Pencils, Pencil Sharpeners, and Erasers

DRAWING PENCILS

Traditional, wood-encased graphite pencils have been around for quite a while—the first graphite pencil was made in 1662—and are certainly the most commonly used drawing implement. Nineteen grades of graphite are currently available and are expressed from hardest to softest as: 9H, 8H, 7H, 6H, 5H, 4H, 3H, 2H, H, F, HB, B, 2B, 3B, 4B, 5B, 6B, EB, EE. The hard grades contain more clay and the soft grades more graphite. Costume designers generally use mid-range grades, often choosing HB for general drawing and sketching and 2H and H for work with tracing paper.

Two reliable drawing pencil brands are Eagle Turquoise and Venus. Drawing pencils are inexpensive, so have a good supply on hand and keep them sharp.

FIGURE 5-8. Colleen Muscha's sketch for the Sergeant and the Recruiter from *Mother Courage and Her Children* by Brecht. A Milwaukee Repertory Theater production. Sketch rendered in ebony pencil on watercolor paper. *Photograph by Frances Aronson.*

DRAFTING OR CLUTCH LEAD PENCILS

Clutch lead pencils, or holders, are designed and manufactured for precision drafting as well as for drawing. The barrels operate with a push-button action which holds and dispenses graphite leads in the full range of grades.

Clutch holders may be of metal or plastic construction. Some people prefer the heavier weight of the metal model. If you are not familiar with pencils of this type, it is a good idea to try several varieties before deciding which one to purchase.

AUTOMATIC MECHANICAL PENCILS

A less expensive version of the drafting pencil is the automatic mechanical pencil. Most brands have a quick-click mechanism which self-feeds the leads from a storage chamber which holds about twelve extra leads. The leads come in four sizes— from thin to less thin: 0.3mm, 0.4mm, 0.5mm, 0.7mm—which do not need to be sharpened. There are only a limited number of graphite grades available, usually from 2B to 6H, and not all grades may exist in each size. These pencils are excellent for rough sketching. Pentel makes several inexpensive models.

SKETCHING PENCILS

Some designers prefer wood-encased pencils especially manufactured for sketching. Some, like the Eberhard Faber Ebony #6325, have soft graphite leads that are very black; others, such as General's Sketching Pencil or Koh-I-Noor's flat sketching pencil (commonly called carpenters' pencils), have broad rectangular blocks of graphite that are excellent for shaded drawings. Carbon pencils, like Eberhard Faber's Koal Blak or Wolff's Carbon Pencil, will give a somewhat different line and texture to your sketch.

PENCIL SHARPENERS AND LEAD POINTERS

All pencils, except for automatic mechanical pencils, have to be sharpened regularly. Wood-encased pencils require one sort of sharpener and leads held in a clutch holder require another.

The lead pointer, either electric or manual, sharpens all varieties of clutch drafting pencils and can produce needle-sharp points on all grades of graphite. All the pointers operate on the principle of rotating the pencil around a stationary grinder. Two excellent manual varieties are the Tru Point Lead Pointer and the Berol Turquoise Lead Pointer.

FIGURE 5-9. An assortment of drafting and automatic pencils. *Photograph by Colleen Muscha.*

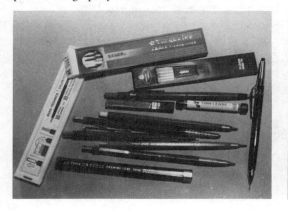

FIGURE 5-10. Sketching pencils. *Photograph by Colleen Muscha.*

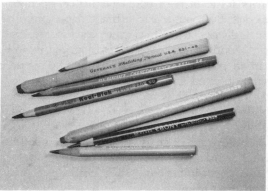

FIGURE 5-11. Pencil sharpeners and lead pointers. *Photograph by Colleen Muscha.*

You can also sharpen leads on a sandpaper block, which is simply a small stack of sandpaper sheets fastened to a wooden handle.

Ordinary school-room pencil sharpeners are satisfactory for wood-encased drawing and sketching pencils, although some very soft leads and carbon pencils don't fare so well in them; the leads tend to break. You can purchase mechanical pencil sharpeners that can be screwed down to a wall or a table as well as a suction variety that adheres to most surfaces quite well. An electric pencil sharpener is a luxury but many designers praise them to the skies. Electric pencil sharpeners come in both cord and battery-operated models. Boston is a reliable brand name for both manually operated and electric pencil sharpeners.

Oddly enough, soft sketching pencils and carbon pencils sharpen best in the little plastic, hand-operated gadgets you can buy at the stationery stores. These are very inexpensive but the blade dulls quickly, so keep several on hand. Along with the usual utilitarian shapes, these sharpeners are often disguised as automobiles, Mickey Mouse characters, or spaceships. Staedtler manufactures small, efficient manual sharpeners made of metal.

ERASERS

It is said that there are designers who don't own erasers. Whoever they are, they must be either very deft or they must have an inexhaustable supply of paper. For most designers, erasing is part of the process. If you are ever inadvertently caught without an eraser on hand, don't forget that you can erase pencil lines with a ball made from bread. Bread was the original pencil erasing material. It was used for centuries before the development of all the types of erasers that are available today.

FIGURE 5-12. Erasers. *Photograph by Colleen Muscha.*

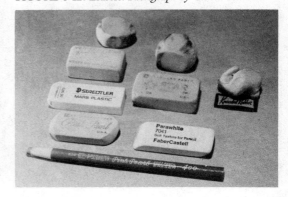

The two most popular erasers for costume design work are *putty* or *kneadable* erasers and *art* or *gum* erasers. Kneadable erasers can be moulded into any shape and are therefore good for small, detailed areas. They are soft and non-abrasive and are excellent for pencil and charcoal. Gum erasers crumble as they erase, never scratch, and almost never smudge. If you erase a large area, the crumbs you produce will make a prodigious mess. Gum erasers are particularly effective when you need to remove sketching lines from a painted sketch.

Some soft pencil erasers effectively erase graphite lines and smudge very little. Eberhard Faber's Pink Pearl is very soft and the Ruby is medium soft. Anything harder than a medium soft eraser may distress your paper surface. Plastic and ink erasers have limited use for designers. Not only is it virtually impossible to erase ink lines completely, but you could not do so without damaging the paper surface.

FIGURE 5-13. Liz Covey's sketch for Leontine in *13 Rue de L'Amour* for the Indiana Repertory Theatre. Technical pen and black ink on multimedia vellum. *Photograph by Frances Aronson.*

Pens and Inks

DRAWING PENS

The most common drawing pens combine a light-weight penholder made from aluminum, plastic, or wood and a flexible pen point which may come in a large variety of widths and types. The flexibility of the nib makes it possible for the pen line width to be varied according to the pressure placed on it by the hand. The crow quill point is extremely popular. Esterbrook, Hunt, and Gillott all make reliable points.

It takes some practice to use a drawing pen, to gauge how often it must be dipped in ink and how much pressure must be applied to maintain a steady line. (Speedball makes a fountain body for their reservoir top pens; this eliminates the need for periodic dipping.) There are advantages to using a drawing pen: it is far less temperamental than a technical pen and, for many designers, the flexible line width is highly desirable.

FIGURE 5-14. Michael J. Cesario's sketch for the Old Man in *The Chairs*. Ballpoint pen, colored pencil, watercolor wash, and enamel spray point on illustration board. *Photograph by Frances Aronson.*

Some designers enjoy working with hand-cut bamboo pens. You purchase them with nibs already shaped but you can whittle the point to your own specifications with a pen knife.

FOUNTAIN PENS

Fountain pens are also made with flexible nibs which respond, although not as sensitively as drawing points, to pressure. Most are made for writing rather than for drawing, although one model, the Osmiroid #75 Sketch Pen, is very versatile and an excellent drawing instrument. It has piston-type filling and a visible ink supply.

TECHNICAL OR DRAFTING PENS

These pens are precision instruments designed specifically for drafting and line reduction techniques, and they are widely used for drawing. They have tubular points and cartridge ink-reservoir assemblies.

There are nine internationally recognized line widths—intended for standardized line reduction—available in all the brands. These are expressed in millimeters from smallest to largest: 0.13, 0.18, 0.25, 0.35, 0.5, 0.7, 1.0, 1.4, 2.0.

Somewhere on each nib package you will find the standardized size designations, although the individual manufacturers each market pens under their own size designations, these sizes being usually color coded somewhere on the pen casing. And, of course, each manufacturer offers more than the nine standardized nib sizes. So try not to be confused when you realize that a Castell T.G. size 3×0 is actually a finer point than a Rapidograph size 5×0. You can, if you search through the fine print, find the exact point size expressed in millimeters. Good point size choices for new users of technical pens are 0.35mm, 0.7mm, and 1.0mm.

Technical pens have either stainless steel points or jewel (sapphire) points. The jewel points are almost three times the price of the stainless steel points but they last much, much longer.

Technical pens can be temperamental and they require constant care and careful usage in order to function smoothly. Neglected or ill-used pens dry up, clog, and leak. You must always replace the pen's cap firmly after use. When starting to write, shake the pen gently in a horizontal direction, taking great care that this shaking does not occur anywhere near your

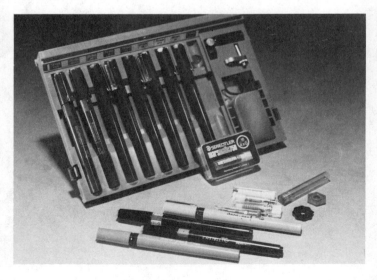

FIGURE 5-15. An assortment of technical pens. *Photograph by Colleen Muscha.*

drawing. Always draw at an angle of about 80 degrees to the horizontal and always draw in the direction of the line. Technical pens must be disassembled for cleaning, and the parts must be held under cool running water. Soak the parts periodically in water or in a commercial cleaning solution. The most effective way to clean technical pens is in a sonic cleaner with commercial cleaning solution.

The best and most widely available brands of technical pens are: Koh-I-Noor Rapidograph, Staedtler Mars 700 series, Castell T.G., and Standardgraph.

INKS

You may use any kind of drawing ink with a dip drawing pen, any brand, any color, waterproof or nonwaterproof. Fountain pens require inks made especially for them, such as the Pelikan 4001 Fountain Pen Inks or the Artone Fountain Pen India Inks. There are special inks for technical pens as well, although some artists feel that Pelikan Ink for Fountain Pens works best in them, since it tends to clog less frequently. There are a number of brands and types of ink for technical pens; most are waterproof but some are

not. If, as in the case of Rapidograph and Staedtler Mars, the company that manufactures the pen also manufactures ink, it might be safest to stick with the same brands in combination.

Rapidograph makes a black drawing ink and an assortment of nine colors; Pelikan offers a similar variety. Colors are, in general, translucent; black and white are opaque. Higgins makes a good nonwaterproof black ink that is suitable for brush washes as well as in technical pens and a particularly good waterproof black called Higgins Black Magic. Steig FW India Inks, Winsor & Newton, and Dr. Martins Technical Waterproof Inks are reliable. Also, Winsor & Newton makes both gold and silver inks that can be used in a pen or applied with a brush.

FELT AND NYLON TIP PENS

There are many different brands and styles of felt and nylon tip pens on the market; most are nonrefillable. The convenience of using these pens and the fact that they require so little care often outweighs their expense and the rapidity with which they run out of ink. The inks are waterbase and may be waterproof or nonwaterproof. Some reliable brands are Papermate

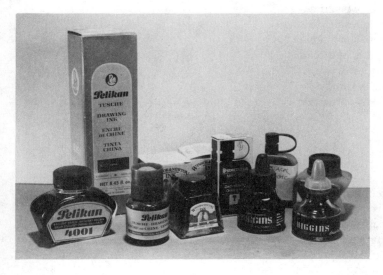

FIGURE 5-16. An assortment of inks. *Photograph by Colleen Muscha.*

Flair, Berol Flash 30 and 32, Pilot Razor Point, Pentel, and Marvy Ultra Writer.

The line produced by felt and nylon tip pens is neither as flexible as the line you can get with a drawing or fountain pen nor as precise as a technical pen line.

DON'T OVERDO PEN AND INK LINES ON COSTUME SKETCHES

Pen and ink lines can add detail and clarity to costume sketches. However, a very heavy line, particularly if it is outlining a figure and a garment, can be misleading. Costumes on the stage are not surrounded by black outlines and must manage to stand out from the scenic background by means of color, fabric choice, and skillful use of the design elements. Keep pen lines light so you can judge what the costume will look like.

Papers and Boards

Costume designers seldom feel bound to traditional paper choices. They will apply watercolor to charcoal papers, gouache to tracing papers, and colored markers to anything. Sometimes these experiments have questionable results, but other times they are very successful. The following remarks about artists' paper and boards tend to be traditional in nature in order to give you an idea of how these materials may normally be expected to behave. Don't read them as rules or curbs to ingenuity.

PAPER WEIGHTS AND TOOTH

The number that expresses paper weight designates the weight of a standard sized ream of that paper. A ream may consist of 480 or 500 sheets; usually drawing or watercolor paper comes in reams of 480 sheets and bond or typing paper in 500 sheet reams.

Some papers are inherently heavier than others. A 70 pound watercolor paper is light weight and a 140 pound watercolor paper is moderately heavy. In drawing papers, the light range is around 16 pounds, medium 32 pounds, and heavy 80 pounds.

Although you will probably purchase paper by how it feels to your fingers and how it reacts to your paints and other color media, it's a good idea to know the approximate weights of your favorite papers so you can save time shopping and, when it's necessary, order paper by mail.

Tooth refers to the surface textures of artists' papers. There are no standardized designations for tooth. A paper that "has tooth" possesses a surface texture and one that has little or no tooth is smooth.

FIGURE 5-17. Sketch by Ann Wallace for Mrs. Peachum in Brecht's *Threepenny Opera*. Felt pen and gouache on newspaper background. *Photograph by Frances Aronson.*

PAD SIZES

Most papers can be bought in pads with sheets either bound together or fastened in a wire spiral holder. The following is a list of normal pad sizes; specific sizes will vary slightly from brand to brand. These sizes are expressed in inches.

8½ × 11	12 × 18 (or 19)
9 × 12	14 × 17
11 × 14	18 (or 19) × 24

COLORED PAPERS

White or slightly off-white paper is always acceptable for costume sketches, but there will be times when you want to work on other colors as backgrounds. Creams, buffs, and greys are often particularly effective. Think twice before you put sketches on bright orange or green papers, and make sure your reasons for doing so are consistent with the production scheme and the effect you wish to achieve. Also beware of using dark papers since it's difficult to indicate detail accurately and have the costume resemble what it's going to look like on stage. Besides being difficult to read, sketches on dark papers are almost impossible to photocopy (a consideration which is discussed on page 122). When you work on dark papers you will usually need to add detail in a white medium: ink, pencil, or paint.

FIGURE 5-18. Costume sketch by Susan A. Cox for *Servant of Two Masters*. Gouache and colored pencil on dark paper. *Photograph by Frances Aronson.*

GENERAL DRAWING PAPERS

All the inexpensive papers normally used for preliminary and rough sketching, as well as for research sketching, are grouped together under this heading.

Newsprint is the cheapest and most fragile of the general drawing papers and is only suitable for very rough and temporary work. It is soft and pulpy and appears in a variety of warm and cool beige tones. The surface is most appropriate to soft pencil and charcoal. A hard pencil or pen may tear the surface, and ink from felt tip markers or pens will spread. Newsprint is available in pads, sheets, and rolls and can often be bought for a very low price as end rolls from newspaper offices.

15X White *butcher paper* is available from craft suppliers in 36" wide rolls. It is considerably stronger than newsprint and has a smooth, slightly hard surface. It is excellent for soft pencils, crayons, markers, inks, and gouache.

Layout papers, available in pads and on rolls, come in various weights and surface finishes. Layout is very white and normally accepts markers, pencil, charcoal, pen, and ink. A particularly nice layout paper for rough sketches is Strathmore Aquabee, 16 pound. Layout paper is translucent, and the 16 pound weight can be used for some tracing without the aid of a light board.

Most art supply shops carry a large selection of *drawing* and *sketching papers.* There are many weights and many surfaces, and you will ultimately make your choice by the way the paper feels to you. Note what is said on the front of the pad about the paper surface. Some are especially treated to accept certain media, and this information can help guide your choice.

CHARCOAL AND PASTEL PAPERS

Charcoal and pastel papers come in a wide variety of colors and qualities, in pads and by the sheet. All of them have some tooth to catch and hold color material from the charcoal or pastel stick as it passes over the surface. A particularly nice charcoal or pastel paper is Mi Teintes, available in many colors, in 19" × 25" sheets as well as in rolls.

TRACING PAPER AND VELLUM

Tracing paper is thin and translucent. It has a dry, crackling surface and tends to shrink up in humid conditions. Vellum is tracing paper that has been treated with oil, causing the surface to be smoother and more substantial. Vellum is somewhat more opaque than tracing paper but much less susceptible to humidity. Vellum is an excellent paper on which to trace and keep costume research.

FIGURE 5-19. Lowell Detweiler's sketch for *An Undiscovered Country,* a Hartford Stage Company production. Watercolor and pencil on tracing paper. *Photograph by Frances Aronson.*

FIGURE 5-20. Tracing papers and acetate. *Photograph by Colleen Muscha.*

There are many weights and qualities of tracing papers. K&E Albanene and Hudson are both reliable brands which offer papers in pads or on rolls. Vidalon is an excellent vellum, imported from France and available in three weights: medium, heavyweight, and extra heavy.

When you are showing preliminary sketches in ink or pencil on tracing paper or vellum, be sure to bring along a sheet of white paper to lay under the sketches; otherwise they may be difficult to read.

TRANSFER PAPERS

You will often need to transfer, rather than redraw, a sketch from one paper to another. This is easily done with a piece of transfer paper which acts just like the carbon sheet in multiple copy forms. Some transfer papers are coated with graphite and others an oily material not unlike that on fabric tracing papers. Both types of transfer papers leave enough oil on the copy lines to repel watercolor. It is always a good idea to press down as lightly as possible when you are making a transfer.

WATERCOLOR PAPERS

Watercolor paper is the most expensive paper regularly used by costume designers. Although every designer should experiment with many different kinds of watercolor paper, their surfaces and qualities, it is a good idea to find a middle-priced paper that satisfies you; then stick to it for the bulk of your work. Costume designs are subject to change and alteration until the production is up and running, and there is no doubt that it's easier to discard sketches if they were painted on modestly priced paper rather than on paper costing several dollars a sheet.

As stated earlier, the normal weight range for watercolor paper is from 70 to 140 pounds, with very heavy weight paper at 300 pounds. A 90-pound paper is suitable for costume sketches which will be mounted or matted. A 140-pound paper is stiff enough to stand without mounting.

103

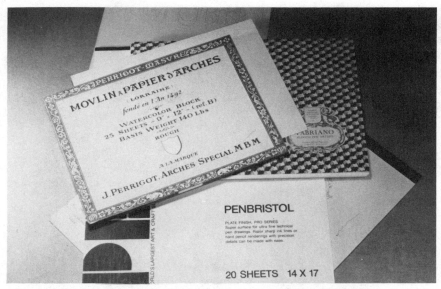

FIGURE 5-21. Watercolor papers and bristol board. *Photograph by Colleen Muscha.*

Watercolor paper surface texture, or tooth, comes in three general grades: *hot press* (H.P.), which is relatively smooth; *cold press* (C.P.), which is a medium texture; and *rough* (R.), which is heavy texture.

Watercolor paper is available in pads, in sheets (usually 22″ × 30″), and in blocks. The sheets are less expensive than the pads, and you can cut them up to whatever sizes you need. Blocks are more expensive than pads.

Watercolor paper will curl and wrinkle when it is wet. Watercolorists, whose methods of painting tend to be wet to the extreme, wet and stretch each sheet over a frame and tape it down, allowing the paper to dry completely before they begin to paint. Watercolor paper that is sold in a block is already stretched and bound. On one side of the block there is a break in the binding through which a knife can be carefully inserted and used to peel off the top sheet once the painting is dry. Very few costume designers stretch individual sheets of watercolor paper before painting. It is a time-consuming process, particularly when there are fifty to a hundred sheets necessary, and most costume designers don't work in an overall wet style. For those that do, watercolor blocks are well worth the extra expense because of the time and effort they save.

Strathmore produces an interesting paper called Aquarius. It is made on a fiber base which prevents the sheets from warping or buckling when they are wet. The paper has little tooth, is quite soft, and only modestly expensive.

Strathmore Artist and Fabriano watercolor papers, available in a full range of textures and weights, are all excellent and moderately priced choices. D'Arches papers and blocks, imported from France, are high quality and rather expensive. Watercolor papers produced by the Royal Watercolour Society in England are exceptionally high in both quality and price.

BRISTOL BOARDS

Bristol boards are composed of lightweight sheets of permanently layered card stock. One to five layers are available; two and three are most widely used.

PLATE 1 Rose Pickering and Ellen Dolan in *Mother Courage*
at the Milwaukee Repertory Theatre.
Costume design by Colleen Muscha. Photograph by Colleen Muscha.

PLATE 5 (right). Bruce Somerville as La Fleche and Jill Tanner as Frosine in the McCarter Theatre production of *The Miser.* Costume design by Liz Covey. Photograph by Frances Aronson.

PLATE 2 (above). A scene from Robert Ingham's *Custer* at the Kennedy Center. Costume design by Rosemary Ingham. Photograph courtesy of the Folger Theatre.

PLATE 3 (right). Henry Strozier as Billboard Man in *Fighting Bob* by Tom Coles. Costume design by Susan Tsu. Produced by the Milwaukee Repertory Theatre. Photograph by Colleen Muscha.

PLATE 4 (below). A scene from the Milwaukee Repertory Theatre production of *Romeo and Juliet.* Costume design by Susan Tsu. Photograph by Colleen Muscha.

PLATE 7 Colleen Muscha's sketches for Hotspur in *Villainous Company* by Amlin Grey at the Milwaukee Repertory Theatre.
Photograph by Colleen Muscha.

PLATE 6 Michael Tezla as Hotspur in *Villainous Company.* Costume design by Colleen Muscha. Produced by the Milwaukee Repertory Theatre.
Photograph by Colleen Muscha.

PLATE 8 Ann Wallace's sketch for *The Critic.*
Photograph by Frances Aronson.

PLATE 9 (left). Liz Covey's sketch for Amanda in *Private Lives* at Pennsylvania Stage Company.
Photograph by Frances Aronson.

There are two general surfaces available: the kid or medium surface that is matte finish and slightly rough and the plate or high surface which is smooth and glossy. The kid surface will accept a wide variety of media: pencil, ink, dry brush, washes, acrylics, and markers; the plate surface is suitable for pencil or fine pen work.

Two-ply Strathmore, kid surface bristol board is an excellent, moderately priced board.

Good bristol board will take a great deal of abuse. If you are careful, you can even scrape off ink or gouache with a knife or razor blade. It is available in single sheets or standard sized pads. Bristol is always white or cream colored.

ILLUSTRATION BOARD

Illustration board is widely used for costume sketches. It is composed of a high-quality rag paper mounted on a relatively thick cardboard back which provides an excellent surface for watercolor and pen and ink, as well as several other mediums.

There are three general grades of illustration board: student grade, commercial grade, and high grade. The commercial grade is recommended for costume sketches.

Surfaces will be designated in the same manner as watercolor papers: hot press (smooth), cold press (medium texture), and rough (heavy texture). A good all-purpose board is Bainbridge 90-R (that is, a 90-pound paper on cardboard with a heavy surface texture) which comes in 20″ × 30″ and 30″ × 40″ sheets. D'Arches and Strathmore also make excellent illustration boards.

POSTER AND RAILROAD BOARD

Poster (showcard) board is made of thin white or colored papers mounted on lightweight, inexpensive cardboard. It comes in 28″ × 44″ sheets. The surface has an oily quality that is incompatible with most water-based media. Poster board is primarily useful for mounting sketches which you have done on lightweight papers.

Railroad board is similar. It is 6 ply board, the same on both sides, and is usually available in 22″ × 28″ sheets. Railroad board is less expensive than poster board.

MAT BOARDS

Art shop customers who don't know the difference sometimes mistake mat board (mounting card) for illustration board. It is made in a similar fashion with colored papers mounted on cardboard. The papers that are used, however, are thin and soft and will absorb water color and gouache, producing a dull and generally lifeless sketch. Acrylic paints, because they dry rapidly, work relatively well on mat board. Mat board is the material of choice for mounting and for framing, subjects that will be discussed later in this chapter.

PROTECTIVE PAPERS

It is always a good idea to cover your final sketches with some protective paper before you go shopping and drop them in the snow or before they go into the shop and have coffee spilled on them. Clear acetate in .003 or .005 thicknesses is a good covering and so is Glassine paper. Both are available in sheets or on rolls. Clear-Pak cellophane is a thinner but quite adequate protection; it is less expensive than acetate or Glassine paper.

RICE PAPERS

Many designers have, at one time or another, enjoyed experimenting with sketches on Japanese rice paper. There are many types, qualities, and textures. Some have very apparent fibers and others have been impregnated with wax to give the sheet translucence. Sumi papers are slightly more refined than ordinary rice papers and are made especially for printing. The soft, fibrous surfaces of all these papers make them unsuitable for detailed pen work, but they are excellent for loose brush strokes.

FIGURE 5-22. Sketch by David Murin for the Manhattan Theatre Club's production of *Translations* by Brian Friel. Felt-tip pen, watercolor, and Magic Marker spray on rice paper. *Photograph by Frances Aronson.*

FROSTED OR MATTE ACETATE

Frosted or matte acetate is not often used for costume sketches; it is both unsuitable and too expensive for protecting sketches. It is designed specifically for pen and ink drawings for reproduction. Some of the illustrations in this book were prepared for the camera on frosted or matte acetate. A similar version of the same surface is available as *plastic vellum* or *multi-media vellum* (neither should be confused with tracing paper vellum). Multi-media vellum will accept markers, pastels, and oils as well as inks.

To correct ink mistakes on acetate or plastic vellum, use a sharp X-Acto knife and scratch away the ink. Remove other media carefully with a hard eraser.

FIGURE 5-23. X-Acto knife blades and holders. *Photograph by Colleen Muscha.*

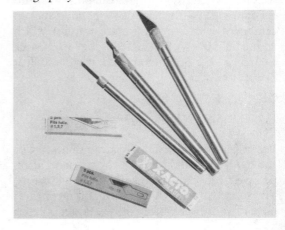

106

Color Media

The color on costume sketches may be paints, colored inks or markers, colored pencils, or pastels. Many designers combine media for specific effects. In order to use any color medium effectively, it is helpful to know something about its composition and characteristics so that you can predict what behavior might be expected from it.

PAINTS

There are three constituents in all paints:

1. colored pigment particles;
2. the medium that carries the particles; and
3. a diluent, normally water or turpentine.

The first pigments came from the earth, from chalk, and from burnt pieces of wood. Somewhere between 2000 and 1000 BC, the Egyptians discovered mineral pigments: azurite, malachite, cinnabar, and white made from lead. The ancient Greeks added indigo, a dye, and a green called verdigris which they produced by the controlled corrosion of copper plates. The thirteenth and fourteenth centuries brought a good many new pigments to the painter's palette, and the nineteenth and twentieth centuries saw the advent of synthetic pigments developed from complex technological processes involving metals and petroleum.

Nowadays art supply stores display a wide variety of paints, ready mixed and suitable for immediate application. It's hard to realize that a century ago painters had to combine their own pigments and mediums, a tedious and time-consuming process.

OIL PAINTS

Oil paints consist of pigments in media of linseed, poppy, or walnut oils. The diluent is turpentine. Oil paints dry slowly and the dried paint takes on a particularly rich glow. The long drying time makes oil paints generally unsuitable for any design work, and costume designers almost never use them.

WATERCOLORS

Watercolors are a common color medium for costume sketches. Watercolor is made by combining very finely ground pigment with gum arabic. The gum dissolves readily in water, the diluent, and adheres firmly to paper. Most modern day watercolors also contain other additives that effect the paint's behavior.

Watercolors are transparent, a characteristic which allows the paper under the paint to play an important role in the total effect of the sketch. When you are using only watercolor, you must work from the lightest to the darkest tones.

You may choose watercolors in tubes, cakes, and jars. Tube watercolors have the consistency of a thick custard. Watercolor cakes are dry and solid, and jar water colors are liquid. Both tube and cake colors are generally available in "artist" and "student" grades with the student grade being the less expensive of the two. Insofar as your pocketbook will allow, try to always purchase artist grade watercolors; the hues and the performance are infinitely superior.

Windsor & Newton Artists' Water Colours are particularly high quality paints, thoroughly consistent and reliable. There is a less expensive but still very good Windsor & Newton watercolor line called London Water Colour which is also recommended.

There are dozens of colors available in watercolor tubes, many more than you will ever need. Over a period of time you will discover which colors suit your own color sense, with an occasional new addition for variety. Here is a list of eleven colors which will provide you with a good basic palette from which you can mix an exciting array of colors.

cadmium red	burnt umber
alizarin crimson	Payne's grey
yellow ochre	ultramarine
monastral (phthalocyanine) blue	Hooker's green
	cadmium yellow
viridian	ivory black

FIGURE 5-24. Sketch by Carol Oditz for the Milwaukee Repertory Theater's production of *Dead Souls*. Rendered in Winsor & Newton watercolors and #2 pencil on watercolor paper. *Photograph by Frances Aronson.*

FIGURE 5-25. John P. Connolly as the Secretary and Larry Shue as Chichikov in *Dead Souls. Photograph by Mark Avery.*

There are two major liquid watercolor brands, Luma and Dr. Martins. Luma Brilliant Concentrated Water Colors come in 80 colors and a Luma Bleed-Proof white which is opaque. They are packaged in eyedropper bottles. There are two types of Dr. Martins: Dr. PH. Martins Synchromatic Transparent Water Colors and Dr. PH. Martins Radiant Concentrated Water Colors. The Radiant Concentrated type is somewhat more brilliant than the Synchromatic Transparent type and slightly more opaque. Dr. Martins also offers an opaque white.

You can create different color values by varying the amount of water you mix with the liquid color. Liquid colors mix differently with each other than tube watercolors do, and you should experiment with simple color wheel mixing before you put your new Lumas or Dr. Martins to work on a sketch.

Cake watercolors are more trouble to use than either tubes or liquids. It's difficult to get enough water into the cake to achieve a stable solution that will allow you to do a good wash. Some designers, however, prefer to work with watercolor cakes and can handle them with great finesse. Pelikan produces a good cake watercolor and Windsor & Newton's moist cake colors are excellent.

WATERCOLOR TECHNIQUES

There are three fundamental watercolor techniques: *wet on dry, wet into wet,* and *dry on dry.* All of these techniques aid costume designers as they strive to represent the sheen of satin, the depth of velvet, the airiness of chiffon, and the weight of stage jewelry.

Watercolor is normally laid on the paper in successive layers and the painting develops from the lightest to the darkest values. A largish expanse of watercolor is called a *wash,* which may be applied wet on dry or wet into wet. A *flat wash* is a single color; a *graduated wash* is made up of

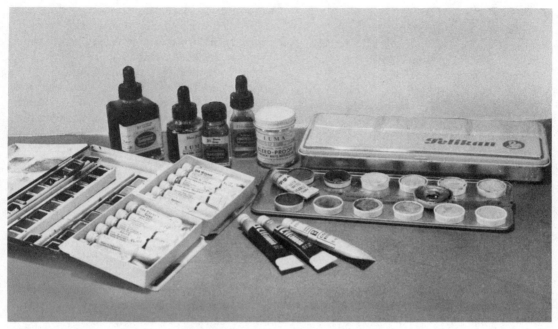

FIGURE 5-26. Watercolors in different forms. *Photograph by Colleen Muscha.*

different values of the same color; and a *varigated wash* is of different colors. All washes should be applied and allowed to dry before any next step is taken. Overworking a wash can be disastrous.

Line and wash watercolor sketches are particularly suitable for representing costumes. Lines are used to draw in major shapes and features while washes amplify or unify the whole. The lines may precede the wash or be imposed over it and done with either a brush or a pen.

Other methods of applying watercolor are *stippling, scumbling,* and *dry brush application.* Stippling is putting dots of color on the paper, oftentimes on top of a dried wash. Scumbling is the application of pigment with a slight scrubbing motion. Dry brush application uses a minimum of water so the paint goes on in little feathery strokes. Practice these methods and see if you can put them to use when representing print cloth, pile textures, and fur.

Brushes are not the only vehicles for putting paint on paper. You can use small natural sponges to apply a watercolor wash and to overpaint texture in a dry on dry manner. You can also create texture in a fine spatter by scraping a kitchen knife over a toothbrush saturated with paint.

Sometimes it's necessary to completely mask off an area in the sketch. You can make an effective mask with masking tape or frisket paper, cut to size and shape, and simply stuck onto the paper. Or you can use a substance called maskoid which is painted onto the paper and which, when dry, seals off the area it covers. Dry maskoid has a rubbery texture, not unlike rubber cement, and can be rolled off with the finger.

If, once the sketch is dry, you want to reduce the amount of color in certain places, you can do so by gently scrubbing up the excess with a sponge, blotting paper, or wad of tissues dipped in clean water. You can also scratch in highlights with a sharp-pointed knife or razor blade, working very carefully so as not to damage the surface of the paper.

109

GOUACHE

Gouache is also called *opaque watercolor* and *designer color*. It is most commonly available in tubes of custard-consistency paint. Tempera and poster paints are crude types of gouache prepared in liquid form and sold in jars. The pigment in gouache is coarser than the pigment in watercolor. The medium is the same, gum arabic, but it is extended with white pigment which makes the paint opaque. Dried gouache is less luminous than watercolor and has a denser surface quality. The colors are slightly chalky. Gouache is used extensively for commercial illustration, particularly for work that requires areas of flat color that will reproduce well. Gouache is highly suitable for detailed painting and is the paint most commonly used by commercial artists in air brushes.

The biggest difference between using gouache and watercolor is that, because of its opacity, gouache allows you to lay a light value over a dark value. Opaque watercolor washes are generally laid down in a middle value from which you can go both lighter and darker. A good gouache wash depends upon getting the correct consistency of paint with water. Always try your mixture before you put the wash on your sketch. Remember also that wet gouache is darker than the color will be when it's dry. If your paint lightens up too much as it dries, don't apply a second layer until the first is quite dry.

WATERCOLOR AND GOUACHE

Since watercolor and gouache contain the same medium the two paints may be used together and very often are. Many costume designers use watercolor for washes and gouache for highlights and details. Transparent watercolor technique is difficult to master completely, and the judicious assistance of opaque water colors, especially white, can simplify the process a good deal. There is nothing, however, to equal the pride you will feel when you display a delicate watercolor sketch with gleaming highlights that emanate from the paper and not from a jar or tube of opaque white.

ACRYLIC PAINT

Acrylic is the common name for a recently developed paint which combines natural and synthetic pigments with a polymerized resin binder, usually acrylic, sometimes polyvinyl acetate (PVA). The common diluent is water. Acrylics came on the market in the United States in the 1950's, although the resins were available twenty years earlier, and many artists were mixing their own paints. PVA based colors became available in the 1960's. PVA colors are less reliable and permanent than acrylic based colors.

Acrylic paint dries as fast as the water in the mixture evaporates, which occurs in minutes because the porous structure of the paint allows for quick and complete evaporation. The acrylic medium is a strong adhesive that binds the paint

FIGURE 5-27. Sketch by Ann Wallace for Nagg and Nell in Samuel Beckett's *Endgame*. Colored pencil and gouache. *Photograph by Frances Aronson.*

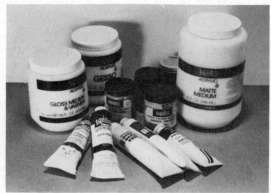

FIGURE 5-28. Sketch by Lowell Detweiler for the Public Theatre production of *More Than You Deserve*. Acrylics and pencil on gray fashion pad paper. *Photograph by Frances Aronson.*

FIGURE 5-29. Acrylic paints and additives. *Photograph by Colleen Muscha.*

to a great many surfaces. As a matter of fact, acrylics can be used on all surfaces except oil-based or emulsion-based grounds.

You can use acrylic paint like oil paint *and* like watercolor. You can apply it in thick layers to canvas or board with a palette knife and as a delicate wash on watercolor paper. All acrylic surfaces, when dry, are waterproof.

You can purchase acrylic paint in tubes and in jars; in both cases the paint is quite thick. In its original state it is opaque, but it can be diluted with water to transparency. Unadulterated acrylic paint in tubes dries with a low sheen while most acrylic paint in jars dries with a matte finish.

There are various additives on the market to mix with acrylic paint. Each one has a different effect on the paint's behavior. The addition of *polymer medium* provides transparency and a glaze to the finish; a *matte medium* adds both transparency and a matte surface; *modeling paste* added

to the paint gives it a putty-like texture used when an artist is working the acrylic as impasto; *retarding medium* slows the drying time of the paint without changing its color; *gel medium* adds a heavy gloss finish and also retards drying; and *gesso* is a white primer which adheres to virtually all surfaces and provides a good ground for acrylic paint.

If acrylic paint is being used like oil paint, oil paint brushes are suitable; if like watercolors, watercolor brushes are the proper choice. Brushes can be cleaned with water but it must be done quickly since the paint dries so rapidly. If, by accident, a brush full of acrylic paint does harden, it can be reclaimed by soaking it in methylated spirits (ordinary or ethyl alcohol denatured with methanol) for 24 hours.

The most widely available brands of acrylic paint are Liquitex, Hyplar (manufactured by Grumbacher), and Windsor & Newton.

111

Acrylic paint has many advantages. For costume designers, it not only combines many good features of watercolor and gouache but also offers the waterproof feature which makes over-painting and the addition of detail so uncomplicated. In general, inexperienced designers find acrylic paint easier to handle than either watercolor or gouache. On the other hand, there is a certain plastic quality to the colors and few people can achieve the expressive subtleties with acrylic paint that they can with watercolor.

MARKERS

Felt composition, nylon, and fiber-tipped markers have come close to revolutionizing commercial art work and have had a great effect on theatre design sketching as well. Markers dispense either spirit-based (permanent) inks or water-based (nonpermanent) inks of great brilliance. Most brands offer at least three nib styles: a flat, angled nib, two degrees of points, a chisel shape, and a wide variety of colors.

The great advantage of using markers is that they eliminate the need for brushes, pots of water, and mixing pans. You can pick one up and apply it with no advance preparation, and it dries instantly. The main disadvantage lies in the in-ability to mix colors (although a certain amount of mixing can be done by applying one color over another). This means you have to buy lots of markers and, even then, accept the fact that many colors are simply impossible to achieve with markers.

Markers are also available in metallic colors, gold, silver, and bronze in both fat and thin varieties.

Markers are especially useful for quick sketches, thumbnails, and the presentation of color ideas. They are also useful in combination with acrylic paint and ink. Markers and watercolor or gouache are not always compatible.

Reliable brands of art markers are Pantone, Design Art Markers, and AD Marker Products. Stabilo Boss Markers and Berol Magic Markers have good quality color, but the broad nib styles in each brand come in container shapes that are awkward to handle.

When you're using markers it's important that you use a paper with a suitable surface in order to discourage bleed-through and spreading. Many layout papers and some drawing papers are available with surfaces specially treated to accept markers. This information will be on the pad cover.

FIGURE 5-30. A variety of markers.
Photograph by Colleen Muscha.

FIGURE 5-31. Colleen Muscha's sketch for Joe in David Mamet's *Lakeboat*. Produced at the Milwaukee Repertory Theater's Court Street Theatre. Drawing pen and brush in gray inks.*Photograph by Frances Aronson.*

COLORED INKS

You can use colored inks the same way you use liquid watercolors, thinning them with water to alter value. The major difference is that most inks contain shellac, are waterproof, and therefore permanent when dry. Colored inks are especially effective in line and wash sketches. Ink types and brands were discussed earlier.

PASTELS

Sometimes, for a change of pace or for a particular effect, it's interesting to use a medium that is not commonly used for costume sketches. Pastels may be just the thing.

Pastels are combinations of powdered pigments with just enough gum or resin to bind them. They come in sticks that are either round or square; the square ones are recommended because they won't roll off your drawing surface. Pastel pencils which may be sharpened and used for fine detail are also available.

A pastel sketch combines the qualities of both drawing and painting. Colors are pure and fresh and can be worked into a variety of surface techniques. If you would like to study the possibilities of pastels, take a look at the pastel work of the following artists: Quentin de la Tour (1704–88), Perronneau (1715–83), Chardin

FIGURE 5-32. Pastel sticks, pastel pencils, and charcoal. *Photograph by Colleen Muscha.*

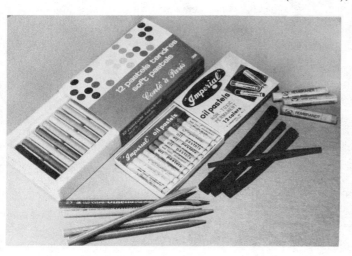

(1699–1779), Degas (1843–1917), and Mary Cassatt (1845–1926). You may well find yourself inspired to experiment with this medium which is often underrated and thought of as best suited for elementary school children.

Pastels are available in soft, medium, or hard varieties; they are rated according to the amount of gum in the sticks. The most brilliant colors come from the softest sticks. There are about 600 colors manufactured in pastel sticks, far more than you will ever need. A 24-color set will allow you to achieve a good deal of subtle color mixing on the page; a 48-stick set is absolutely sufficient. Grumbacher soft pastels are excellent. Nupastel color sticks are harder and a bit less expensive.

Pastel costume sketches must be "fixed" in order to prevent them from smudging as they are handled. Most fixatives darken color slightly and will probably add a faint shine to the work. Grumbacher Tuffilm or Krylon Crystal Clear provide permanent protective sprays. Grumbacher's Myston and Blair's Spray Fix are "workable" fixatives, which means that you can continue to work on the sketch on top of the fixative.

Pastel sketches should be done on the proper paper and are often especially effective on tinted papers: grays, fawns, and buffs. You may also be interested in combining pastels with watercolor or gouache.

CHARCOAL

Except for occasional rough sketches, you will seldom use charcoal in costume work except for special effects. Nevertheless, it never hurts to know something about every possible medium. If you would like to see an especially beautiful charcoal sketch, look at James McNeill Whistler's *Maude Reading*.

Charcoal is essentially burnt wood. It is available in three forms. *Stick* or *vine charcoal* is usually thin, burnt willow twigs. It is very soft and crumbly and will brush off readily. *Com-*

pressed charcoal is burnt wood combined with a medium and formed into round or squared sticks. It is much more permanent than stick charcoal. A thin core of charcoal may also be encased in wood as a *charcoal pencil*. These are, of course, less messy to use but the range of strokes possible with them is limited. The charcoal core in pencils is available in various hardnesses. For the best results with charcoal sketches, use paper that is intended for pastels and charcoal.

COLORED PENCILS

Colored pencils are used most often in costume sketches for detail work. Occasionally a particular project might be effectively executed wholly in colored pencil, particularly light colored costumes that will be built in soft, airy fabrics.

There are two kinds of colored pencils: waterproof and nonwaterproof. The colored leads in waterproof pencils are made from a mixture of chemical pigment and kaolin and are available in a wide range of colors. The leads are relatively hard and can be sharpened into good points for drawing and for detail work. Color mixing is achieved by working one color on top of another. Eagle Verithin and Prismacolor are two good brands of waterproof colored pencils.

Nonwaterproof colored pencils or watercolor pencils have soft leads. A brush full of water

FIGURE 5-33. Colored pencils. *Photograph by Colleen Muscha.*

drawn over a line on the paper will produce a wash effect that can be very handsome. The Swiss-made Caran D'Ache Supracolor II water soluble, soft pencils are among the best water-color pencils now available.

Brushes

Good brushes are frightfully expensive and inexpensive brushes are almost always unsatisfactory in the long run. Always purchase the very best brushes you can afford; take excellent care of them and they will last for many years.

The best brushes to use with water-based pigments are called *sable*. Modern, modestly priced sable brushes are made from weasel hairs. Top quality, expensive red sable brushes are made from the tail hairs of the Siberian mink. Sable brush hairs can carry a lot of pigment from palette to paper for washes. The hairs cling together and maintain the brush shape. If they are well cared for, sable brushes will last for many years and are well worth the initial investment.

Brushes made from squirrel, bear, or pony hairs are much less expensive but much less satisfactory. It is frustrating to use brushes which hold too little paint to complete a stroke and from which hairs tend to stick out at odd angles, to say nothing of their infuriating tendency to shed hairs at the most inopportune times.

If you must purchase inexpensive brushes, try Sablon watercolor brushes, manufactured by Simmons. Sablon is a white synthetic filament which is remarkably soft and resilient, and the brushes made from it behave surprisingly well.

Brushes made from ox and hog hair are quite stiff and suitable for oil based pigments and acrylic paint used like oils.

Brushes come in a variety of shapes: pointed, round, flat, chisel, and fan. Pointed brushes make clean-edged strokes and are excellent for detail work. Round brushes are especially good for carrying pigment and doing washes. You can make broad single strokes with a flat brush, and the chisel shape is made especially for lettering, although it is also useful for stripes and texture on cloth. The fan brush is often called a blending brush and is used for soft details.

FIGURE 5-34. An assortment of brushes. *Photograph by Colleen Muscha.*

A typical size range for watercolor brushes is from 000 (the smallest) to 14. If you are just beginning, a good selection might be: pointed sables, numbers 2, 6, 10; round sable, number 12; and flat sable, number 14. If economy is necessary, substitute Sablon for the round and flat brushes. If extreme economy is called for, purchase all sizes and types in Sablon and plan to replace them with sable one at a time.

CLEANING BRUSHES

While you are painting, never leave brushes standing head down in water for long or you will harm their shape. Rinse the brush vigorously in a large quantity of water after each use and either return it to the brush container or lay it on paper toweling. Clean all brushes thoroughly immediately after each painting session, especially when you are using acrylic paint.

All brushes that are used with water-based paint should be washed with soap (*not* detergent) and cold water. Never use hot water because it will soften the glue that is used to hold the brush hairs in place and greatly shorten the life of the brush. Work up a gentle lather in the palm of your hand to remove all traces of pigment and rinse under running water. Shake excess water from the brushes, reshape the heads with your fingers and stand the brushes upright in a glass or jar to dry. Between periods of painting, it is all right to leave the brushes upright and in the open. If, however, they are to go unused for a long period of time, store them in a flat box with a mothball or two for added protection.

Tapes and Adhesives

Masking tape has innumerable uses. Some have already been mentioned: to mask off areas of a sketch, to help organize swatches. You will probably also use masking tape to fasten your sketch

FIGURE 5-35. Adhesives, tapes, and staplers. *Photograph by Colleen Muscha.*

to the drawing surface while you are working and to mount the sketch once it is complete.

There are actually two sorts of tape that are commonly referred to as masking tape. One is properly called drafting tape. It's thinner than actual masking tape, and slightly less sticky. It is especially designed to hold drawings, tracings, and blueprints to drawing surfaces and it lifts off of most surfaces without harm. Masking tape is a bit thicker and will adhere to more surfaces. Costume designers tend to use these two tapes interchangeably.

Scotch Magic Transparent Tape has two excellent properties combined: you can see through it and you can write on it. It is excellent for joining two pieces of paper together, almost invisibly, and irreplaceable for mocking up wig and beard patterns with plastic wrap.

Brown paper tape is the cheapest and most permanent tape for mounting and covering sketches. It comes in various widths and in both a self-adhesive variety and one that has to be moistened. If you don't enjoy licking the tape yourself, you can put a sponge in a shallow bowl, fill it with water until the sponge is saturated and a bit of water stands in the bottom of the bowl, and then pass the strips of tape over the sponge.

Rubber cement is almost as indispensible to costume designers as masking tape. Use it to mount paper onto cardboard and to attach swatches and trim to the finished sketch. It is a latex-based adhesive that is suitable for all light-weight boards and papers. Best-Test is a familiar brand. Purchase a can of thinner since the adhesive tends to get too thick after a while. A rubber cement dispenser with a brush is very handy.

Spray adhesives are also good for mounting. They are convenient and, therefore, more expensive. The type called spray mount sets up quickly but does allow for some adjustment in position before final bonding takes place; the one called photo mount bonds in seconds, so be sure to put your sketch in the right place the first time. 3M manufactures good spray adhesives.

White glue has many uses in the costume shop but not so many in the costume designer's studio. It is not the best adhesive with which to bond paper to card or to attach swatches to sketches. Papers mounted with white glue tend to buckle and wrinkle, and the glue may even show through. White glue, even when set up, may soften in warm, humid conditions and should never be considered permanent.

Miscellaneous Equipment

There is no end to the amount of equipment a costume designer can collect and use, all of it contributing in some way to getting the work done more efficiently. Once you own the basics, start saving for the treats and don't forget to let your friends and family members know what you're saving for so they can surprise you with useful gifts on holidays. What follows may help you get started on what may prove to be a lifetime of acquisition.

STAPLER

Any desk model stapling machine is adequate for tacking papers together or for fastening swatches to sketches. A particularly good model for costume designers is the Bostitch Stapling Plier-Model B8P. This stapler can be used in the conventional fashion and also as a tacker. It will drive both ¼″ and ⅜″ staples.

PAPER CUTTER

Although most art supply stores have paper cutters available for cutting your boards and papers, it is certainly convenient to have one of your own. You should not consider anything smaller than a 24″ cutter. Bradley is a reliable, moderately priced brand. Beware of secondhand paper cutters and test carefully before you buy. A paper cutter that doesn't cut absolutely straight is worse than none at all.

FIGURE 5-36. Paper cutter. *Photograph by Colleen Muscha.*

RULERS

A metal ruler will serve you both for measuring and as a straight edge for drawing lines and cutting cardboard. Twenty-four inch metal rulers are particularly handy. Choose a metal ruler with a cork bottom which raises the metal edge up off the paper and prevents smudging when you use it for drawing lines. If your ruler doesn't have a cork strip, tape pennies to one side of the ruler you have to get the same effect. Plastic, see-through rulers are also very useful when you are drawing.

TRACING TABLE

Tracing tables, also called light tables or light boxes, are somewhat expensive but may be well worth the investment if you draw slowly and are often under pressure to work quickly. A tracing table consists of a box frame, either wood or metal, a glass top, usually frosted, and fluorescent tubes inserted under the glass. The drawing to be traced is laid on the glass, and the paper on which the tracing will be drawn is placed on top of that. When the light is turned on, the lines are clearly illuminated and you can trace them onto the fresh paper with ease and accuracy. A tracing table can be a great boon when you have several drawings to redo and a short time in which to do them. It is also a helpful device for designers who use stock figures.

If you're handy with tools you can build a light table for a fraction of the cost of a commercially manufactured one. Make sure you use fluorescent fixtures because incandescent bulbs will heat up the glass so much you can't work on it.

You can create a spur-of-the-moment light table by turning a square or rectangular glass baking dish upside down over a low wattage

FIGURE 5-37. Tracing table. *Photograph by Colleen Muscha.*

light bulb set in a small lamp or a dime store fixture. Prop the dish up on books or bricks. The dish will eventually get too hot to work on but, in the meantime, you can get lots of emergency tracing done.

MAGNIFYING GLASS, REDUCING GLASS, AND MIRROR

Costume designers often find that their thumbnail sketches are better and more lively than their larger, finished sketches. Something happens in the process of enlarging the figure that makes it stiff and may even throw off its proportions. If you sometimes have this difficulty, you may find a magnifying glass a useful tool. Study the pleasing proportions in the preliminary sketch while you enlarge it by moving the glass further away from the sketch. What you see may help you to reinterpret the thumbnail accurately on a larger scale.

You may also find a magnifying glass helpful when you are examining problem areas in the sketch. Basic drawing and design problems often reveal themselves when you look at them magnified.

Examine your sketches in a mirror also. It's amazing how many flaws will show up when you see the sketch reversed and distanced. Use the mirror for looking at preliminary sketches and for checking the progress of final sketches as you work.

A reducing glass has the opposite effect of a magnifying glass; it makes things smaller. When you use it to examine a sketch you can get some notion of how the costume may look from a distance, from way up there on the stage. Carry your reducing glass with you on swatching trips. It will often help you determine if a fabric pattern will "read" from the stage.

MAT CUTTERS

These are handy little tools that greatly simplify the cutting of mats. An inexpensive variety is the Dexter Mat Cutter; a more costly one, with a straight edge attached, is the X-Acto Mat cutter. Both types can be adjusted to make either straight or beveled cuts.

What Information Should the Final Costume Sketch Include?

Although the costume designer will generally have the opportunity to go over all sketches with the technicians responsible for constructing the garments and accessories and will, in most instances, visit the shop regularly to attend fittings and keep up with the building progress, the

FIGURE 5-38. Liz Covey's sketch for Kate in the McCarter Theatre's production of *Taming of the Shrew*. Technical pen, sepia ink, and colored pencil on Somerset Cream paper. Note details given on the sketch and window mounting. *Photograph by Frances Aronson.*

designer cannot be in the shop every moment; therefore it is necessary to include certain basic information on all the sketches in order to prevent mix-ups and mistakes.

Each sketch should have the name of the play, the character, the actor, and the scene or scenes for which the costume is intended. In a large show it is a good idea to number the sketches consecutively, and if individual characters have several costumes, to number these also. For example:

MACBETH	MACBETH
Sketch #5	Sketch #6
Lady Macbeth, Jane Smith	Lady Macbeth, Jane Smith
I-5, 6, 7, & II-2	II-3
costume #1	costume #2

and so on.

Embellish the sketch as necessary with drawings of back views, decorative detail, and accessories. Write any notes and instructions that will help the technicians make correct decisions, such as pattern sources, fabric treatments, explanation of sword rigging, and the like. Describe or draw undergarments if they are necessary to the silhouette. Be sure to include any special closings the garment should have to facilitate quick changes. List unseen costume props such as a pocketwatch or a wallet (these items may also turn up on the prop list but it never hurts to have a double-check) and costume accessories like cuff links and tie pins.

It is not a good idea to put this explanatory information on the back of the sketch. Far too many notes on backs of sketches get overlooked. Devise ways of making notations on the sketch itself, ways that can be both handsome and practical. In most instances it is preferable to print or write in your own hand in a subdued ink or pencil. Fancy printing or labelling with press-on letters takes focus away from the costumed figure.

Mounting Sketches

Finished costume sketches ought to be able to stand on their own, actually as well as aesthetically. Few fitting rooms have pin-up boards and there is seldom an extra person around who can be spared for the single purpose of holding up the sketch. A sketch that wilts in the middle when

FIGURE 5-39. Michael J. Cesario's sketch for *Cabaret* produced by the Nebraska Repertory Company. Figure rendered in colored pencils on light gray paper, cut out, and flat mounted on black board. *Photograph by Frances Aronson.*

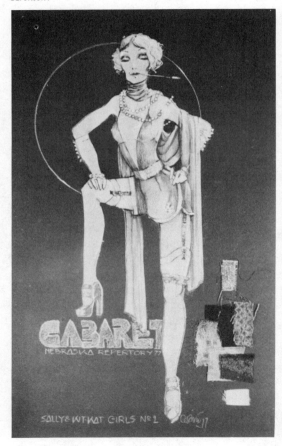

you try to prop it up is maddening. Therefore, if you have not done your final sketch on very heavy paper or illustration board, it should be mounted.

The simplest way to mount a sketch is to bond it to poster board, railroad board, or mat board with either rubber cement or a spray adhesive. The board may be cut the same size as the sketch or a bit larger to create borders. If you are leaving a border, be sure to calculate the placement of the sketch and make pencil marks to indicate where each corner should fall.

To use rubber cement, spread a thin layer of the adhesive on the back of the sketch and on the cardboard. Allow the surfaces to dry slightly. A large sheet of tracing paper laid between the two surfaces will help you to match up your corner marks exactly. Slip the tracing paper out and press the two surfaces together. Remove any excess rubber cement with your fingers or with a gum eraser. If you are using a spray adhesive, follow the directions on the can—carefully.

WINDOW MATS

Mounting with a window mat is a bit more complicated but often much more handsome. Use mat board (mounting card) for window mats. Determine the size of the mat by adding the width of the desired borders to the size of the sketch. (Don't forget that the window has to be cut a bit smaller than the outside dimensions of the sketch paper.) Cut out the window with a sharp knife or with a mat cutter and be sure you are not cutting directly into your dining room table! Mount the sketch behind the window mat with masking tape or brown paper tape. If the sketch is on very flimsy paper, you may want to mount it on board before placing it behind the window mat.

When you are creating a border around your sketch, either by mounting it on a larger piece of board or behind a window mat, be sure to have the bottom border slightly wider than the top and sides. If all four sides are equal, the sketch will appear to be too low down and look as though it is falling out of the mat. With a window mat that is to have 3″ borders, for example, make the top and sides 3″ and the bottom 3½″. When you pin up the matted sketch, all borders will appear to be equal.

Use restraint when you are choosing a color to border a sketch. Anything that will detract from the costumed figure should be avoided.

Be aware as you are mounting your sketches that you will have to carry them around with you—don't add too much cardboard to the total weight. Borders may be of modest width. Lightweight cardboard is quite suitable for mounting, just as long as it's firm enough to stand up when it needs to.

COVERING SKETCHES

When the sketches are complete, most costume designers spray them lightly with a fixitive for protection. In addition, since costume sketches get handled so much in transit and in the shop, it is always a good idea to use one of the protective papers discussed earlier and cover them completely.

You may use clear acetate, Glassine paper, or cellophane; you may even use kitchen weight plastic wrap in a pinch. If you are mounting your sketch in a window mat, you may place a layer of protective paper behind the window before you tape down the sketch—or you may cover the whole sketch, no matter how it is mounted. Cut a sheet of protective paper two or three inches larger in all four directions than the mounted sketch. Lay the protective paper over the sketch and fold the excess to the back. Create neat corners and tape in place. Be careful when you are folding acetate; it has a tendency to crack if creased too hard.

Photocopies

Once the costumes are designed and the construction of them is underway, various people involved in the production will probably want photocopies of the sketches. A set of photocopies may go to the costume shop to be placed in the costume "bible," the book in which the construction history of that show is recorded; another set may go to the stage manager so the actors can refer to them during rehearsals; the scene designer and/or property artist may also want a set; you may even prefer to take swatched photocopies of the sketches with you on shopping trips rather than struggle under a load of cardboard.

Regular photocopies come in two sizes: 8½ × 11 and 8½ × 14. If your sketches are larger than that and if there is a photocopy center available to you, you may be able to find a machine that reduces as it copies. Drawings up to 12 × 14 can be reduced to either regular photocopy size. Since reduction is much more expensive than ordinary copying, you can save a bit by having only one set of sketches reduced and copying the other sets from the reduced set. An interesting side effect of the photocopy reduction process is that the drawings may look clearer and better in the reductions.

If there is no reducing copy machine available, you will have to copy the sketches in two halves and tape them together with Scotch Magic Transparent tape.

It is possible to photocopy in color but the process is too expensive for ordinary use, especially since the reproduced color is far from accurate.

Many theatres have their own photocopy machines and sometimes you may even encounter a copy machine with its own operator who will do the job for you. Dry copy processes are far superior to wet copy processes and I.B.M. machines seem to copy costume sketches better than the other brands.

Swatching

Before your sketches are turned over to the shop, be sure each one is accurately swatched with the actual fabrics from which the costumes will be built. Check to see that the correct side of the fabric is clearly indicated. Swatch proportionately; that is to say, if one fabric only represents a small area of color, such as a skirt border or a necktie, put only that proportionate amount of the swatch on the sketch. Arrange swatches both attractively and sensibly, and securely. Display bits of trim, lace, and other decoration on the sketch along with the fabrics.

FIGURE 5-40. A nicely swatched sketch by Ann Wallace for Trouble-all in *Bartholomew Fayre*. Gouache on a background of brown paper bags. Brown paper bags were crumpled up, bleached, gessoed, and then varnished to board. Background painting done with watercolor in a plant sprayer. *Photograph by Frances Aronson.*

From the Drawing Board
Into the Street

Although most of you will have been doing some shopping during the process of preparing final sketches, it is when the last sketch is complete that the demands on the designer change drastically. Once all the sketches are approved by the director and are ready to go into the shop, the designer leaves the peace and quiet of reading, researching, drawing, and painting and plunges headlong into the task of purchasing everything the shop will need to build the costumes. Telephones, traffic, and shopkeepers dominate the next phase of designing costumes for the theatre.

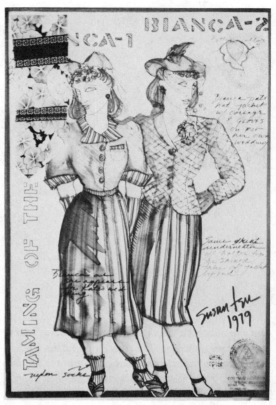

FIGURE 5-41. Susan Tsu's sketch for Bianca in the Milwaukee Repertory Theater's production of *Taming of the Shrew*. Ready to be shopped. *Photograph by Frances Aronson.*

6

The Pre-Production Period

Ordinary clothes automatically become extraordinary on the stage or screen. The frame around the events invites intensified attention to what is being worn; we know it is there intentionally even though it represents something worn casually....

ANNE HOLLANDER
Seeing Through Clothes

The show is designed. You have sketches in hand. You are well aware that the director and the actors may make discoveries in rehearsal that will call for changes but, because you have explored the script fully and in careful collaboration with the other members of the production group, you are confident that these changes will be minimal.

Now it's time to change gears, to begin the practical pre-production work that will allow your designs to move smoothly from sketches to dresses, suits, and poke bonnets. As soon as the costume technicians have begun to cut and stitch garments, the designer must be available to oversee the work at regular intervals, to interpret drawings, answer questions, and participate in all fittings. You can accomplish all this during the production period only if you have scheduled your time well, know exactly what has to be found, pulled, rented and built, and have the bulk of the shopping done.

You may have two weeks in which to do your pre-production work or you may have two days. Some of it will inevitably spill over into the production, or building, period. Whatever time you have, do as much as you can before the shop puts scissors to cloth. This is, for example, the best time to make lists.

The following discussion is divided into four sections:

1. Planning
2. Finding, Pulling, Renting
3. Shopping and Buying
4. Recording.

The order in which they are presented is not necessarily the order in which you will be able to proceed, since each situation will determine its own order. Learn early to be flexible and don't ever wait around to complete one phase of the process before starting on the next. A time may come when you are called on to plan, pull, buy and record all at the same time in less than three days in a blinding snowstorm. If you know how to plan, how to organize your work, and how to make wise decisions quickly, you will probably succeed.

124

Planning

Revised Costume Plot

Many of you took a rough costume plot with you when you had your first conference with the director (discussed in Chapter 2). It was made up as part of the initial script work. This plot reflects only the needs of the text and does not include decisions made for this particular production; nor does it reflect your designs. Now is the time to update the original costume plot; in many cases you will want to write it up anew. Choose a roomy, double-spaced form in which to record the plot since there will be more changes, additions, and subtractions during the course of the production period. No costume plot is considered final until the curtain goes up on opening night.

Look at your sketches as you compose your costume plot. List every item of clothing and every accessory required by each costume. Do not overlook underwear. Include collar studs, cuff links, pocket watches, padding, handkerchiefs, and wedding rings. Don't bother to describe the items on the plot. It is enough to list them.

FIGURE 6-1. A scene from Arena Stage's production of *A History of the American Film* by Christopher Durang, a play that requires an exceptionally complicated costume plot. *Costume design by Marjorie Slaman. Photograph by George de Vincent.*

Here are lists that include items you might put on revised costume plots for a female and a male actor.

Women

wig or hairpiece
hair decoration
corset
petticoat
understructures such as bustle, hoop skirt, pannier, etc.
dress/jacket/skirt/blouse
apron
tights
shoes or boots
belt
handkerchief
coat/cloak/cape
gloves
hat
purse
jewelry such as hat pin, brooch, ring, necklace, earrings, etc.
accessories such as parasol, umbrella, fan

Men

wig
facial hair such as beard, moustache, sideburns, mutton chops, etc.
shirt
collar
collar studs
cuff links
tie
tie pin
handkerchief
arm garters
suit/jacket/trousers/vest
suspenders
belt
socks
shoes or boots
overcoat/cape/cloak
gloves
hat

spats
jewelry such as ring, watch and chain, etc.
accessories such as cane, umbrella, etc.

When the costumes are finished—certainly by the time they are turned over to wardrobe—you can give this final costume plot to the wardrobe supervisor who will use it as a dressing list for each actor in the production. At that time you can add descriptive details to help the dressers identify individual garments.

Meet With Costume Shop Personnel

It is no secret that the relationship between a costume designer and the technicians who build the show has a great deal to do with the quality of the work that is done. A designer who treats shop personnel as automatons and does not allow them to feel involved in the work they are doing can only expect to inspire run-of-the-mill workmanship. The best work is usually done for a designer who takes the time to explain sketches, describes the effect he or she hopes the designs will have, welcomes cutting and construction advice and considers it seriously.

Treat your first official meeting with costume shop personnel as an occasion to set the stage for a good working relationship. This should be your goal even if you know the members of the staff and have worked with them before, since each building period takes on its own character. Make sure there is adequate time to go over all the sketches in detail. Remember that you have been looking at them for days; the shop technicians may be seeing them for the first time and cannot be expected to see everything at once.

Talk about each sketch. Describe how you envision it in motion, point out closings, delineate layers carefully. If fabric has not been shopped, explain what kinds of fabric you are looking for. Be as specific as possible, especially about detail and trim.

FIGURE 6-2. Frank Hamilton as Captain Shotover and Jeanne Ruskin as Ellie
Dunn in the McCarter Theatre production of *Heartbreak House* by G.B. Shaw. Mr.
Hamilton is wearing a false moustache, full beard, and sideburns. His own hair
was bleached and treated to match. *Costume design by Andrew B. Marlay. Hair
design by Paul Huntley. Photograph by Cliff Moore.*

After you have talked about the sketches, invite comments and suggestions. Listen to what is said. The shop staff will be interested mainly in how the garments are to be built and might suggest methods that may be more effective than yours. Young designers often worry that taking suggestions is tantamount to losing control of their design. Try not to take this position. All theatre is collaborative. You will never lose control of good, strong designs; sometimes they turn out even better because a draper or a craftsperson makes a valuable contribution to the work.

If you have not worked with the shop before or if there have been personnel changes since you worked there last, be sure to find out exactly how the staff is organized. Who drapes, who cuts, who stitches, and who is responsible for accessories? How many hours per day does the shop work? How are stock supplies charged and who is responsible for recording expenditures? Is there a shopper on the staff? And so on. Ask personal questions as well. If you smoke, ask if smoking is permitted in the shop. Is a desk or work space provided for designers? Is there a refrigerator in which to store lunches, and do they have tea, coffee, or soft drinks available?

A costume shop staff is a unique blend of personalities and the costume designer coming in needs to be sensitive to the individuals and to the nature of the working unit. Once you perceive the climate in a shop, you can decide how to make appropriate contributions in order to inspire the best craftsmanship possible during the time you are all working together.

Schedules and Deadlines

Now that you are acquainted with the way the shop operates, you can make a schedule for the production period and establish deadlines.

Sit down with the shop supervisor and plan the overall fitting schedule. This is particularly important if you do not live near the shop and must make periodic trips to oversee the work. Decide at the outset when you will come to the shop so the technicians can plan accordingly and be ready for your visits. Remember that a full day of fittings is exhausting for the designer and for the technicians, so try to space them to allow for rest time. In an Equity company, three separate fittings is the rule for each costume: a muslin fitting, the first fabric fitting, and the final fabric fitting. In most cases you will not see the completed costume with all its accessories until the dress parade or the first dress rehearsal.

As you make up the fitting schedule be sure you know what Actors' Equity Association regulations are in force at that theatre. Different theatres operate under different contracts with Equity, and each contract has its own rules that dictate the frequency and length of fittings as well as rules that regulate what parts of the costume the theatre is responsible for and what, if anything, is the responsibility of the actor.

If you are in doubt about Equity regulations and the shop staff cannot answer your questions, ask to talk with the stage manager or to see the theatre's Equity rule book. Should you, even inadvertently, violate an Equity rule by keeping an actor in a fitting longer than allowed, the theatre will have to compensate the actor at the overtime pay rate. Try to anticipate situations in which the normal number of hours allotted to fittings is insufficient for the work that has to be done and discuss the matter with the stage manager. Additional fitting time may be taken from rehearsal or, if this is impossible, overtime pay might be included in the budget.

On page 129 is an excerpt from the Actors' Equity Association Rule Book that applies to contracts between Equity and the League of Resident Theatres (LORT) from July 1981 through July 1984. Contracts are renegotiated at regular intervals and the rules do change, so it is a good idea for costume designers to stay up to date.

If you need to contact Equity to ask about LORT contract rules or the rules that govern other types of contracts, you may write or phone any of the following offices:

National Office:
165 West 46th Street
New York, NY 10036
(212) 869-8530

Branch Offices:
360 N. Michigan Avenue
Chicago, IL 60601
(312) 641-0393

6430 Sunset Blvd.
Los Angeles, CA 90028
(213) HO 2-2334

465 California Street
Suite 210
San Francisco, CA 94104
(415) 781-8660

Many shops keep work charts on the wall that list all the costume pieces for which they are responsible; spaces are provided on the chart in which work steps can be checked off as they are completed. Such charts are supposed to reflect exactly where the work on the show is at any given time. Unfortunately, this is not usually the case—as soon as the technicians begin working at a good clip, they forget to check off the various tasks as they finish them and the chart may rapidly become useless.

In all this planning don't forget to set personal deadlines as well. Assign yourself a completion date for shopping, pick a date on which to visit the rental company, note which rehearsals you expect to attend, and schedule a meeting date with the milliner. Each production makes many, many demands on you and the only way you can meet them all is by apportioning your time carefully.

Section 12. from the Actors' Equity Association Agreement and Rules Governing Employment in Resident Theatres, July 1981 through July 1984.

12. CLOTHING AND COSTUMES.

A. The Theatre shall provide all costumes and clothing except modern conventional undergarments. The Theatre shall also provide properly fitted footwear which, if for dancing, shall be new. All other footwear shall be clean, sanitary, and in good repair. All footwear used for dancing shall be furnished at least one week prior to dress rehearsal. Such footwear shall be of suitable construction for dancing when used for Contemporary Theatre Dance Movement, i.e., classical, ballet, modern, jazz, ethnic, etc. During rehearsals, the Theatre shall furnish at least one pair of toe shoes for each member of the Chorus called upon to dance in toe shoes.

The Theatre shall furnish kneepads when necessary for rehearsals and/or performances.

B. <u>Make-up</u>. The Theatre shall provide all make-up except ordinary and conventional make-up.

If the Actor is required to use body make-up, the Theatre shall furnish a regular linen towel service for removal of such make-up.

C. <u>Rental</u>. No Actor shall rent or lend any wardrobe to a Theatre for use in any production unless the terms of the rental, based on the schedule agreed upon in writing between Equity and LORT, are stated in the Actor's contract of employment or in a rider thereto. The agreed upon payment shall be made to the actor with the Actor's weekly salary.

D. <u>Cleaning</u>. Costumes or clothing, including wigs and hairpieces used in a production, shall be freshly cleaned when delivered to the Actor and cleaned thereafter whenever necessary. Spot cleaning, when required, shall be completed in time to allow at least four (4) hours for drying and airing prior to the half-hour call.

Stockings, shirts and other "skin parts" of costumes and/or clothes shall be laundered or cleaned at least once a week, and more often should the Deputy and Stage Manager deem it necessary. Laundered items shall be completely dry and delivered prior to the half-hour call.

E. <u>Change of Hair Color</u>. The Actor may not be required to change the color of his/her hair unless he/she agrees in writing. If he/she agrees, the Theatre shall pay the expense of changing the color and of its upkeep during the run of the engagement, and of the restoration to the original color at the close of the engagement.

F. <u>Change of Hair Style</u>. The Actor may not be required to cut or change the style of his/her hair in any way, or to shave his/her head, unless he/she agrees in writing. He/she may, however, be required to let his/her hair grow, or he may be required to grow a beard provided he agrees in writing. If he/she agrees, the Theatre shall pay the original expenses and the expenses of the upkeep of said hair or hair style.

Structure the Budget

By now you know exactly how many dollars you have to work with. Once again, be very sure that you know exactly what the producing organization expects the budget to cover. Some items that may or may not be included in the costume budget are: wigs and facial hair, basic stitching supplies, dry cleaning, maintenance materials, transportation costs for you and for your assistant, postage or shipping, and phone calls. You must know what you are responsible for before you can structure the budget. Remember that certain items, such as muslin for draping compli-

cated period patterns, can add up to shocking totals if you have not estimated the cost as carefully as possible. Paying for actors' haircuts or perms can also put your budget seriously out of joint during the days just before dress rehearsals if you have neglected to add in these costs from the start.

Estimate all fixed costs with the help of the shop supervisor and subtract them from the budget at the start. Next, set aside ten percent of the total budget and earmark it for tech week emergencies and last minute changes. For a show that is primarily shopped off retail racks, up this figure to fifteen percent.

FIGURE 6-3. Original budget estimate for a production of *Custer* by Robert Ingham.

```
                    Custer - budget notes

       7 uniforms
             $150 ea for materials              $1,050
       7 prs boots
             2 prs cavalry type $200 ea
             5 prs short or ordinary riding
                   boots $50 ea                    650
       3 dresses
             12 yds fabric ea @ app. $10/yd        360
       3 prs high laced, heeled ladies' boots
             $50 ea                                150
       beaded necklace for Wooden Leg              20
                                                $2,230


       silk screening process:

       photography expenses                        300
       screening supplies, equipment               400
       half-tones                                  300
                                                $1,000

                              TOTAL   $3,230
```

BUDGET BREAKDOWN -- "BIOGRAPHY"

	Item	Amount	Subtotal
MINNIE	dress fabric	20.00	
	collar and cuffs	5.00	25.00
	shoe rental (own shoes)	12.00	37.50
	dress fabric (2nd dress)	16.00	53.00
	garter belt	4.99	57.99
	collar fabric	6.00	63.99
	3 prs. seamed stockings	6.00	69.99
SLADE	hair appointment	50.00	
	shoes	25.00	75.00
	blouse fabric	22.50	97.50
	girdle	7.49	104.99
	gloves	6.99	111.98
	gloves (2nd pair)	4.99	116.97
	coat	60.00	176.97
	suit fabric & interfacing	64.18	241.15
	3 prs. stockings	6.00	247.15
	purse	15.00	262.15
	earrings	1.00	263.15
	garters	2.57	265.90
	coat decoration fabric	2.00	267.90
	fur and fastenings	22.97	290.87

	Item	Amount	Subtotal
MARION	gloves	4.99	
	gloves (2nd pr.)	4.99	9.98
	purse	24.99	34.97
	purse (2nd one)	14.99	49.96
	wig	225.00	274.96
	coat fabric	79.80	354.76
	muslin and lining	23.00	377.76
	garter belt	4.99	382.75
	girdle	4.99	387.74
	shoes	39.95	427.69
	smock fabric	20.00	447.69
	evening dress fabric	60.00	507.69
	coat lining	9.75	517.44
	dress silk	60.00	574.44
	draping mock-up fabric	12.50	589.94
	trouser rental (own)	15.00	604.94
	dress fabric (3rd dress)	67.00	671.94
	coat	60.00	731.94
	blouse	18.00	749.94
	shoes (2nd pr.)	36.00	785.94
	coat cuffs	21.00	806.94
	leotard for dress base	15.50	824.44
	evening gloves	7.00	831.44
	3 prs. stockings	6.00	837.44
	2nd leotard	17.50	854.94
	shoes (3rd pr.)	62.00	916.94
	jewelry	23.00	939.94
	straps for evening dress	25.00	964.94
	piping fabric for dress	13.00	977.94
	purse (2nd one)	10.80	988.74
	shoes (4th pr.)	21.00	1009.74
	fur trim for coat	25.50	1035.24
	trim fabric for 2nd coat	4.00	1039.24
	bra	5.40	1044.64

FIGURE 6-4. (continued)

Item	Amount	Subtotal
MISCELLANEOUS ITEMS		
shipping for borrowed costumes	13.50	13.75
shopping bag	.25	23.75
Tintex dyes	10.00	24.29
Xerox	.54	28.79
Ivory Snow and Tintex dyes	4.50	50.79
costume collection rental	22.00	58.52
envelopes and heel cups	7.73	59.05
Xerox	.53	59.55
phone call and Xerox	.50	48.55
costume collection refund	11.00	56.06
muslin and linings	7.50	58.05
linings	2.00	74.90
shoe dyes	16.85	77.88
Tintex dyes	2.98	79.38
tea for dipping down	1.50	80.08
hat pins	.70	93.58
dress shields	13.50	96.33
tape	2.75	96.61
hat pins	.28	107.61
Greyhound shipping	11.00	136.46
cufflinks and rings	28.85	144.71
thread or Tintex dyes	8.25	178.86
buttons	34.15	181.86
rings	3.00	191.91
barge cement and magix	10.05	

MINNIE	69.99
SLADE	290.87
MARION	1077.83
FEYDAK	182.49
WARWICK	65.76
KINNICOTT	107.00
NOLAN	12.00
KURT	64.85
MISCELLANEOUS	191.91
TOTAL	2062.70

Item	Amount	Subtotal
bra (2nd one)	7.00	1051.64
purse (3rd one) & belt	14.99	1066.63
earrings	2.15	1068.78
ring	1.05	1069.83
buttons and clasp	8.00	1077.83
FEYDAK		
shoe rental (own shoes)	12.00	141.60
suit	129.60	157.59
ties and handkerchiefs	15.99	182.49
shirts	24.90	
(all other items from stock)		
WARWICK		
white gloves	3.00	16.50
3 wing collars	13.50	22.50
wrist watch	6.00	28.50
hat rental (own hat)	6.00	65.76
shoes	37.26	
(all other items from stock and borrowed free of charge.)		
KINNICOTT		
ensemble rental (actor's own)	90.00	107.00
shirt	17.00	
NOLAN		
shoe rental (own shoes)	12.00	12.00
(all other items from stock and borrowed free of charge.)		
KURT		
shoes	39.95	64.85
shirts	24.90	
(all other items from stock and borrowed free of charge.)		

Beyond these rather obvious steps, there are no hard and fast rules for structuring a costume budget. Instinct and experience both play a large role in successful budgeting and you will get better at it every time you do it.

STARTING POINT.

For those without sufficient experience to have a starting point, begin by dividing the money that remains after you have deducted fixed expenses and the tech week emergency fund among the costumes required for the show. If you have five-hundred dollars left and there are ten costumes to produce, start off by allotting fifty dollars to each costume. What follows is a process of robbing Peter to pay Paul. The set of peasant rags will certainly cost less than the leading lady's silk dress, so you will subtract from one and add to the other. If you can pull the rags from stock, subtract even more from the cost of that costume and apply it to still another costume. Continue this juggling act until the arrangement looks sensible on paper. Remember that you should have been aware of the budget figure while you were designing the costumes and you should already have made some instinctive adjustments concerning the garments and their probable cost.

ESTIMATING.

After the initial breakdown has been established, begin to price individual items. Go through your revised costume plot and estimate, piece by piece. If specific garments or accessories have to be purchased, get on the telephone and find out exactly what you will have to spend. Don't trust memory. Prices of most things have a way of escalating; the top hat you got for sixty-five dollars three years ago might well cost ninety dollars now. If you cannot calculate the exact cost—having fabric pleated before you know exactly how many feet of pleating you will need—make a slightly higher estimate. Under-estimating leads to rude shocks.

You cannot accurately estimate fabric costs until you have worked out the yardage each garment requires. It is often a good idea to do this in collaboration with the draper. When the budget is really tight you will not want to overbuy, but you certainly don't want to run out of cloth when there are two skirt panels left to cut.

Once you have established the number of yards a costume will take, you can divide that number into the amount of money you have apportioned to it (taking out for trim, linings, buttons, etc.) in order to see what your per yard ceiling price will be. If this calculation tells you the fabric must cost no more than eight dollars per yard to fit within your budget, you will save a lot of time by not looking at more expensive choices.

Figure 6–5 contains some yardage estimates. Be sure to note fabric widths. Remember that you need extra fabric to match plaids or patterns. If the plaid or pattern is relatively regular, add one extra yard for every five purchased. One-way plaids or distant repeats may require more.

Estimate tight ruffles at a ratio of 3:1, looser ones at 2 or 2½:1. Knife pleating, such as you might use to trim an 1870's dress, is also a 3:1 ratio and eats up fabric at an amazing rate. When the fabric you are considering is silk taffeta at eighteen dollars per yard, pleating may turn out to be an extremely expensive trim; you should know this information in advance.

If, after you have finished estimating the cost of realizing the costumes you designed, you discover that the cost exceeds the budget, go back and see where corners may be cut.

1. Consider reworking certain stock garments instead of building them from scratch. Give some thought to borrowing from nearby theatres or renting, if the fee is less than the cost of building.

```
MEN
Contemporary Suit (single-breasted):
   Coat - 2 yds (54"-60" wide)
   Trousers - 1-1/2 yds-1-3/4 yds (54"-60" wide)
   Vest fronts - can be gotten out of the 3-1/2 yds.
   Suit coat lining - 1-3/4 yds (40" wide)
   Inner structure:
       3/4 yd pocketing
       1/2 yd wigan
       2 yds stay tape
       1/2 yd haircloth

Long-sleeved shirt - 3-1/2-4 yds (40" wide)

3-piece frock coat suit - 5-6 yds (54"-60" wide)

Frock coat, 19th C. - 3-1/2-4 yds (54"-60" wide)

Tailcoat, 19th C. - 3-3-1/2 yds (54"-60" wide)

Vest fronts only - 3/4 yd

Vest fronts and backs - 1-1/2 yds

Add extra for plaids and napped fabrics.


WOMEN
Tailored coat - 1-3/4 yds (54"-60" wide)

Tailored skirt - 1-1/4 yds (54"-60")

Trousers - 1-1/4 yds (54"-60")
           2-1/2 - 3 yds (40" wide)

Blouse with long sleeves - 3-1/2 yds (40" wide)

Dress, 1860's - 12 yds, exclusive of trim (40" wide)

Dress, 1880's - 10 yds, exclusive of trim (40" wide)

Skirt, turn of the century - 6 yds (40" wide)

Add extra for plaids and napped fabrics.
```

FIGURE 6-5. Yardage estimates.

2. Think about using old fabric that the costume shop has in stock. It may not be exactly what you had in mind but a little dye and paint could transform it completely.

3. Think about using really cheap fabric and treating it with decorative techniques that will give you the look you want without the expense.

4. Reconsider using wigs and facial hair since they are particularly expensive items. As a matter of fact, you should make it a rule of thumb to avoid using a wig unless it is absolutely necessary. Unless it is a very good wig indeed, it will never look as nice as the actor's own hair. Short hair wigs for men tend to be particularly unsatisfactory. If a wig is absolutely necessary, renting it may be cheaper than purchasing it, particularly if you can arrange to rent it from another theatre. Go through every wig and beard in the shop and see if you can make them serve, perhaps by trimming or dyeing them. Hair rinses that will wash out, such as Fancifull, are excellent for wigs because the hair can be restored to its original color and not have to remain bright red or jet black forever.

5. Scheme to save on trim by reusing braid, fringe, or appliques from old costumes. Check with the shop manager, however, before denuding stock garments. Create metallic trim by painting cotton lace and braid with bronzing powder in an FEV or lacquer solution, a process that is generally much cheaper than purchasing the real stuff.

FIGURE 6-6. Andrew B. Marlay's sketch for Lady Utterword in the McCarter Theatre production of *Heartbreak House* by G.B. Shaw. *Photograph by Frances Aronson.*

FIGURE 6-7. Charlotte Moore wearing the costume made from the sketch in Figure 6-6. Dress fabric includes two antique shawls and antique lace found in the theatre stock. *Photograph by Cliff Moore.*

FIGURE 6-8. *Cabaret* at Marriott's Lincolnshire Theatre. The actress in this photograph is wearing a good-looking but very inexpensive synthetic wig. *Costume design by Arnold S. Levine. Photograph courtesy of Marriott's Lincolnshire Theatre.*

FIGURE 6-9.
Katherine McGrath as Ilona Szabo in the McCarter Theatre production of Molnar's *The Play's the Thing*. Ms. McGrath wears a becoming wig, and her dress is trimmed with antique appliques. *Costume design by Robert Morgan. Photograph by Cliff Moore.*

6. Consider labor as you trim the budget. Even if the costume budget does not pay for labor directly, you must consider the number and the quality of labor hours available to you for building the costumes. Plentiful labor, even if it is semi-skilled—beginning students or the members of volunteer stitching groups which help out in many regional theatres—may supply you with hours that will save you dollars. Perhaps you can have your pleating done in the shop rather than send it out. Volunteers have been known to produce sets of hand-knit chainmail, mufflers, and masses of oversized crocheted lace. Willing shop workers with minimal skills can paint trim, add highlights to a dull brocade, and string ropes of beads. They can save you cold, hard cash if you plan the work with them in mind.

If, after all these reconsiderations, you cannot structure the cost of the show within the budget figure, go immediately to management and present your paperwork. Don't simply cross your fingers and hope it will work itself out. It probably won't, and you will save yourself a lot of grief by speaking up at this point rather than having to explain to an angry business manager why you spent more dollars than were allotted. It's easier for the producing organization to find a bit more money for costumes early on than to make up for losses later.

Make Lists

Sit down with the shop supervisor and make lists of what you propose to build, find, rent, and buy. Don't forget anything. Even if your greatest concern is finding brocades and velvets in just the right hues, you are also responsible for providing the technicians with bones, boning tape, millinery adhesive, and shoe dye. The staff shopper may purchase them but you must be sure they are on a list, complete with brand name if you have a preference. You will never be able to anticipate everything—new needs will arise in the course of building—but the more complete you can be in the beginning, the less time will be wasted later in repetitive shopping trips.

FIGURE 6-10. Max Wright as Balance in the Long Wharf Theatre production of Farquhar's *The Recruiting Officer*. Notice the delightful prop soldiers. *Costume and scene design by John Conklin. Photograph by William L. Smith.*

Be sure you have a list of all the property items directly related to costume which the prop shop is responsible for making, finding, or buying. You will want to okay canes and cigarette lighters and supervise weapons and weapon rig-gings that the property technicians are building from your designs. Make regular visits to the prop shop to look at everything that affects costume.

Finding, Pulling, Renting

Finding

Knowing what you need to find is only the first step in actually finding it. The following comments refer both to finding items you expect to acquire for free and finding extraordinary or unusual items to buy.

If you are designing a production whose run will be limited, it is often possible to borrow (for free) certain types of garments: modern policemen's uniforms, lab coats and nurses' uniforms, restaurant garb (chef's hats and waitress uniforms), choir robes, clerical outfits, football, baseball, and basketball uniforms, academic gowns, fur coats, and formal wear. It is easier to borrow in a city than in a small town and easiest in a medium-sized city where the local theatre is relatively well-known, respected, and has a reputation for reliability.

Never expect to find what you want to borrow on the first phone call. And don't generalize. That is to say, if one restaurant won't loan you a chef's hat, don't presume that the next one you call won't either. One young designer had the experience of calling seventeen hotels before finding one that would loan out six maid's uniforms. This designer's persistence paid off, all six uniforms were borrowed for free and the designer was therefore able to divert a large chunk of the small budget to ten yards of silk crepe for another character's evening gown.

Figuring out how to get in touch with the person who can actually loan you what you want is often a challenge. When you are contacting a hotel to inquire about borrowing, for example, you may fare better with the director of public relations than with the kitchen manager. If you are working at a regional theatre, see if there is anyone on the board of directors who can help you, a physician who can lead you to a lab coat (or provide you with one himself) or a college president who is willing to help you find an academic outfit.

Some businesses, furriers, and formal wear renters in particular, will often loan garments in exchange for free advertisement in the program. Make sure such an exchange is consistent with theatre policy before you agree to it and follow up to see that the advertisement actually appears. Some will loan items to you in exchange for a pair of tickets to a performance. Again, check theatre policy before saying yes.

Whenever you borrow, make sure the person or organization you borrow from knows exactly what use you will be making of the item and how long you will keep it. Don't promise to return a policeman's uniform on the day after

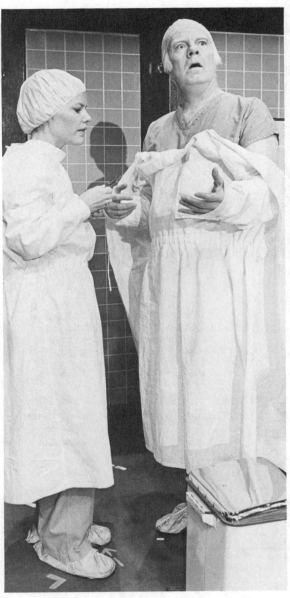

FIGURE 6-11. George Ede as Dr. Boyd and Pamela Payton-Wright as his nurse in *The National Health* by Peter Nichols at the Long Wharf Theatre. Their costumes are good examples of the kind of items costume designers must learn to find. *Costume design by Whitney Blausen. Photograph by William L. Smith.*

strike because it will have to go to the cleaner's first.

Most established theatres carry insurance that covers loss of and damage to borrowed items. In most cases, in order for the borrowed items to be protected by the insurance, you must present management with a list of exactly what you have borrowed and what its value is—*before* the items are used. Some theatres have special insurance forms you must complete on all the props and costume pieces you borrow.

Finding the unusual, the rare, and the scarce is a task costume designers do regularly. The process can be frustrating and fascinating. There are no rules for finding what is hard to find, and the best advice is to follow every lead doggedly and don't give in to despair. Every designer has a tale of such a search. The objects searched for range from wearable World War I gas masks to turn-of-the-century fireman's boots and high button shoes for a child of 8. Such searches are made even more difficult if time and/ or money are scarce.

Always ask the shop supervisor for assistance since there is often a staff member who is good at finding things, enjoys talking with strangers on the telephone, and is not daunted by refusals. If there is, enlist that person's aid at once.

Don't put off a difficult search hoping that the object may turn up all by itself. It won't. Besides there is always the possibility that you won't find the item anywhere and must therefore allow yourself time to come up with a second best.

Pulling

Some costume designers have a genius for pulling dull, drab garments off the storage racks and reworking them into exciting costumes. This takes a special eye for seeing potential. Not everybody can imagine an ensemble created out of a skirt from one frock, a bodice from another, a cut-down jacket from a suit, and a belt sprayed just the right shade of brown. If *you* can, your small budget shows will be particularly successful.

Many designers consider pulling from stock a penance and go at it with a grumpy attitude, wishing they had the money and the labor to make everything from scratch just as they envisioned it. If you can avoid being grumpy and approach a pulled or partly pulled show as a process in which you are creating new costumes from diverse elements, you may be able to transform a burden into a challenge. It is not unusual for a costume designer to have a reworked costume singled out for special praise in a production in which all the others were made from scratch in the shop.

If you know from the start that you will have to incorporate pulled garments in your show, you should go through stock before drawing completed sketches. It is not unusual, however, to find yourself adding more items from stock during the pre-production period either to lighten the budgetary pressure or to relieve the load on the shop.

The stocks of costumes in regional and university theatres that have been in operation for a number of years are the best hunting grounds for reusable costume pieces. These collections will probably include both old costumes and clothing donations from local people or even from small shops that have gone out of business. There will inevitably be men's shirts, ties, trousers, 1950's prom dresses, and piles of 1950's and 1960's hats. Costumes from past shows may well include some knee breeches, long skirts, shirtwaists, and vests.

Consider anything that has even the vaguest possibility for being reworked. You can conjure up some quite amazing things with the homeliest items when you add imagination and a sprinkling of inexpensive goodies. Every piece you pull from existing stock is something you will not have to purchase.

Since millinery work requires especially skillful hands and is very time consuming, get in the habit of looking at every hat in stock with an eye to reshaping, covering, spraying, and retrimming. Build hats from scratch only if there is absolutely nothing suitable to use as a base.

If you have a lot of pulling to do for a show, organize the items you are looking for in garment categories. Group suits together with notations about color and sizes, then shirts, hats, shoes, and so on. Costume storage is usually arranged by types of garments. Suits and jackets will be close together with trousers nearby. Shirts may be stored together in boxes or drawers or hung in another part of the storage area. Shoes may be at the far end of the room on shelves or in another room altogether; the same may be true of hats. You can speed up the pulling process if you are prepared to choose all the shirts at one time, all the shoes, hats, etc.

There is no such thing as a thoroughly clean costume storage area. Most are crowded,

FIGURES 6-12 and 6-13. Mostly pulled costumes from an Old West *Taming of the Shrew* at the Dallas Shakespeare Festival. Leslie Gerasi as the chair-wielding Kate (above), with Rene Moreno as the cowering piano player. John Mansfield as Petruccio (right), dressed up for his wedding. *Costume design by Susan Rheaume. Photographs by J. Allen Hansley.*

and the choicest things may be tucked away in hard-to-reach areas. Dress for the occasion in jeans and a sweat shirt, not in your best dress or new high-heeled shoes. Be prepared to climb ladders, rummage underneath racks, and emerge quite grubby at the end of the day.

Pulling costumes from storage takes a long time, especially if the area is not kept in good order. You may have to take many garments out to examine and measure, sometimes putting them on tailor's dummies for a really good look. You may find that three-piece suits have been split up and it will take you additional time to reassemble trousers, vest, and jacket. Make sure you allow yourself enough time to look at everything you need to see. Usually a member of the shop staff will be able to help you, a timesaver indeed. There are occasions, however, when you will want to search in solitude. If so, say so.

Before you leave the stock area in a theatre where you are designing, be sure to rehang and shelve the things you have considered and rejected. Your neatness will be noted and appreciated.

Renting

The biggest challenge in using a few rented costumes in a show is incorporating them in such a way that it doesn't look as though a strange and alien group of characters just stepped on the stage. This problem is at its most intense when you have rented sight unseen and the costumes arrive the day before first dress. Suddenly, with the intrusion of half a dozen suits and waistcoats, the subtle color range you labored on for so long over the dye pot is out the window. In most instances you have no recourse but to grin and bear it. There are a few precautions you can take to try and avert such disasters but you will probably not escape them altogether.

FIGURE 6-14. Rented uniforms for Arena Stage's production of *Sergeant Musgrave's Dance* by John Arden. *Costume design by Nancy Potts. Photograph by George de Vincent.*

Whenever you are renting from a commercial firm, make every effort to go in person to select the costumes you will use, or send a trusted associate. This is the only way to avoid surprises and, even if you don't find exactly what you want in color or in silhouette, you have a better chance of successfully incorporating it into your total scheme if you know what it looks like a month before dress rehearsal rather than a day before.

RENTAL COMPANIES

Eaves and Brooks Costume Company, Inc. (New York) and Western Costume Company (Hollywood) are currently the largest costume rental firms in the country. If you are in the midwest and can't travel to either coast, perhaps you should rent once from each in order to try them out. In general, Eaves and Brooks is more eager to rent an entire set of costumes for a production and Western pays closer attention to those who only want a few costumes. Western's stock comes largely from the film industry and Eaves and Brooks' from the commercial New York theatre. Rental fees are about the same at both, with Western coming in a bit lower for one or two outfits. If you're in Lincoln, Nebraska the air freight cost is equally exorbitant from either side of the continent.

Most cities have one or more local costume rental firms. The bulk of their business is in outfitting large amateur productions—the community theatre Gilbert & Sullivan show and the annual high school musical—and in individual costume rentals for masquerade parties and Halloween, not to mention the annual traffic in Santas and elves. Local firms are not always sensitive to the needs of regional theatres and university theatre training programs and they may charge more than Western or Eaves and Brooks to rent you a single costume for a four to six week period, even when you include the cost of shipping from Western or Eaves and Brooks. If you have a talk with your local costume renter,

and if the stock is broad enough to be useful to you on a fairly regular basis, you may be able to create a suitable renting relationship. There are advantages in working with a local firm, the chief one being that you can see what you're getting before you've got it.

The Costume Collection in New York City is a particularly interesting and unique costume rental organization. It is part of The Theatre Development Fund which, among other things, makes half-price tickets for Broadway shows available to people who are willing to stand in line in Times Square on the day they wish to go to the theatre. The Costume Collection serves only not-for-profit organizations which of course include all colleges and universities, most regional theatres, Off-Off Broadway, and some summer stock.

Rental fees at The Collection are considerably lower than commercial rates and you may barter for costumes. That is to say, you can trade stock garments of a sort that The Collection can use for rental credit. You must have all costumes cleaned before you return them or have a cleaning charge added to your rental bill. Even though the stock at The Costume Collection is not as comprehensive as the stocks at Western or Eaves and Brooks, there are many interesting things to be found at a cost that is easy to bear.

The best way to use The Collection is to make an appointment and select what you want to rent in person. At the time of this writing, you are allowed to take the costumes three weeks before your show opens because The Collection leaves alterations up to you. You are also welcome to make repairs and add trim although you may not cut things away, distress, or dye costumes. You can also take more garments than you actually need, try them on your actors, and make final choices. No rental charges will be made on costumes returned before your opening night, although there is a small handling fee.

According to Costume Collection Administrator Whitney Blausen, the following information must be provided by the renting organization before costumes can be taken:

1. A copy of the organization's tax-exempt certificate, IRS code 501 C-3.
2. A deposit check for fifty percent of the rental, made payable to Theatre Development Fund.
3. A letter of financial responsibility from an officer of the renting organization, on letterhead stationery written as follows:

(organization) authorizes (designer) to rent costumes in our name for (production) to be done on (dates). The seating capacity of our theatre is (_____). (organization) assumes financial responsibility for payment of the rental, cleaning costs, and for any loss, damage or late return of the costumes. We are aware that late fees of $7.50 per costume per week are charged if costumes have not been cleaned and returned by the due date in the contract and The Collection has not been notified of extenuating circumstances.

(signed by the officer and his or her title)

Whenever you rent long distance from a commercial firm, be sure to send them as much information as possible about what you want: complete and accurate measurements, clear photocopies of your sketches with any notes necessary to explain them, and a range of swatches. Always phone ahead to make sure that what you want is available and to settle on a rental fee.

RECIPROCAL RENTALS

Many regional and university theatres rent costumes to and from each other either on a cash or reciprocal basis. The practice is more lively between groups within the same general area. A free-lance costume designer who works in many regional theatres will get to know what stock is where and may even begin work on a show with a specific item in mind to rent.

FIGURE 6-15. Storage racks at the Costume Collection. *Photograph by Janet Beller, Courtesy of Theatre Development Fund.*

When designers rent costumes from other theatres, they assume the responsibility of making sure those costumes are returned at the end of the run, a job often neglected simply because the designer is off working on another show at another theatre. Unless you are absolutely certain that the shop staff *never* forgets to return rentals promptly, note on your calendar the date the production closes and phone to make sure the things are being sent back. Renting or borrowing from another theatre is usually such a financial boon to your budget that you should make every effort to keep the process as simple and as business-like as possible. It goes without saying that costumes rented from another theatre should be cleaned before they are returned.

When you rent, be sure to calculate costs other than rental fees. There is shipping. Western Costume Co., for instance, will only ship to you by air freight, which is expensive. The Costume Collection uses United Parcel Service, which is less costly. If the rental is local you may still incur gas and mileage expenses when picking up and returning the costumes. And remember cleaning costs if you are renting from The Collection or from another theatre.

Shopping and Buying

As a costume designer, you will have to buy such things as fabric, notions and trims, old clothing, and new, modern clothing. By the time you have produced the costumes for half a dozen productions in any city, you will have explored more byways than thoroughfares, poked about in a variety of curious shops, and met many interesting and unusual people. Your copy of the telephone company's yellow pages will be well thumbed and your city map will be coming apart at the folds. The work that began in solitude at your drawing board takes you far afield indeed.

Fabric

Fabric is the basis for most costumes and, like automobiles, ranges from silks and wools with the exquisite performance of a Rolls Royce or a Mercedes Benz to the sturdy cottons and cotton/synthetic blends which, like Volkswagen Rabbits and Toyota Corollas, do their jobs well but without a lot of flair. Fabric costs range as widely as the price tags on cars. You may pay forty-five dollars for a yard of silk and eighty dollars for the same amount of a wool and cashmere blend. Cotton broadcloth may, on the other hand, be tagged at three dollars and ninety-eight cents per yard and a cotton/polyester gauze at one dollar and ninety-eight cents per yard. How you choose between the extremes, and from every possibility in between, will be determined by your budget and by everything you know about fabric performance. Car purchasers don't expect a Toyota to perform like a Rolls. Costume designers have to know that polyester chiffon will not behave the way silk chiffon does. An important part of every costume designer's background is a thorough study of the fibers from which fabrics are created and the ways in which these fibers are made into yarns and the yarns woven, knitted, or pressed into pieces. Silk cloth is not desirable only because it is expensive. You want it for what it will do, for its drape and lustre. If your costume doesn't require silk performance, you won't choose silk no matter what your budget is.

Your first task, then, is to choose the fabrics

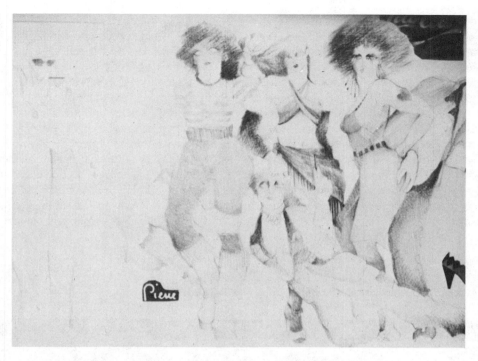

FIGURE 6-16. Sketch of costumes in the 42nd Street sequence in *On the Road to Babylon*. Many of these pieces were bought rather than built. *Costume design by Susan Tsu. Photograph by Frances Aronson.*

FIGURE 6-17. Scene from *On the Road to Babylon* at the Milwaukee Repertory Theater. *Photograph by Mark Avery.*

that are appropriate for the garments you have designed. The second consideration, often as important as the first, is to find those fabrics in the colors you want. It is with these two goals in mind that you set out to buy cloth.

Insofar as it is possible for you to do so, try never to pay a full, retail price for a yard of fabric. Virtually every city in the country has discount fabric shops, and in cities where garments are manufactured you will find shops selling both mill ends and factory ends. If you must buy from the most expensive fabric store in town, request a discount for the theatre. You may well get it.

New York City is, of course, the mecca for fabric shopping. If you know where to go and how to look, you can sometimes save enough on your cloth to pay for a round trip airplane ticket between New York and Lincoln, Nebraska.

There is a list of New York fabric shops at the end of this book, grouped according to their locations in the city, with a note about the types of fabric each carries and their relative costs. Some of these shops will charge purchases to the institution you are shopping for if you arrange for this service in advance (important when you are buying for a college or university theatre department). Others deal only in cash. In those shops where you may be able to practice the fine art of bargaining, always make sure you have cash in hand.

FIGURE 6-18. Unique fabric choices for the young men of Verona. Shakespeare's *Romeo and Juliet* at the Milwaukee Repertory Theatre. *Costume design by Susan Tsu. Photograph by Mark Avery.*

If cost is the most exasperating part of fabric shopping, the most bewildering part for the young designer is training your eyes to see the one piece of cloth you want when it is wrapped on a bolt, jammed on a table with dozens of other bolts, sitting in the midst of a room lined, hung, and draped with fabrics of every color, weight, description, and fiber content. Learning to see well takes practice, but here are a couple of hints that may help you in the early stages.

When you first come into a shop in which fabric blossoms in unkempt profusion, revealing no order of color, content, or cost, take a little while to walk slowly around the store. Don't look for anything. Decline offers of help from the shopkeeper and simply allow your eyes to take in the territory. Soon you will discover that you are able to look past the things you don't want to see and isolate cloth you might want for your show. Choose a few for closer inspection, feel them, hold them up to see how they drape. The whole process is one of learning to block out the wrong things so you can see the right ones.

Don't forget that most fabric shops have fluorescent lighting which distorts color, particularly blues and pinks, and makes everything look duller than it will under stage lights. Take your possibilities to the front of the store and look at them in natural light before you make up your mind.

Also, don't be lured by a print that's too small. Examine the fabric with squinted eyes, from a distance or with a reducing glass. Unless you choose a print only to alter color or add a slight overall texture, stick with relatively clear, large-scale prints that can be seen from your particular stage.

Even when you have definitely decided to buy a certain fabric, shop around a little more. Chances are, especially in New York, that you may find that fabric in three different shops—for three different prices!

If your costumes require linings, make sure you get them at the same time. Purchase underlinings and interfacings if they are not supplied by the shop.

Sometimes you will depend upon assistants to do your shopping for you. This may happen when you're doing two shows at almost the same time or when the theatre you're working for employs a design assistant to work with all guest designers. You may choose to do your own swatching during the design phase of your work and then send the assistant to purchase yardage for you. Or you may have the assistant swatch within the color, weight, and texture limits you designate. Since it is usually difficult to make final choices from swatches alone, you should try to see the fabrics on the bolts or, if your budget permits, have the assistant buy a quarter or a half yard of the fabrics so you can handle them before making up your mind.

Not every costume fabric you acquire will be new and off a bolt. Sometimes you may discover exactly the right thing in an old tablecloth, curtain, or slipcover. These items are available in most thrift shops and tend to be inexpensive. Bedspreads and sheets have also been pressed into costume service as well as mattress pads and spinnaker cloth from a set of sails. Make it a habit to consider every possibility you can think of in your quest for interesting and workable fabrics.

Wrapping and Shipping Fabrics

If you shop in one city for a show being done in another, you face all the complexities of shipping. The easiest way, of course, is to have the store do it for you, and there are many fabric shops that will comply with this request, charging you little more than the actual cost of sending the packages. Most understand that you need the goods quickly and send them out as soon as possible.

FIGURE 6-19. Sometimes you may discover exactly the right thing in an old tablecloth. Larry Ballard as Chrysalde and Michael Santo as Arnolphe, in Moliere's *School for Wives* at the Intiman Theatre. *Costume design by Susan Tsu. Photograph by Chris Bennion.*

Many times, however, you have assembled your fabrics from a variety of shops that cannot ship for you, leaving you on your own to box, wrap, tape, and deliver the parcels to the appropriate carrier.

Box fabric as though you expected the worst possible handling. Fill cartons snugly so things won't shift around and work their way out. If your fabrics don't come to the top of the box, add crumpled papers; they make an excellent filler without adding lots of additional weight.

You may decide to wrap your fabric without putting it in a box. If you do this, be sure you are using at least two layers of very stout brown paper. (Top quality grocery store bags make excellent wrapping paper for small and middle-sized parcels.) Sometimes the most convenient way to ship a large quantity of fabric is on the roll or tube it came on. You can wrap two or more tubes together or roll several lengths of fabric onto a single tube. Fabrics shipped on tubes will be free of creases, which more than makes up for the work it takes to separate the layers. You can purchase special paper sacks to cover fabric roles.

Tape your packages with brown Kraft tape or with strapping tape. Masking tape is *not* stout enough for shipping, and the U.S. Post Office will no longer accept parcels with masking tape on them. Modern package sorting machines have made the use of twine unacceptable.

Always put a label with your address inside the parcel in case the outside label comes off in transit. An inside label can be your most important means of recovering a lost package.

SHIPPING SERVICES

United Parcel Service (UPS) is the most inexpensive and reliable transport for medium weight and medium size parcels. Packages cannot weigh more than fifty pounds or be more than one-hundred-twenty inches around the four longest surfaces. It isn't easy to carry a package larger than these limitations so they aren't usually a problem. UPS will pick up and deliver. They can tell you exactly how long it will take for the parcel to make the trip: five days from New York City to Milwaukee, Wisconsin; four days from Washington, D.C. to Dallas, Texas. The quicker Blue Label Service is available between certain cities but costs more. If you are using UPS to ship to an organization—a theatre, college, or university—you can ship collect. Make sure you inform the receiving group how much money they must have on hand when the parcel is delivered.

The U.S. Post Office parcel post service is a bit more expensive than UPS but it is very convenient to be able to drop packages off at your local Post Office. If you do much shipping through parcel post, get a copy of the official instructions that tell you how to package and wrap and what the size and weight regulations are. Parcel post service is a little slower than UPS and its loss and mix-up rate seems higher. Be sure to insure your packages at a realistic rate. Sending your package priority mail, special handling, or special delivery will speed up the process and add protection, as well as expense.

Greyhound and Trailways bus companies transport packages, often sending them out on the next bus if you pay a small surcharge. Your goods will arrive in the length of time it takes the bus to make the trip but someone at the other end will have to pick them up at the bus station. Be sure to put a contact phone number on the outside of any packages you send by bus. Bus shipping is more expensive than parcel post or UPS; the rates have risen sharply in the past few years.

The quickest, surest, and most expensive shippers are the air freight companies. Emery Air Freight is used widely by theatres. Air freight companies will pick up the packages on the promised day, even if it is midnight before they get to you. In most cases the items will be delivered the next day. If money is no object, this is certainly the way to go. Check your yellow pages for local and national air freight companies.

If you will not be in the shop when your packages arrive, be sure you have labelled the contents of each package carefully. Attach notes saying which costume the fabric is to be used for, which side will be used if this is not obvious, whether or not it needs to be washed or dyed before it is cut. Careful instructions will prevent serious mistakes being made in your absence.

Notions and Trim

Most designers combine notion and trim shopping with fabric shopping so items can be matched up on the spot. Sewing notions, such as zippers, thread, tape, etc., are usually part of the stock items provided by the shop. You will, however, be responsible for purchasing buttons, decorative clasps, and any braid, lace, or appliques called for in your designs. Before you shop, don't forget to go through all the trim tucked away in the theatre shop's stock, including that on old costumes.

Shopping for trim anywhere outside New York City or Los Angeles can be extremely frustrating. Small selections and high prices are the rule in places where trim is not sold in large quantities. You will often be forced to dye, paint, combine, or simply create the trim you need from bits. If you are able to shop trim in New York, you might, if your budget can stand it, purchase a bit more yardage than you need so it can be added to the shop stock. Perhaps you will be lucky enough to find it again when you return to that theatre to do another show.

Old Clothes

Shopping for old garments can be both tedious and lots of fun. Every town and city in the country has thrift shops and often one or two that carry vintage clothing as well. Stores run by Goodwill, Salvation Army, Volunteers of America, the Saint Vincent DePaul Society and similar organizations are good places to start shopping for ordinary old clothes of contemporary vintage.

Shops that sell high-quality second hand clothes are often run on a consignment basis, and it is in places of this sort that you might be lucky enough to stumble upon a slightly out-of-date mink coat that can be altered for your leading lady, a comfortably worn Harris tweed jacket for your leading man, and, possibly, a nearly new designer frock for yourself. Consignment shops are particularly rich hunting grounds for good shoes, men's ties, purses, belts, and shirts.

Most vintage clothing shops price their garments just as high as the traffic will bear. They cater to particular customers who will pay what seems to be outrageous sums for well-padded gabardine suits and broad-shouldered crepe gowns from the forties. When you are shopping in vintage clothing shops always explain that you are looking for theatrical costumes and don't be too shy to suggest a lower price. The shop owner may be willing to part with pieces that have hung on the rack for several months for an amount considerably less than the one on the tag.

Check antique garments for wearability before purchasing them. Examine seams and tug slightly at the cloth (not, however, hard enough to produce great rips in a dress you have not yet purchased!). Make sure there are no areas where the color has faded noticeably. Beware dresses that were designed to have matching belts and don't. Unless there is enough hem allowance to make a new belt, you may have a hard time finding something to match.

Visit flea markets and rummage and garage sales for all kinds of old clothes at rock bottom

FIGURE 6-20. Andrew B. Marlay's sketch for Tracy Lord in *Philadelphia Story* produced by the Pennsylvania Stage Co. The dress was purchased from an antique clothing shop. *Photograph by Frances Aronson.*

FIGURE 6-21. Mildred Dunnock, Frank Langella, and Michael Higgins in the last act of Eugene O'Neil's *Long Day's Journey into Night* at the Long Wharf theatre. Robe and wedding dress purchased from an antique clothing shop. *Costume design by Rosemary Ingham. Photograph courtesy of Long Wharf Theatre.*

prices. Many designers go regularly to such sales to look at and sometimes buy interesting items, knowing they will turn out to be useful sooner or later.

New Clothes

It often seems to be an unwritten law in theatre that contemporary plays requiring costumes bought off the rack are set in the season opposite the one you are in. You find yourself trying to buy ear muffs in July and sun dresses in December. About the only thing you can do is announce your problem to store managers and owners who may, if it is possible, allow you to examine whatever out-of-season clothing they have in stock. Remember also that cities with garment factories are producing garments two or three seasons ahead. A sympathetic sales manager may make it possible for you to buy half a dozen wool skirts long before they will appear in the shops.

Sometimes you are lucky enough to be shopping in season, and off you go to Macy's or Gimbel's or any number of small men's and women's shops. Most of them will allow you to take several garments out for fitting and approval. It is often easier to show your choices to your leading lady or leading man in the theatre fitting room rather than in the store where either may see and want something highly unsuitable for the play.

When shopping for shoes or boots you should have the actor accompany you if at all possible. You will save a lot of time and the frustration of exchanges.

Whenever you purchase anything you think may have to be returned, be sure that it can be returned, and for cash. Many shops will exchange for another size or another item in their stock. If you cannot find what you want in that store, the theatre will be left with credit and no certainty that they can use it in the near future.

Some situations require that you purchase costume pieces through catalogues—Sears, Penney's, Montgomery Ward, and L. L. Bean are a few of the most commonly used ones. Before you order, be sure to find out exactly how long

151

delivery will take and then add a few days more. Establishments that do mainly mail-order business, such as L. L. Bean and the Dixie Gun Works (a wonderful Tennessee company that sells a wide variety of authentically reproduced military gear), require cash or a credit card number before they will ship any goods. Both companies ship promptly upon payment and both ship with UPS unless you request, and pay for, air freight.

Wigs and Facial Hair

Wigs and facial hair are very special purchases. The most satisfactory pieces for the stage are custom-made and hand-tied, with real rather than synthetic hair. Synthetic hair wigs, which you will not always be able to avoid because of cost, never look quite as real on stage and they are not easy to re-style. An investment in well-made wigs of real hair will always be a good one

FIGURES 6-22 and 6-23. Wig sketches by Lowell Detweiler for the Hartford Stage Company production of *The Beaux Stratagem*. These sketches went to the wig maker along with the appropriate measurements. *Photographs by Frances Aronson.*

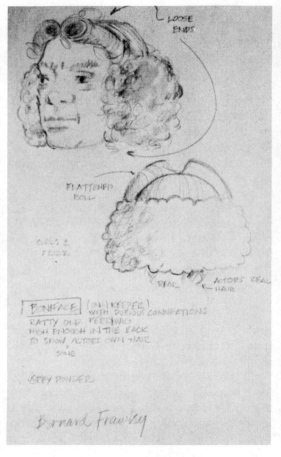

because they can be reworked and used over and over with changes in color and style.

When you are having wigs and facial hair made for a production, be sure to find out exactly how the wigmaker wants measurements taken. (This will also be true if you are renting wigs.) Carry out these instructions with care. If it is called for, send a sample of the actor's own hair for matching purposes. Send copies of your sketches showing exactly how the pieces should

be made and styled. False hair of any sort is a major investment and you want to do all you can to make sure it looks the way you want it to look.

If you have not had a great deal of experience with wigs and false beards, read Chapter 17, Beards and Moustaches, and Chapter 18, Hair and Wigs, in Richard Corson's *Stage Makeup* before you place your order.

Don't forget that the best beards and moustaches are grown by the actor on his own

FIGURE 6-24. Rachel Gurney as Hesaone and Robert Nichols as Boss Nagan, in *Heartbreak House* at the McCarter Theatre. Ms. Gurney is wearing a wig, and Mr. Nichols has a false moustache and sideburns. *Costume design by Andrew B. Marlay. Photograph by Cliff Moore.*

FIGURE 6-25. Three views of the wig worn by Katherine McGrath in the McCarter Theatre production of *The Play's the Thing*. *Costume design by Robert Morgan. Photograph by Cliff Moore.*

face. If there is time and if he is willing, always opt for natural face hair.

WORKING WITH A HAIR DESIGNER

When you are working on a production that demands many wigs and/or fancy hairstyles and have an adequate budget, you may be able to engage a hair designer. They are usually employed on Broadway shows, and the larger resident theatres have begun to use them on occasion. The advantages for a costume designer are obvious.

The hair designer enters the production after the costumes have been designed and meets with the costume designer to go over the sketches and discuss what each actor needs in the way of wigs, styling, and face hair. Usually the hair designer will want to attend a read-through of the play and, subsequently, see each actor individually for head measurements, hair samples, etc.

Many hair designers have their own stock of wigs from which to pull. If wigs and facial hairpieces must be built or rented, the hair designer will take care of all the arrangements and oversee wig fittings that take place during the production period.

The hair designer will be present for dress rehearsal to put on wigs, dress hair, and help the actors in any way that is needed. During the dress rehearsal the hair designer will consult with the costume designer about necessary changes and execute these changes between rehearsals.

Often the hair designer will have an assistant who takes over maintenance and styling of the hair once a show has opened and who is present at every performance to assist the actors with their wigs and hairpieces.

A few of the large regional theatres employ a full-time wig and hair specialist. This person often builds wigs and hairpieces which, after their initial use, can be placed in stock. The savings inherent in building up a stock of usable wigs, having the wig and face hair stock well cared for, and avoiding the last minute emergencies for which local hairdressers must often be engaged make a strong argument in favor of employing such a specialist.

Your Shopping Spirit

The impression you make on shopkeepers when you are shopping a show reflects on you and sometimes on the theatre where you are working. Be as polite and as businesslike as you can. Make sure garments taken out on approval are returned promptly. Be certain you understand the state's requirements for tax exempt purchasing, if the theatre falls within that category, and have all the appropriate information with you, plus forms if they are required. A shopkeeper who finds you pleasant to deal with will remember you and treat you as a valued customer, and you may smooth the way for other shoppers from the theatre.

Recording

Keep Records Up-to-Date

Detailed recordkeeping along the way will eliminate hassles during the final, frantic days before the show opens.

Your costume plot appeared early in the process and has gone through a number of changes. Keep it up to date and make sure it includes everything. Your show reference book is also in progress and should be kept close at hand

FIGURES 6-26 and 6-27. Rough sketch for Sybil in *Count Dracula* (left) for the Pennsylvania Stage Company production. *Costume design by Andrew B. Marlay. Photograph by Frances Aronson.* "Bible" page (below) for the costume sketched in Figure 6-26. This costume was built entirely out of fabric pieces from stock garments and scraps, some of which were overdyed. *Photograph by Frances Aronson.*

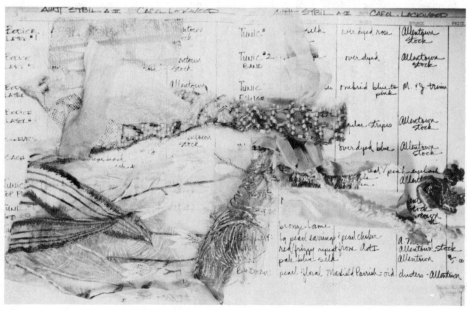

FIGURE 6-28. A record of expenditures.

"OTHELLO" COSTUMES $2,000.00 PAGE 1

RECEIPT #	DATE	ITEM/SOURCE	PETTY CASH Amount	Sub-total	P.O.'s CHARGES Amount	Sub-total	TRANS./TRAVEL Amount	Sub-total	COMBINED TOTAL Amount	Sub-total
1	2/5	STERN - SHIRTING/EMILIA U/SKT	9.00						9.00	9.00
2	2/5	XEROX	.50	9.50					.50	9.50
3	2/5	TRANSP. - FARES - SHOPPING					3.00		3.00	12.50
4	2/7	LERATEX - BIANCA O/SKIRT	8.00	17.50					8.00	20.50
5	2/7	ZUPNIK - IAGO CLOAK&TUNIC	12.00	29.50					12.00	32.50
6	2/7	EUR.WOOL - RODERIGO VELVET	6.00	35.50					6.00	38.50
7	2/9	THUR - OTHELLO O/ROBE	15.00	50.50					15.00	53.50
8	2/9	PATERSON - OTHELLO LINING	10.98	61.48					10.98	64.48
9	2/9	INTERC. - BIANCA/MONTANO	21.50	82.98					21.50	85.98
10	2/9	JONAS - DES. NIGHTG./U/DRESS	8.00	90.98					8.00	93.98
11	2/9	TRANSP. - SHOPPING					3.75	6.75	3.75	97.73
12	2/9	U.P.S. SHIPPING	4.27	95.25					4.27	102.00
13	2/9	CAB TO UPS & SUBWAY					5.75	12.50	5.75	107.75
14	2/10	GLADSTONE - OTHELLO ROBE			21.50				21.50	129.25
15	2/10	P&T - DES. CAPE/ASS/GTUNIC	31.50	126.75					31.50	160.75
16	2/10	ART-MAX - BIANCA SLEEVES	7.25	134.00					7.25	168.00
17	2/10	C&F - GRATIANO O/GOWN/SHIRT			29.56	51.06			29.56	197.56
18	2/10	TRANSP. - FARES - SHOPPING					3.00	15.50	3.00	200.56
19	2/12	COST. ARMOUR - HELMETS			90.00	141.06			90.00	290.56
20	2/12	TRIMEX. BUTTONS & CORDING			24.21	165.27			24.21	314.77
21	2/12	OSGOOD - OTHELLO/DES/CASS.			61.00	226.27			61.00	375.77
22	2/12	TRANS. CAB TO STN.					4.25	19.75	4.25	380.02
23	2/12	ROUND-TRIP TRAIN TKT					31.50	51.25	31.50	411.52
24	2/13	CAB FROM STN.					4.50	55.75	4.50	416.02
25	2/14	XEROX	.25	134.25					.25	416.27
26	2/15	DYES	3.60	137.85					3.60	419.87
27										
28										
29										
30										

always. Never go shopping without it and use it as a repository for all bits of information that are pertinent to the production: stage manager's notes, a city map, and the name and address of a cobbler who is willing to repair a fragile pair of period shoes for you.

The shop may also be keeping a record of the show's progress. In New York workrooms and in many regional shops as well, this is called the "show bible." Show bibles contain fabric samples, fabric swatches that have been dyed and/or painted with recipes and instructions for the dye or paint process used, records of yardages bought and actual yardages used, addresses of places where work was jobbed out and how much it cost, etc. These books are particularly valuable for productions that might be done annually (*A Christmas Carol* or *The Nutcracker*) or revived during a future season.

Keep up with your accounts. Every day after shopping, be sure to enter the monies spent. Be sure to enter charges as well as cash purchases. Charges are sneaky things that can add up quicker than the dispensing of bills. (Figure 6-28 illustrates a method of recording expenditures.) Find a recording method that works for you but remember that no system will work unless you feed it regular information. Once again, don't forget to keep a portion of your budget (ten to fifteen percent) set aside for tech week.

The action is about to begin. Your plans are made, shopping is either done or well underway, and the shop is ready to start to work. Get some rest if you can because you are about to embark on the most concentrated part of the work of a costume designer and you will need all your physical, mental, and emotional resources to cope with the days and weeks ahead.

7

The Production Period

...neither a setting nor a costume is good if the actor is uncomfortable. Part of the designer's job is to give the performer every physical and psychological, as well as visual, assistance.

JOE MIELZINER
Designing for the Theatre

During this last period, the costume designer's work becomes more and more integrated into the total production effort and there will be increasing contact with the other people who are working on the show. This may be daily if you are in residence at the theatre or at regular intervals if you are not. In a university or regional theatre where shops, offices, and rehearsal spaces are normally located either in one building or in buildings that are relatively close together, it is fairly easy to keep up with everything. Other circumstances may make contact and communication difficult. If you are doing a New York show for which the set is being built on Long Island, the rehearsals taking place uptown, the production offices operating in midtown, and the costumes being built downtown, you will be hard put to stay in touch and will have to expend real effort, many taxi fares or subway tokens, and a lot of shoe leather to be every place you have to be.

The following discussion presumes you are working in a theatre where the distance between shops, stages, and offices is no great problem. If the situation is vastly different, you must find ways to adjust to it that will allow you some degree of contact with the developing production. One designer tells a story of designing costumes for a show for which the costumes were built on the East Coast while all the other activities were carried out on the West Coast. Transcontinental trips were out of the question during the production period since the designer had to be in the shop. Contact was maintained through long distance phone calls, key fittings were carried out by a West Coast assistant on garments sent back and forth by Express Mail, and runthrough rehearsals were seen on video cassettes! This was a cumbersome and expensive way to work but one which did allow the costume designer some participation in the overall process.

The production period should be the most exciting part of the process for everyone involved in it. Individual pieces of the production construct begin to fall in place. The director gets to see the acting company working together, dialogue moves from page to mouth, the

158

groundplan is taped—in scale—on the floor and real distances discovered, a painted surface becomes cloth and a brushstroke a feather. Everything that has been flat on the page, flat on the sketch and tiny on the set model comes up to life size and begins to breathe. There is nothing more exhilarating than watching all the pieces fit together, creating a total theatre experience. But between page and stage there is much to do, many seams to sew, shoes to dye, and trim to tack in place.

Much of what a costume designer does during the production period happens concurrently rather than sequentially and an actual sequence is difficult to predict. This chapter is divided into three major sections:

1. Working With Actors and Director;

2. Working With the Costume Shop; and

3. Working Through Dress Rehearsals.

There will be times during the production period when you feel as though you have too much to do, too many decisions to make, and too many people to please. It is during these times that you will be glad you have a well-read, well-researched, well-designed, and well-planned play and production scheme to follow. It is far easier for you to be flexible and to make whatever changes the production period demands if your work has been thorough.

Working With Actors and Director

Read through and Design Presentation

It is generally the custom for all designers to be present at the first rehearsal; they are often called upon to make short presentations of their work to the company. Afterwards the cast may do a relaxed, sit-down read-through of the script. This initial meeting between company members often sets the tone of the work to follow.

In regional theatres the actors may have just arrived and may be meeting their fellow actors for the first time. Introductions must be made between newcomers and permanent staff members with careful identification of people and their duties. Everybody should know members of the stage management staff, the publicity director, the business manager, and others who will have to be consulted on specific matters.

During the first meeting of a professional company, the actors will assemble privately to elect an Equity deputy who will serve as their representative to management.

After business matters have been tended to, the director often talks to the company about the play and what he hopes to achieve in the production. Some directors enjoy this opportunity to chat, others have little to say and seem eager to get on with the rehearsals. Designers' presentations usually come next.

You may be asked to pin up the costume sketches on a display board or pass them around to the company. In many situations this is the first time the actors have seen any indication of what they will wear, and it will be helpful to them if you can say something about the choices you have made—how they were made and what effects they are intended to create. Answer any questions that arise and make sure the actors know you will be available for further discussions.

FIGURE 7-1. Costume designer Liz Covey, scene designer John Jensen, actors Herb Foster and Portia Patterson examine costume sketches in the rehearsal hall at the McCarter Theatre. *Photograph by Cliff Moore.*

Remember, at this point in the process the costume designer is much further ahead in character development than the actor who has not yet started to rehearse. It's quite possible that the actor's first impressions of the character will be very different from your visual interpretation. Don't be upset if an actor takes exception with his or her costume at this point. Be tactful and wait until rehearsals get underway. As the character develops, the actor may discover the costume is absolutely appropriate. If changes do occur through rehearsals, you will make adjustments—but that comes later.

After the designers have been heard from, you may expect a short break and then the read through of the script. Most read throughs take two to three hours and you should make every effort to stay. Up to now you have only imagined the play. Hearing the play aloud, even though the actors are not yet "acting," will reveal things to you that you may not have seen in the script. One of the most common realizations designers have after hearing a script read is, "I didn't know it was so funny." Humor is particularly hard to read in on the page; it leaps out at you when spoken.

While the read through is going on, take the opportunity to study the actors' faces and bodies. Imagine them in the costumes you have designed. In most cases they will not be absolute strangers to you; at the least, you will have had photographs and measurements to work with while you were designing. But this may be the first time you have had more than a few minutes to look at them objectively. You may discover that one woman's shoulders are a bit wider than you'd thought, that another's hair looks quite limp and will probably need a perm before it accepts a style the period requires, that one of the men always slumps in his chair—you may note that you want to check his posture when he's on his feet because it will effect the way his tailcoat hangs.

Perhaps the most important effect your presence at the first rehearsal has, however, is that it lets the actors know you are concerned about the play and about them. Actors meet many costume designers who are more interested in clothes than they are in plays. By involving yourself in the actor's rehearsal process, you are identifying yourself as being part of the collaborative production process. An informal chat during coffee break on the first day can create the foundation for a friendly and productive working relationship between designer and actor.

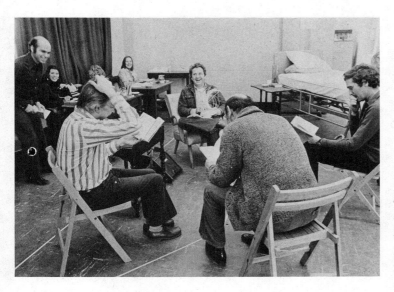

FIGURE 7-2. Rehearsal in progress at the Long Wharf Theatre. Director Arvin Brown, stage manager Anne Keefe, and actors Louis Beachner, Christina Whitmore, Richard Venture, John Braden, George Taylor, and Emery Battis. *Photograph by William L. Smith.*

Measurements

The initial visit the actor makes to the costume shop, usually during the first day or two of the rehearsal period, is to have measurements taken. Preliminary measurements may have been sent ahead so the drapers could begin muslins or the actor's measurement sheet might be on file from an earlier production. Nevertheless, you will probably want to take a more complete set of measurements or update and recheck old ones. This visit also affords you and the draper another opportunity to look at the body you are costuming.

Since early rehearsal days are particularly busy ones, measurement sessions are usually brief; fifteen minutes is normal. Two people taking measurements can speed up the process; one for the tape, the other to write. In some shops the draper prefers to do all the measuring; in others, measurements are taken by whomever is free at the moment. If time is really short, the shop staff may measure two or three actors at a time.

The person who records the measurements should ask the actor for height, weight, commercial clothing sizes, presence of fiber allergies, etc.

Ask if the actor has any special physical problems that will effect costume; a request for arch supports is quite common. Notice physical irregularities such as a low shoulder or a leg or arm significantly shorter than the other. Some actors will point these things out to you but others will wait for you to notice.

Costume designers should be present for measurements, helping out if necessary. Chat with the actors and make them feel welcome in the costume shop. You can help make a sometimes tedious process more pleasant and, when an actor's body is relaxed, the measurements taken are much more accurate.

Rehearsal Clothes

Although directors work in many different ways, it is the normal procedure to get the show "on its feet" and actors "off book" within the first week or so of rehearsals. (The normal rehearsal period for New York and professional regional theatre productions is four weeks for a straight play and five or six for a musical. Universities may rehearse for six weeks but seldom longer.) At this point in the proceedings you will be asked to provide rehearsal garments.

FIGURE 7-3. It may take some ingenuity to come up with a rehearsal suit for this crocodile. *Costume design by Ann Wallace. Photograph by Frances Aronson.*

FIGURE 7-4. William Leach as Cyrano in the Milwaukee Repertory Theater production of *Cyrano de Bergerac.* An appropriate rehearsal costume was helpful to this actor. *Costume design by Susan Tsu. Photograph by Mark Avery.*

Rehearsal garments fall into two categories, both of which are very important to the actor in rehearsal. Some garments will be used to simulate restrictions, such as long skirts, boned bodices, suitcoats, high-heeled shoes. Others will help the actor work out stage business, such as handling an overcoat which has to be taken off or put on while on stage, or doffing a hat. Rehearsal fans are always a must. Try to anticipate the need for rehearsal garments so you will be prepared when the requests come.

One of the real pitfalls of providing rehearsal clothes is that the actor may become so fond of and used to the substitute hat or purse that he or she may want to use it in performance rather than the item you designed and are having built in the shop. Make sure the actors know that the pieces they are using are only for rehearsal, and always try to choose things that are not nearly so wonderful as what will appear on the day of dress rehearsal.

If the costumes have long skirts, actors should never rehearse without long skirts. Some actors have their own long rehearsal skirts which is a help to everyone and a practice to be encouraged. If long rehearsal skirts are not available in the costume stock, you should consider finishing up the petticoats first and allowing them to be used.

Skirt understructures such as bum rolls, bustles, and panniers present special problems for the actors who must sit down and negotiate doorways in them. Approximate the shape as best you can for early rehearsals and put the real items in as soon as the shop has finished them.

Hats are especially necessary for rehearsals since they are the objects of much stage business. Men's hats are easier to find appropriate substitutes for than women's hats. This is a time to be creative with the stacks of old 1950's felts

which, when pinned up here and there, will do admirably until the perky straw number makes its appearance.

Try to allow actors ample time to break in new shoes and adjust to heel height. A week or so before dress rehearsals get underway is usually sufficient but be considerate if actors ask to wear their shoes earlier than that. If you take a moment to think about your last pair of new or unfamiliar shoes and how long it took for them to be really comfortable, and how many sore heels and toes and blisters you got in the process, you will be sympathetic to their requests. Imagine having to stand on stage trying to act when your feet are killing you!

FIGURE 7-5. Undergarment sketches by Lowell Detweiler for the Hartford Stage Company production of *The Beaux Stratagem*. The hoop and the corset will certainly be needed in rehearsal. *Photograph by Frances Aronson.*

FIGURE 7-6. David Murin's sketch for Lucienne in *A Flea in Her Ear* produced by the Hartford Stage Company. A hat similar to this one should be available for rehearsal. *Photograph courtesy of the Touchstone Gallery, New York.*

Someone on the stage management staff must take responsibility for rehearsal garments. Before a single item is issued, have a chat with that person. Explain how the garments are to be used on stage and how they should be cared for between rehearsals. Sometimes rehearsal garments are kept in cabinets in the rehearsal hall and sometimes they are returned to the costume shop after each rehearsal. It is seldom a good idea to issue a rehearsal costume directly to an actor to keep in his or her possession; actors have too many things to think about to add rehearsal costumes to the list.

If actors are using shoes, petticoats, or understructures in rehearsal that they will actually wear with their costumes, don't forget to call the items, along with the actors, for fittings.

If the show includes costume pieces that are especially difficult to get used to (straight jackets, plaster casts, or a standing ruff), plan to complete them so they can go into rehearsal early. This may eliminate a certain amount of first dress panic.

Watch Rehearsals

Whenever you can be away from the costume shop for a few minutes—when it is all right with the director—pop into rehearsals for a look at how the show is progressing. By doing so, you may be able to anticipate a potential problem and the actors will enjoy your interest. You may also find that the stimulation of seeing what is going on in the rehearsal hall increases your own excitement about the production.

Begin these visits after the first week of rehearsal and try to make them once or twice a week thereafter. In some theatres there will be periodic run throughs, either of an act or of the whole play, to which the technical staff is specifically invited. Go to these rehearsals with note pad in hand and watch closely for every bit of business and blocking that can affect costume.

Your pad will contain comments such as: "Her boned bodice will not permit her to bend that way;" "He appears to be taking something out of a pocket that doesn't exist." These rehearsals are perfect times for troubleshooting, so be alert.

Communicate with Stage Management

Once rehearsals are underway, the most important channel of communication for the costume designer is the one with stage management. In most instances this contact needs to be made on a daily basis.

Many stage managers issue a bulletin after each day's rehearsal with notes for all the design departments about that day's changes, additions, requests, and problems. Keep all these notes in your show reference book and refer to them regularly. It's easy to forget that a character needs a pocket added to the inside of his coat. It is also quite reassuring to have all this information in writing.

Good stage managers are worth their weight in gold and can make your life consistently easier. Cultivate their good will at all times.

Handling Disagreements

There will undoubtedly be times when an actor absolutely disagrees with the costume designer about what he or she should wear on stage. The structure of most theatre production in this country makes it a virtual necessity that costumes be designed, and sometimes be in the shop, before rehearsals begin. In effect, the designers and the director have already gone through a "design rehearsal process" prior to the start of the actor's rehearsal process. It would be unreasonable to suppose that differences in opinion would never arise.

As stated earlier, don't be too concerned about the exceptions an actor may take before rehearsals begin. But if, after two and a half weeks of rehearsal, the actor has strong feelings that his or her costume is wrong for the character that is developing, it's time for a conference.

You will usually sit down with the actor, director, and stage manager to talk it out. *Don't be defensive.* Your talent and ability are not in question, only the appropriateness of the costume you have designed for one character. Explain your choices and listen to the actor's objections. If you understand and perhaps even agree with the objections, you will happily set out to make whatever changes are necessary to bring actor and character into a mutually satisfactory visual relationship. If you do not understand or agree, or if you think the actor is dead wrong, the director will decide whose choice prevails.

When your choice is not supported by the director, it may be because he or she simply doesn't agree with you. It may also be because the director needs to protect a sensitive relationship with the actor, something that is often crucial to the actor's performance. If this is the case, and the director decides that the actor's feelings are more important to protect than yours, don't be bitter. You must learn to take such decisions as a part of your professional life and not as an attack on your person. Accept the new choice, work hard to fit it into the visual construct of the show, and try to solve the problem in such a way that the shop will have a minimum of extra work.

At other times, it is the director who will ask for changes because he or she has discovered that certain choices you both made early on are not right for the show as it is being discovered in rehearsal. Once again, if you agree, your only problem is to make the changes possible. If you disagree, make sure you discuss the matter thoroughly. What you must avoid are situations in which you feel as though you have been thoughtlessly dictated to and not heard. Your opinions may not prevail in the end but, for your own mental health, make sure you express them clearly.

Always remember that theatre is a collaboration and not a place where individual artists make individual statements. All collaboration requires some degree of compromise. Remember also that there are many ways to create a single visual effect and, when one of your choices has been rejected, do everything you can to find another that will be integral, even if you never come to like it.

Working with the Costume Shop

You have begun your work with the costume shop in the best possible way: your sketches were on time, you presented them clearly and articulately, your shopping is all but complete, and you have consulted with the shop supervisor and the draper in setting up the work schedule. Now it's time for costume construction to begin in earnest and, whether you are there all the time or only at intervals, your manner in the shop, your attitudes about the work, what you do and how you do it, will have a lot to do with how successful the final product is.

Keep Your Eyes Open

Watch the work being done so you can catch mistakes early and prevent larger tasks from having to be redone. You must do this in a way that will prevent the technicians from feeling that you are breathing down their necks or being unduly critical. You can correct a mistake without allowing the person being corrected to feel that he or she is an idiot. The best way to learn to do this is to imagine yourself in the place of the person being corrected. The Golden Rule should always prevail in costume shops.

WORKING WITH THE DRAPER

In the early stages of the work, pay particular attention to the drapers and cutters. If a garment is badly patterned and/or badly cut, no amount of beautiful stitching can save it. A gifted draper, like a gifted stage manager, is worth his or her weight in gold and will not only make the garment fit accurately but will interpret your sketch with sensitivity, transferring proportions and details from the paper to the cloth in such a way that it is not just any frock coat but the very frock coat you designed.

You must not expect to find a gifted draper in every shop but you can do your best to inspire the finest work each draper is capable of producing.

Ideally, every costume designer ought to know how to drape any costume he or she designs and most do have at least a basic notion of how to proceed. The more you know, the more you will be able to participate in discussions about how garments are to be cut.

Don't dictate to the draper. If you know that you want something done in a particular way, say so, but also listen to alternative methods and try to allow the final decision to be a mutual one. Learn how to deal with different personalities and degrees of proficiency. An inexperienced draper may accept all your ideas and instructions word for word while a draper with a great deal of experience may want to fall back on his or her own familiar, tried and true ways without listening to you at all. You can, if you choose your words well, encourage the inex-

FIGURE 7-7. Costume designer Marie Anne Chiment and technician Noel Borden discuss the construction process of a costume for Arena Stage's production of *A Midsummer Night's Dream. Photograph by Joan Marcus.*

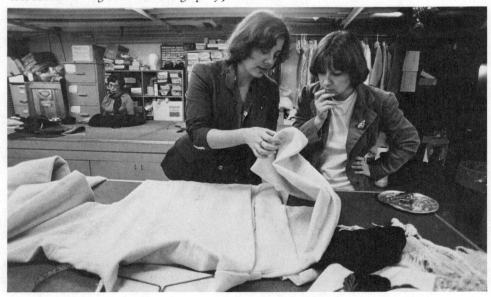

perienced draper to work out parts of the pattern independently and the less flexible one to try out a new method.

Always explain both what you want and why you want it. Thanks to your text analysis and period research, you are the resident expert on the play, the period, and the style of the costumes. Don't expect the shop technicians to know what you know. In far too many instances, they will not even have read the play! Share what you have discovered. Explain the period, tell why the doublets are cut just so and why the buttons are where they are.

If appropriate, choose authentic period patterns that may be used by the draper as guides to general shape, seam and dart positions, etc. Discourage the drafting up of period patterns verbatim since they are nearly always impossible to fit on a modern actor's body. Present knowledge of patterning and fit is far superior to what was known in the past, and it is better for the draper to begin with modern techniques and

adapt them to period shapes rather than the other way around.

DESIGN GUIDES

Be certain you have a very sure visual sense of the period silhouette you have designed since you will need it to guide you through dozens of decisions having to do with proportion, width of panniers, size of hoop, depth of cleavage, etc. You will have to make many of these decisions when the garment is being mocked up in muslin and it will take all your good sense and imagination to mentally turn that vast expanse of stiff, off-white cloth into the crisp black taffeta gown, *circa* 1876, that it will eventually become. You cannot, however, wait for the real black taffeta to be cut before you decide precisely how wide the bustle will be.

Along with your own sketches, keep research books and pictures within easy reach. Look especially at period paintings in which figures in period clothing can be compared in

FIGURE 7-8. Costume designer Susan Tsu and draper Barbara Murray in conference at the Milwaukee Repertory Theater. *Photograph by Mark Avery*.

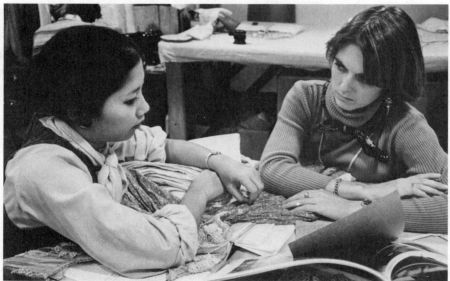

proportion to furniture, fireplaces, doorways. Recheck the proportions within the costume. Is the hoop twice as wide as the body inside it, or three times as wide? How much bodice to skirt or doublet to length of leg?

You will also take the size and scale of the stage and of the set into consideration as you guide the creation of actual silhouette and proportion in your costumes. On a tiny stage you may have to scale down a bustle or shorten a train if it threatens to get tangled up in the furniture. And always remember that actors have to fit through the set doorways—that includes their skirts, their cloaks, and sometimes their hats and parasols!

Keep an eye on general construction techniques, especially if the stitchers are relatively inexperienced. Make sure they understand the construction steps involved in each garment and why the steps should be done in a certain order.

If the draper or the shop supervisor gives a stitcher instructions with which you disagree, make sure you talk with the one who did the explaining before asking the stitcher to do it differently. Try never to say the original instructions were wrong. Always admit that there are many different ways to accomplish any stitching operation. Say firmly, however, that you dote on one particular method and would dearly love to have it done that way. If you intervene gracefully and tactfully you may even have the satisfaction of seeing your superior method adopted as standard operating procedure in that shop.

Let the stitchers know you admire skillful stitching. Try to inspire high quality workmanship without being so nit-picky that the costumes never get assembled.

Compliment Good Work

If you feel that a task has been particularly well done, say so. It could be the cut of a whole handsome garment, construction of a fabulous hat, a well-set collar, or even a neatly done continuous lap closing. Costume technicians work very hard and for modest pay. You can add immeasurably to their sense of satisfaction in work well done if you simply remember to acknowledge it.

Think Ahead

Don't ever allow the costumes to be started until you have planned for quick changes, adequate movement, and upkeep. These considerations began at your drawing board and now they should be communicated to the drapers and stitchers.

If quick changes are necessary, work out the location and nature of each closing in detail. Find out how much assistance the actor will have with the change and incorporate this into solving the problem. If a costume has to be overdressed, make sure the layers will fit on top of each other without obvious bulk. All of this should be mocked up in muslin.

If an actor wearing a tight garment has a great deal of movement, make sure to ask for gussets. Put gussets in dancers' costumes as a matter of course. If you are costuming a group of dancers, be sure to talk with the choreographer before deciding on the amount of fullness to cut into the skirts. If there are turns, the skirts will probably be very full at the bottom but gored in order to reduce bulk at the waist. Nothing on stage looks worse than a dancer doing turns in a skimpy skirt. Work out a basic formula for the full skirts and make sure all of them are cut alike, especially if more than one cutter is involved.

Anticipate maintenance problems. Ask for double-stitched seams at stress points. Make sure that collars, cuffs, and washable insets are made easily detachable so make-up can be removed from them between cleanings. Check to see that there are enough pairs of dress shields in the shop to protect all costume underarms. If a garment is to be washed during the run of the show, make sure the fabric is washed before it is cut. As a matter of fact, it isn't a bad idea to wash all washable fabrics before cutting them just in case you decide later that a costume needs to be washed or dipped down. If zippers are used in the costumes, be sure that they are sturdy metal ones. If the zipper is there for reasons of convenience and is not in period, see that the closing is contrived in such a way that the audience is spared even so much as a glint of metal teeth.

Plan for Volunteers

If the shop has the help of local volunteers, give them jobs they will enjoy and make sure their tasks are organized for them when they come in.

FIGURES 7-9 and 7-10. Sketches by Lowell Detweiler from *Fables* at Central City Opera. Notice the garments in Figure 7-10 (below right) that go over the garments in Figure 7-9 (below left). The figure on the right is created by an overlay rendered in watercolor and colored pencil on tracing paper. *Photographs by Frances Aronson*.

Find out what each one can do and likes to do. A volunteer who can't stitch may really enjoy making bows, dyeing shoes, or pinning trim in place. Do your share to see that volunteers feel welcome and have a good time while they are in the shop. Happy volunteers return another day.

Be Present
and Do Your Share

Try and spend as much time as you can in the shop so you are available when needed to answer questions and make decisions. Never miss a fitting. If the shop must work late, think twice before you go off to the movies. You will be much more appreciated if you stay and help.

Between conferences, supervising, and fittings, pick out a task or two that you do well and take it for your own. It can be demoralizing for the technicians if you stand around for great chunks of the day drinking coffee. Every designer has some bit that he or she does especially well and likes to do—putting trim on hats, doing hand-rolled hems, or combing wigs. Whatever your speciality is, pitch in and do it! If you really can't do anything, at least offer to run errands or fetch the pizza for supper.

First Fitting
for a Modern or Pulled
Costume

Designing contemporary plays with costumes bought off the rack is not the piece of cake you may expect it to be. Because you have little or nothing to build, you might think you're going to get off easy. Far from it. Choosing a contemporary costume inevitably gets complicated by everybody's personal prejudices. While the costume designer can usually get away with being the expert on a period show, everybody involved with a modern play has definite opinions about what the characters should wear, especially the actors—"I would never wear a plaid skirt in the garden." "Denim makes me feel dowdy." "I think elbow patches are pretentious." "I loathe striped ties!"

Your job—and a difficult one it will be—is to keep costume conversation focused on the characters and the script and not on the actors' own likes and dislikes.

From the start, try to see that you, the actor, and the director are all looking for the same thing. Sketches that reflect the kind of dress or suit you are looking for are a great help. You won't find exactly what you've drawn but, hopefully, you'll find something that has a similar effect.

The stronger your ideas are and the more specifically they can be related to the text, the better your chances are of swinging the decisions in your direction. Tact and patience are usually required in abundance and possibly a series of first fittings before the major choices are made and everyone is pleased.

The first fitting for a contemporary production should deal only with the major garments, choosing them and working out fit and style alterations. It's a waste of time to purchase a shirt, tie, and socks before you are certain which suit will be used.

A pulled costume can be from any period and may require a great deal of reworking before it begins to look like your sketch. Make sure the actor doesn't feel like a second-class citizen if he's being put in a pulled outfit while another actor in the same production is getting three elaborate dresses made from scratch. If you are excited about the possibilities inherent in the pieces you have pulled together, you can transmit your feelings to the actor. Explain what effect you're looking for and how you plan to achieve it. Allow the actor to be involved in the process and he will happily put on and take off a half dozen pairs of trousers until you have found one with just exactly the correct amount of bagginess.

Make sure someone is present in the fitting

to take notes. This may be the design assistant or the technician who is responsible for taking measurements. Any garments that are found acceptable should immediately be tagged and put with the actor's other things. It's a pain in the neck to spend half an hour finding the best pair of trousers only to have them inadvertently returned to a rack of trousers that are all exactly the same color. Rejected costumes should be returned to stock promptly so they will not get mixed up with what is going to be used.

First Muslin Fitting

Imagine what it would be like to be pinned into a slightly scratchy, off-white dress which may or may not have the seams worn inside out, while at least three sets of eyes stare at your body, plucking now and then at the cloth and talking in a semi-foreign tongue that includes words like armscye, gusset, and bust apex. This is what it's like to be an actor at a muslin fitting: uncomfortable, ignored, and spoken of in the third person.

BE CONSIDERATE TOWARDS THE ACTOR

It's easy enough to turn this sometimes ghastly experience into a pleasant one and it is often the designer who must insist upon humane treatment for actors in fittings. Understand that few actors can tell anything about what their costume will ultimately look like when they are swathed in muslin and covered with safety pins. Bring the sketch into the fitting room, refer to it, and take time to explain which parts of the muslin refer to which parts of the sketch. If they are available, have the fabrics in the fitting room and give them to the actor to feel. Talk to—not just about—the actor and be very careful how you refer to his or her body. An actor with a short neck does not need to have it spoken of disdainfully nor will it help the dieting actor to be reminded of pudginess. Aim for a sensitive, tactful objectivity.

FIGURE 7-11. Costume designer Carol Oditz, actor Dilys Hamlett, and draper Katie Duckert in a muslin fitting at the Milwaukee Repertory Theater. *Photogra h by Mark Avery.*

Show that you care about the actor's comfort and pay attention when you are told that tight armholes are cutting off circulation. Ask the actor to display some of the movements that have been blocked in rehearsal, particularly if they involve kneeling, raising the arms above the head, sitting or lying on the floor. If the fitting occurs before blocking is done, simply ask for a range of normal movements.

Muslin fittings should be attended by the draper—the draper may be responsible for actually pinning in alterations—by someone to take notes of the proceedings, and by the designer, who must see everything there is to be seen. You must make sure the muslin fits the body as snugly as the design demands but isn't pulled so tight that the costume, when cut from a bulkier fabric, will be too small. Most important of all, you must decide if the pattern pieces, the seaming, the placement of grain lines, and the proportion of all the parts—one to another—achieve the same effect on the actor in front of you as they did on the costume you sketched. You will make adjustments for a short neck, wide shoulders, and a high waist but your sketch remains the official roadmap to get to your design.

If the draper has worked closely with your sketch, the muslin will not need a radical overhaul. Few costume building schedules allow enough time to produce more than one muslin mock-up, so try to work with what is there unless it's a real disaster. If a second muslin has to be done, supervise it closely.

While you are doing all this looking, you may also be chatting with the actor and giving suggestions to the other technicians present. You may be picking out shoes and other accessories to try on after you have finished with the muslin. It is the combination of intense concentration and simultaneous activity that produces fitting room-related headaches. To prevent them, stay as relaxed as you can and do one thing at a time. Remember that your most important function in this fitting is to make decisions about the muslin

mock-up. The actual garment will be cut out of the real stuff from these adjusted muslin pieces or their paper pattern equivalents. Once the plaid silk is cut, your decisions must stand.

Ask someone to keep you informed of the passage of time throughout the fitting so you won't have to add that to your list of things to think about. If the fitting is to be thirty minutes long, you might ask to be warned at the end of ten and then twenty minutes. You cannot fit a wig, hat, and shoes in the final two minutes of the fitting and you will need to work quickly to get everything in. The more experience you have in the fitting room, the more your internal time sense will guide you and the more easily you will move through the fitting process.

Monitor the Workload and Set Priorities

Usually more time is wasted in a costume shop during the first week or ten days of a building period than at any other time and it is paid for in phenomenal amounts of overtime during the two weeks before costumes go on stage. You have already tried to avoid early time waste by having everything on hand on the day the shop begins your show. Now, while the muslins go back to the cutting tables for adjustments and transformation into real cloth, go back to your original schedule and reconsider it with the shop supervisor.

You have seen the technicians at work and can look at your original expectations in light of the staff's actual capabilities. Is your schedule realistic? Are you on schedule now? Does your schedule ask too much from the technicians on any given working day?

Request more help if you and the shop supervisor feel it is warranted. If none is available and the work load is obviously too heavy, sit down and make a list of all the shortcuts you know that can help decrease the amount of work without harming the way the costumes will look on stage. You may decide ruffles can be serged instead of hemmed and that some skirt hems can be done by machine rather than by hand. Decide to purchase preassembled hair canvas jacket fronts. Determine to set up trim early so it can all be machined. Consider the judicious use of certain adhesives.

Always be sure you are being realistic in your demands on the shop. Many of the technicians are committed to several shows in a season and it is unfair of you to ask them to do unreasonable amounts of labor on yours. Take the lead and encourage everyone to break for lunch, to go outside to eat, sit in the park, get away from the shop. Many costume shops are located in basements without windows and without a breath of fresh air or a beam of sunlight to brighten the environment. A walk outside can do wonders for morale. If there are to be evening work hours, see that everyone goes home or out for supper. Avoid "all-nighters." They might sound somewhat romantic to the newcomer, but they are times of mere drudgery during which little work actually gets accomplished. Sleep always increases efficiency. A shower, clean hair, and breakfast makes nimble fingers.

You and the shop supervisor can see to it that the schedule and the workload stay within the realm of possibility and that they provide for some free time. Within this workload and time frame, it is up to you to set the priorities and determine what gets done first and what may be left till last and what may just possibly never get done at all. Decide what is more important for the play, the actors, and for your own sensibilities and push hard to get those things done the way you want them done. Even if you adore lots of hand stitching and couturier finishes, these are things that may be dispensed with in favor of neat, sturdy closings and all the trim in place. There is usually some small something in everything you design that never gets on the stage and some dress rehearsal note that doesn't get done.

It's up to you to make sure that what doesn't get done is your decision and what the shop concentrates on doing is really priority stuff.

Dyeing

It's the rare production that won't require you to dye at least one piece of fabric to achieve a necessary color and, if the shop doesn't have a staff member who is responsible for dyeing and painting, this task will inevitably fall to you. It's not unusual for a costume designer to spend the first several days of a building period wrapped up in an apron or a smock, sweating over a hot plate, dye pot, and washing machine.

FIGURE 7-12. Sandra Yen Fong working at the dye pot at Arena Stage. *Photograph by Joan Marcus.*

Every costume designer must know the basics of fabric dyeing. Even if there is a staff dyer available, you must give advice and okay the colors. And you must know about the dye potential of various fibers so you will never present the shop with a piece of baby blue one hundred-percent polyester cloth and ask them to make it midnight blue. There is not space here to discuss dyeing processes; let it suffice to say that if you don't know about fabric dyeing, read, experiment, and learn to do it.

Make sure that fabrics are dyed and waiting when the draper is ready for them. You may find that your dyeing schedule is based on the muslin fitting schedule. As soon as a muslin is adjusted, the fabric should be ready to cut. Use your sketches to guide you. Beware of changing a color you painted and/or swatched just because you happened to mix, by accident, a color that you suddenly like better. Colors, as you recall, depend upon relationships for their effect and one change may affect the balance of the whole range.

Do test samples of your dyes before tossing in the whole piece and be sure to use the correct assistant chemicals in recommended proportions so the dye will be as permanent as possible. When you are dyeing, observe safety precautions. Protect your hands and arms with rubber gloves and your lungs with a properly filtered respirator.

Dipping a costume down is another sort of dyeing and is usually done during the later stages of the building period. White costume pieces and accessories, shirts, handkerchiefs, modesties, cuffs, and the like may be dipped to kill the glare they produce under stage lights. Commercial dye, tea, and coffee are all used to dip down costumes.

Personal taste is very much involved in toning whites; some designers seldom dip anything down while others are tormented by the mere presence of a glaring white scrap of lace flashing about in the leading lady's hand. Directors may also request that white, and other bright colors, be taken down if they feel the brightness is working against the desirable stage focus.

Start the dipping process with a light touch. After you see it on stage you may deepen the toning as necessary. The process may take several steps. Since much dipping down happens during dress rehearsals, make sure you have given the garment plenty of time to dry before the actor has to put it on again.

Second Fitting

A second fitting for the actor who is wearing contemporary or pulled garments is necessary to check on alterations and decide on accessories. It will almost always be the final fitting before dress parade or dress rehearsal. Make sure to ask the actor if you might have missed seeing any action in rehearsal that could be impeded by the costume. Explore the whole range of stage movements in the fitting room.

The second fitting for a constructed costume is the first in fabric and it may be very exciting. Your design is beginning to take shape on a real body and you should be able to see your intentions in progress. The actor also begins to understand what part the costume will play in his or her characterization and many actors spontaneously strike poses and take on attitudes that hint at a successful blending of actor, clothing, and character.

There are times when you will be disappointed in what you see. The design isn't working as you thought it would. It hangs wrong here, tucks incorrectly there, doesn't become the actor at all. Try to keep these feelings of disappointment to yourself so the actor does not perceive them. Set about to make what changes you can, keep cheerful, and save the breastbeating for later.

FIGURE 7-13. Costume designer Marie Anne Chiment fastening gauzy fabrics on a costume being modeled by intern Carl Mulert. Notice the sketch from which Ms. Chiment is working. *A Midsummer Night's Dream* at Arena Stage. *Photograph by Joan Marcus.*

Make a list of what you have to accomplish in the second fitting. Fit and style alterations come first. Check all the actor's movements and make sure they are possible. Mark hem lengths but make sure the correct shoes are on the actor's feet. Wigs, hats, and other accessories in progress should be tried on at this fitting. You may also want to discuss individual accessories with the actor since this is about the time in the rehearsal process that you will discover a purse has been cut and a handkerchief added.

Lay on trim, place bows, drape scarves, and look at everything with care. This is probably the last time you will have the actor in the costume before these things are stitched in place. Once again, don't forget to have your sketch with you in the fitting room and don't forget to consult it at every turn.

Invite the director to this fitting. Many directors enjoy seeing costumes in progress and will invite themselves. This might be a good time to chat with the director about making good use of a period costume on stage.

Actors who tend to be troublesome in fittings will often pick the second fitting to be at their worst. These actors may have suffered at the hands of thoughtless costume designers or technicians in the past. They may not have a good sense of clothing and/or be desperately concerned about the work they are doing in rehearsal. Stay calm when an ingénue in a pinned-up-the-back gown which is unfaced, unhemmed, and untrimmed tells you the dress is ugly, ill-fitting, and impossible for her character to wear on the stage. It is certainly a rude thing to say but you will gain little by pointing this out or responding in an equally rude manner. Most important of all, don't allow your own feelings to be hurt. Think of all the reasons the actor might have for taking his or her frustration out on a costume, explain what construction steps remain to be done, refer as you have done before to the sketch, and get on with your work. If you feel the situation is going to persist, ask the stage manager to set up a meeting to talk things out. Nine times out of ten the actor will return to the costume shop later to apologize for the outburst, explaining that it was the result of a particularly bad afternoon in rehearsal. Accept the apology gracefully.

Trim

Once the alterations from the second fitting have been made and before facings and closures are installed, work out and set up any trim that can be machined on. If you wait until the garment is finished, most trims have to be tacked on by hand, a time-consuming operation.

Put the costume on a tailor's dummy and pin your braids and laces in place. Move them about until you approve of the effect. If possible, do your pinning several feet from a large mirror so you can study the trim from a distance as you go along.

This is the time to decide on ruffle widths and on how many rows of lace really make up that inset. Since all the garments being built will be reaching the first fabric fitting stage at approximately the same time, you may spend many hours ankle deep in trim.

Accessories

Actual shoes, gloves, and purses have been chosen. Now you must see that they are correctly colored. Shoes may also need heel taps or dance rubber on the soles. Some shops have the equipment for putting on their own dance rubber; others send the shoes out to a cobbler, a process which might take several days.

Make jewelry selections and see they are put in properly labeled boxes. You may have

FIGURE 7-14. Accessories are very important to Susan Tsu's costumes for the Milwaukee Repertory Theater production of *Taming of the Shrew. Photograph by Mark Avery.*

more than one choice at this point and you may not want to make up your mind until after you have seen each one on stage during dress rehearsals. Make sure all clasps are firm. Earrings should stay on without pinching and, if they are for pierced ears, be equipped to fasten securely. Check ring sizes.

Tights will have been fitted and may need to be dyed. Wash new tights thoroughly with detergent before you dye them, and leave them in the hot dye bath for the shortest possible time in order to protect their elasticity.

Make certain that actors who must wear detachable collars, ties, tie pins, clips, or collar pins know what to do with them. A surprising number do not have the foggiest notion of how to tie a bow or a Windsor knot or where to put a tie clip. Explain cheerfully and photocopy a set of instructions on the tying of ties to put up in the actor's dressing room until he gets the hang of it.

FIGURES 7-15 and 7-16. Figure 7-15 (above) is a sketch by Carol Oditz for *Storyville* at Ford's Theatre, Washington, D.C. Trim and accessories are quite specific. Figure 7-16 (below) is a production photograph from *Storyville*. The costume at the far left was built from the sketch. *Sketch photograph by Frances Aronson. Production photograph by Richard Braaten.*

Final Fitting

Final fittings will occur close to tech week and shortly before dress parade if there is to be one. This is the time to make final adjustments, check the hem before it's put up for good (or at least until after first dress), make sure closings are neat and snug, and check that collars lie properly and sleeves hang accurately. If bodices are to be

FIGURE 7-17. Jim Pickering as Tybalt in the Milwaukee Repertory Theater production of *Romeo and Juliet*. Sword and dagger riggings are important parts of this costume. *Costume design by Susan Tsu. Photograph by Mark Avery.*

fastened to skirts, it's a good time to mark places for the hooks and bars. Check sword and dagger riggings for balance and be sure the hero's cape will stay on his shoulders. Try on the wig with the hat so the actor will get used to the feeling of being a bit top-heavy.

When the costume is all together, take the actor out into the shop for a promenade. Have the actor walk, sit, or even turn somersaults if that is part of what goes on on stage. Try to convince the young actress who is afraid of falling that she really can go upstairs without raising her skirts above her knees. Make sure the ingénue can lift her arms high enough to embrace her lover and check to see that her skirt will not be too long when she gets on the raked stage.

The director might be even more eager to see final fittings than he or she was to look at costumes in a less-finished stage.

Hopefully, the costume will be warmly praised on its first public appearance; this will be very helpful to the actor who is beginning the process of adapting to his or her sometimes quite strange garments.

There are many times when the final fittings, even if scheduled in advance, never happen because the shop is just too busy or rehearsal time is too tight. In these cases you will make the best possible use of measurements and tailor's dummies (and each other!) and do the best you can to be ready for dress parade or first dress rehearsal.

Shading, Ageing, and Distressing

Painting costumes to achieve depth or as part of an ageing or distressing process is a task that has to come last, after building and alterations are finished. Because it happens at the end, it is often done hurriedly. Some designers do it right before first dress and others wait until after first dress to check the lighting.

If ageing and distressing are vital to the look of your show, schedule your time so you can

do it calmly. These processes, if well and properly done, ought to be accomplished in several steps, not in a mad rush. If you are concerned that you will go too far in breaking down a garment, treat it gently at first and plan to increase the amount of distress applied after you have seen it on stage.

There are a great many techniques for shading, ageing, and distressing stage costumes, far too many to go into here. Consult *The Costumer's Handbook* for general ideas and check the *Theatre Crafts'* Index for articles about specific production experiences.

Remember not to put permanent dirt and age spots on costumes you have rented. Use something that will clean out. If the garment is dark, try talcum powder or fuller's earth (a grey powder sold in most drug stores) or deodorant in roll-on or spray containers. All of these will readily dry-clean out.

FIGURES 7-18 and 7-19. Colleen Muscha's sketch for Fireman in David Mamet's *Lakeboat* (top left), and production photograph showing the aged, painted costume (below). Actors Victor Raider-Wexler and Paul Meacham at the Milwaukee Repertory Theater's Court Street Theater. *Photograph by Mark Avery.*

Dress Parade

Many costume designers and technicians detest dress parades and they do not occur in all theatres. They do have, however, a useful and positive side if they are well-organized and smoothly run. Under the best of circumstances a dress parade will give you the opportunity to see the costumes all assembled, individually and in groups, several days before tech week begins; this will enable you to know what you must concentrate on, what problems need solving, and what changes have to be made. The director can give voice to his concerns as well. A good dress parade can make for a more peaceful first dress.

These are the most common complaints about dress parades: 1. A dress parade means you have to get things done earlier than you would without it. 2. They are usually done in rehearsal halls with ghastly lighting. 3. The director and the designers are looking at garments up close when they were intended to be viewed at a distance; and therefore they will see problems that don't really exist. 4. Dress parades are always rushed.

Now consider an ideal dress parade. It is either being held on a theatre stage where there are no union restrictions about stage use, or management considers dress parades important enough to pay union stagehands to run it. If it is not being held on a stage it is in a large rehearsal hall where a couple of lighting instruments,

FIGURE 7-20. Bottom, played by Mark Hammer, tries out the pool that is part of *A Midsummer Night's Dream* set at Arena Stage with the assistance of technical director David M. Glenn. *Costume design by Marie Anne Chiment. Photograph by Joan Marcus.*

FIGURE 7-21. These costumes must allow for maximum movement. Gary Sloan as Tybalt and Jack Wetherall as Mercutio in the Long Wharf Theatre production of *Romeo and Juliet. Costume design by J. Allen Highfill. Photograph by William B. Carter.*

gelled and focused, illuminate the actors, who are a good distance from where the director and designers are sitting. Hand props are available as needed, particularly guns that must fit in pockets, swords that must be drawn, pocket watches, glasses, etc. There is a chair, a stool, and even a step unit in easy reach.

The stage manager has scheduled the sequence of garments carefully so the actors who have to change into second and third costumes have time to return to the dressing room while other things are being looked at. An adequate block of time has been allowed for the proceedings.

The costume crew is all on hand. The wardrobe supervisor has checked over all the costumes and is helping the actors in the dressing rooms. The shop supervisor is armed with safety pins, chalk, tape measures, and any other items thought necessary for on-the-spot chores. Another costume staff member is armed with a large note pad and pencil. Soft music would not be inappropriate.

The stage manager is in charge of the event, calls the actors in order, and keeps track of the passage of time.

Each actor has ample time to display his or her costume, turning so all sides are displayed and going through a complete repertoire of movements, including sitting, kneeling, and so on. If any part of the costume is uncomfortable the actor says so and someone from the costume shop finds out what is wrong. Many problems are simple matters of adjustment: suspenders to let down, drawstrings tied too tight, or dress shoes being worn with heavy socks. If a garment alteration is necessary, it is marked to do in the shop.

The ideal dress parade makes it possible for the actor to put the costume thoroughly through its paces. This is a better place for a seam to rip than on stage. Go through quick changes slowly, step by step, to see if there are any snags that can be cleared up before the change has to be made under pressure. Put on coats, take off hats, buckle on armor, and solve problems calmly.

181

Sometimes, through no one's fault, a costume simply doesn't work. The director and the costume designer usually know it at the same time. In such situations you may simply have to go back to the drawing board and come up with something new. Such occasions are certainly the exception, but isn't it better to know at dress parade that you have a new costume to create rather than several days later and much closer to opening?

If the shop has known from the first day that a dress parade was scheduled, it will be something to aim for, the first goal. Vital construction steps will be done, such as closings on quick change garments and gussets for the character who tumbles. For other than the practical necessities, the dress parade is the time to see costumes from the outside with trim in place and jewelry on. Save inside work such as linings for the days between dress parade and dress rehearsal.

After dress parade the shop staff should sit down together and go over the notes that were made. Decide how alterations and changes will be made and make assignments. Then go out to lunch or dinner, whichever is appropriate.

Working Through Dress Rehearsals

First Technical Rehearsal with Costumes

Count yourself lucky if you are working in a theatre that is able to schedule a tech rehearsal without costumes; this allows the actors to concentrate solely on getting used to the set and handling real props. In some theatres the turnaround period is so short that all design elements are added at the same time, making the rehearsal especially trying for everyone. A first tech, with or without costumes, is usually a ponderous affair that moves slowly and stops often. The actors, if they are in costume, have lots of time to sit around getting wrinkled, drinking—and maybe dripping—tea and coffee in costume, and possibly even spilling a bit of mayonnaise on their frocks in the dressing room. No amount of warning, no set of rules posted on the call board, no threats or bribes have ever been known to completely halt costume abuses under such circumstances. Be the best watchdog you can be and try especially hard to prevent mayonnaise spills which make particularly ugly stains.

Preparation for Dress Rehearsal

When costumes go into a dress rehearsal they should be completely wearable if not completely finished. The actor's work in the rehearsal won't be impeded if a bow isn't in place but he or she cannot concentrate if a hem is coming down or a sleeve is falling out.

Spend whatever time you have just before the first costume rehearsal going through the individual pieces for each actor. Perhaps the wardrobe supervisor will do this with you. Check items against your costume plot and make whatever final alterations there are in the plot. Make absolutely certain that dresses all have perspiration shields.

The stage manager has already made dressing room assignments. Help put the costumes in the dressing rooms and double check that everything is present.

An experienced wardrobe supervisor will have, in addition to the costume plot or dressing list, a list of costume pre-sets and strikes and a list

FIGURE 7-22. Electrician Jamie Gallagher and stage manager Anne Keefe in tech rehearsal at the Long Wharf Theatre. *Photograph by Bill Kelly.*

noting and describing quick changes. Duties are divided up if there are two or more people on the wardrobe staff. Check with the experienced wardrobe supervisor to see if he or she needs anything explained, then get out of the way and watch. If the wardrobe person is young and inexperienced, or, in the case of a university theatre, a rank beginner, make sure you stay close by to give a hand when it's needed, offer suggestions and, in general, be supportive.

Wardrobe should have a sewing kit containing safety pins, needles, thread, adhesive tape, and any other items that might be useful in an emergency. There should also be a pad and pencil available on which wardrobe staff members, and actors in their absence, may write down notes.

You should be backstage or near the dressing area when the actors arrive and are getting dressed for the first rehearsal with costumes. There will inevitably be questions for you. Try not to help with dressing, however, since the wardrobe staff should be doing that. Make notes of things you want to remember. Dress rehearsal

FIGURE 7-23. Actor Emery Battis prepares for a dress rehearsal of Gorky's *Summerfolk* at the Long Wharf Theatre. *Costume design by Bill Walker. Photograph by Bill Kelly.*

is certainly not a time to rely on your memory. Check each actor out when he or she is dressed and see that everything is on correctly. Wish the company and the back-stage crew good luck and make your way out into the house.

During Dress Rehearsal

Sit, at first, somewhere in the center of the house. This should be the best position for viewing the show. Later you will want to check the costumes from far back and from the very front but it is a good idea to get an average perspective first without either blurred details or sweaty faces. Make sure you are equipped to take notes (with a light if necessary) or have someone sitting by you to write down the notes you dictate.

If you are in the center of the house you will be in easy reach of the director in case you are needed while the rehearsal is going on. The set and lighting designers will have a table rigged up nearby and will be in touch with lights, sound, and stage management over headphones.

Look as hard as you can look. See the total effect first and then the details. There will be surprises. Nothing ever looks quite the way you thought it would under lights. For every costume that doesn't look quite as good, however, there will be another that looks considerably better. Don't take notes immediately. Give yourself a real chance to see.

Stage lighting can highlight your colors and sculpt the figure in the stage space or it can wash out everything and create a dull, flat picture. If you are unhappy with the gel colors or the lighting positions, don't hesitate to speak to the lighting designer about the problems you see. Be tactful but don't be shy.

Nothing in the set should be unfamiliar to you but sometimes a throw pillow or a set of curtains do unexpected battle with the leading lady's dress. The set designer will probably see the problem when you do but, if he or she doesn't, don't suffer in silence.

Now, note taking begins in earnest. Write down everything that effects the actors' movements and business. Check hemlengths and sleeve lengths. See if there are white garments which should be dipped down. Check that your shading and ageing reads properly. List everything that needs to be done. No matter that it probably all won't get done. Write it down now and assess priorities later. The shop supervisor may also be taking notes that deal with fitting adjustments. The wardrobe staff will have notes that reflect backstage incidents and actor comfort.

If the rehearsal halts to solve a costume problem, stand ready to go to the stage and assist. Practice overcomes most problems. Show the actor how far to tilt her hat and help another hang up his coat so it is easy to put on again.

Don't leave the theatre unnecessarily during the rehearsal. The director doesn't want to wait for you to be found before he can talk to you. Besides, you might miss something important. Ask someone to bring you a sandwich or a cup of coffee if you are starving, but stay in the house.

At the end of the first phase of the technical/dress marathon, the director will either have notes for you or you will be included in a general note-giving session.

Take your notes and the director's notes back to the costume shop and sit down for a session with the staff. Assemble everyone's notes and make a general work list. Assign individual costume notes to the person who is responsible for that costume, usually the draper, who will parcel out jobs to the stitchers. Make a list of things you must do and things you must shop for. When everything is in neat columns on a series of pads, go home to bed.

Between Dress Rehearsals

Before the next dress rehearsal, make sure you have gone over maintenance with the wardrobe supervisor. Tell her which costumes should be pressed for each performance and which are intentionally wrinkled and grubby. List what is washable and how often things should be washed. Ask about the dry cleaning schedule to make sure it is adequate for the show.

Attempt to solve as many of the problems listed in your notes, in order of priority, as can be handled in the hours you have before the cos-tumes go back on the actors again. If one garment needs a lot of reworking, ask the director to allow you to keep it out of the next rehearsal so it may be complete for the one after that. Be cheerful in the shop even if you are tired. So is everyone else. Let the technicians know you are pleased with their work and proud of them. Bring in a treat, a bowl of fruit or a box of pastries, whichever is appropriate for the group.

Stop work in time for the costumes to get back to the dressing rooms well before the next rehearsal. Grab notebook and pencil and enter the darkened house for another go.

FIGURES 7-24 and 7-25. When actors change, costume designs may change as well. Costume designs by Jennifer von Mayrhauser for Nancy Snyder (left) and for Lynn Redgrave (right) for the Broadway production of *Knock Knock. Photographs by Martha Swope.*

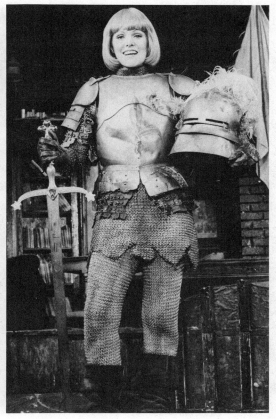

Pulling It All Together

The number of dress rehearsals you have in which to pull the costumes into an integrated whole will vary from theatre to theatre. Three is average but occasionally you will run into a situation in which there is only one dress rehearsal before a preview with an audience. No matter what the front office says about a preview not being a proper performance, actors equate performance with audience no matter what, if any, ticket price the people out there are paying. Nevertheless, you may continue to take notes through preview performances and to make changes and adjustments in between. If all goes well your list will grow shorter although it may never disappear altogether.

You may be called upon to make changes during previews because the script is being cut or rewritten. If you are designing costumes for an untried musical comedy, numbers and scenes may be cut and added several times before everyone concerned is satisfied. Previews, changes in the script, and design changes may go on for many days.

However long a time you have to pull it together, do your best. Listen to good advice, ignore bad advice and hope you can tell the difference. First and foremost, learn to trust your own eyes.

On opening day it must be finished and you deserve nothing more or less than a good dinner before the performance and a good party after it.

FIGURE 7-26. Scene from *A Midsummer Night's Dream* at Arena Stage. *Costume design by Marie Anne Chiment. Photograph by Joan Marcus.*

Epilogue

In regional theatres the visiting costume designer is often due to leave for home, or for the next show, early on the morning after opening. Make sure you arrange some time to have the whole shop assembled beforehand so you can thank them for their work. Don't be afraid of sentimentality. Many costume technicians do their work devotedly; if they did, you should say so. When a designer leaves without any indication of appreciation for the work done, the shop staff is sure the designer was unhappy with what they did. Don't leave this impression if you don't mean to.

It's a nice custom to give small opening night gifts to members of the shop staff. The thought is what counts, however, and a card or a personal note will be as much appreciated as something more costly.

It always strikes costume designers as a bit sad that their work ends just as the production comes to life on stage. On opening night you may have nothing to do and you may feel, just for a moment, quite out of things. But every opening night is exciting and all the more so if the play is good, the production worthy, and the audience full of applause at the end. Be happy and proud of your work. You helped create and build what is on the stage and, if the production runs two weekends in a university theatre, six weeks in a regional theatre, or two years on Broadway, it wouldn't have been the same without you.

FIGURE 7-27. A cast portrait from the Long Wharf Theatre production of James M. Barrie's *The Admirable Crichton. Costume design by Bill Walker. Photograph by William B. Carter.*

8

The Costume Design Business

Competition for costume design jobs is stiff, especially in New York City, in the top regional theatres, and in the film and television industries. No young designer just entering the field can expect to design a Broadway musical right away. Most of you will enter the field as a design assistant or a costume technician. All designers, until they are very well-established indeed, have to explore the job market regularly and present themselves and their work to producers and directors.

Entering The Job Market: Where, What, and How

Thanks to the significant growth of regional professional theatres in the past fifteen to twenty years, jobs for costume designers are not confined as narrowly as they once were to New York and Hollywood. You can now find design opportunities in Milwaukee, Denver, San Francisco, Atlanta, Dallas, Miami, Seattle and other large cities, as well as in a host of smaller cities and in some small towns. New York City, however, continues to be the main proving ground for theatre designers (as Hollywood is for film designers) and the place where significant reputations are made.

When you choose where you will go to begin your professional career, you must consider several things: your personality, your knowledge and experience, and your goals. Don't rush off to the Big Apple just because you think you ought to when, in reality, you would benefit from a season or two working with a regional theatre company. On the other hand, don't let fear and insecurity keep you from moving on when your abilities and ambitions begin to clamour for a larger scope.

Since the focus of this book is theatre design, this chapter concentrates on theatre de-

FIGURE 8-1. David Murin's sketch for John Barrymore for the Broadway production of *Ned and Jack*. Sketch executed in felt-tip pen, Dr. Martin's ink, and Magic Marker spray. *Photograph by Frances Aronson.*

FIGURE 8-2. Jennifer von Mayrhauser's sketch for Grandma, played by Maureen Stapleton, in a television special adapted from a Ray Bradbury story, *The Electric Grandmother*. *Photograph by Frances Aronson.*

FIGURE 8-3. David Murin's sketch for Kitty in the American Stage Festival production of *The Royal Family*. Felt-tip pen, Dr. Martin's ink, and Magic Marker spray. *Photograph by Frances Aronson.*

FIGURE 8-4. Victor Raider-Wexler and Peggy Cowles in *Dance of Death* at the Milwaukee Repertory Theater. *Costume design by Pat McGourty. Photograph by Mark Avery.*

sign jobs. Many theatre designers move easily between the stage, films, and television and many of the suggestions that follow can easily be adapted to finding film and TV employment. These areas, however, are not addressed specifically.

Design teaching jobs are also outside the scope of the chapter. They require, in addition to design training and experience, advanced academic degrees and teaching ability. There is no reason to assume a good designer will be a good design teacher. Some young designers use teaching positions which include regular design assignments to gain experience before they approach the profession. This practice can be advantageous for the designer but not necessarily for the students who are being taught by someone more involved in designing than in teaching. There are, of course, many successful designers who are also brilliant teachers but, in most instances, they established their design careers before becoming teachers. On the other hand, there are brilliant design teachers who never pursued a professional design career.

Regional Theatres

Regional theatre costume shops all over the country hire several hundred costume technicians each year for work seasons that vary in length from twenty-eight to fifty weeks. Many of these positions go to young designers who are looking for opportunities to work with a full season of plays, to observe and learn from the resident or guest designers, and to earn a modest income at the same time.

If you have good draping and flat patterning skills you may well find excellent employment in this area. As stated earlier, good drapers are rare and jobs are available. Increasingly, however, the larger regional shops are hiring drapers whose profession is draping rather than drapers who are making their way into design.

Costume dyeing and painting and building costume props and accessories are particularly good jobs for young designers. Many regional theatres hire one person to carry out all these responsibilities during the season while others job in painters, dyers, and craftspeople as needed. If you are building accessories or painting costumes you will work in close contact with the designer, an optimum position for learning.

More and more regional theatres are hiring costume design assistants to work directly with incoming guest designers. In some instances design assistants are given one or two design assignments, often for the theatre's second or experimental stage. Design assistants are in a position to learn a great deal from the more experienced designers and they may be able to practice their own design skills at the same time.

You can usually create a situation in a regional costume shop in which you learn many things. Keep your eyes open all the time and always show you are willing to do a variety of tasks. Don't let yourself get stuck for long in a nonlearning job. Thirty-seven weeks of running material through a sewing machine that is stuck away in a corner may put food on the table but it won't necessarily help you toward your goal of becoming a self-supporting designer.

Very few young designers working as technicians in regional costume shops get up from their sewing machines to assume design positions and most, after a season or two, move on to another theatre and a position closer to the design process. Sooner or later an ambitious young designer has to strike out on his or her own and face the uncertainties of free-lancing. This may be a difficult transition to make and many of you will continue to do technical work for some time as you seek to establish your design reputation.

WHERE TO LOOK

There is no one central place where all regional costume shop job openings are advertised. Many appear in ArtSEARCH, a publication put out by the Theatre Communications Group, Inc., 355 Lexington Ave., New York, N.Y. 10017. The subscription rate is, at the time of writing, $25 per year, and it is published every two weeks.

A few regional theatre costume shop jobs will be listed in the American Theatre Association *Placement Bulletin* although the publication mainly carries notices of teaching vacancies. Address inquiries about the ATA *Placement Bulletin* to: 1000 Vermont Ave., N.W., Washington, D.C. 20005.

When you are searching for costume shop jobs in regional theatres, your best bet is to write to the theatres that interest you and send them your resume. Unless you know the name of the costume shop manager, address your correspondence to the theatre's managing director. Don't expect answers from everybody. Regional theatres tend to be understaffed and overbusy. Send inquiry letters in the early spring for work the following fall. Theatre addresses and the names of managing directors are available in the *Theatre Directory*, published each year by the Theatre Communications Group and available at the preceding address.

The following is a list of theatre companies that are members, at the time of writing, of the League of Resident Theatres (LORT). LORT theatres are relatively well established, present a full season of plays with professional actors, and employ costume technicians.

A Contemporary Theatre
100 West Roy Street
Seattle, WA 98119

Actors Theatre of Louisville
316-320 West Main Street
Louisville, KY 40202

Actors Theatre of St. Paul
2115 Summit Avenue
St. Paul, MN 55105

Alaska Repertory Theatre
705 W. 6th Avenue, Suite 201
Anchorage, AK 99501

Alley Theatre
615 Texas Avenue
Houston, TX 77002

Alliance Theatre Company
1280 Peachtree Street NE
Atlanta, GA 30309

American Conservatory Theatre
450 Geary Street
San Francisco, CA 94102

American Repertory Theatre
Loeb Drama Center
64 Brattle Street
Cambridge, MA 02138

Arena Stage
6th & Main Avenues, SW
Washington, DC 20024

Arizona Theatre Company
120 West Broadway
Tucson, AZ 85701

Asolo State Theatre
P.O. Drawer E
Sarasota, FL 33578

Barter Theatre
P.O. Box 867
Abington, VA 24210

Berkeley Repertory Theatre
Box 542
Berkeley, CA 94701

Center Stage
700 N. Calvert St.
Baltimore, MD 21202

The Cincinnati Playhouse in the Park
P.O. Box 6537
Cincinnati, OH 45206

The Cleveland Play House
P.O. Box 1989
Cleveland, OH 44106

The Cricket Theatre
Hennepin Center for the Arts
528 Hennepin Avenue
Minneapolis, MN 55403

Denver Center Theatre Co.
1050 13th Street
Denver, CO 80204

Folger Theatre Group
201 E. Capitol Street SE
Washington, DC 20003

George Street Playhouse
414 George Street
New Brunswick, NJ 08901

Geva Theatre
168 Clinton Avenue South
Rochester, NY 14604

Goodman Theatre
200 South Columbus Drive
Chicago, IL 60603

Goodspeed Opera House
East Haddam, CT 06423

The Guthrie Theatre
725 Vineland Place
Minneapolis, MN 55403

Hartford Stage Company
50 Church Street
Hartford, CT 06103

Hartman Theatre Company
307 Atlantic Street
P.O. Box 521
Stamford, CT 06901

Indiana Repertory Theatre
140 West Washington Street
Indianapolis, IN 46204

Intiman Theatre Company
Box 4246
Seattle, WA 98104

Long Wharf Theatre
222 Sargent Drive
New Haven, CT 06511

Mark Taper Forum
135 N. Grand Avenue
Los Angeles, CA 90012

McCarter Theatre Company
91 University Place
Princeton, NJ 08540

Meadow Brook Theatre
Oakland University
Rochester, MI 48063

Milwaukee Repertory Theatre Company
929 N. Water Street
Milwaukee, WI 53202

North Light Repertory Company
2300 Green Bay Road
Evanston, IL 60201

Old Globe Theatre
P.O. Box 2171
San Diego, CA 92112

Pennsylvania Stage Company
837 Linden Street
Allentown, PA 18101

Philadelphia Drama Guild
220 South 16th Street
Philadelphia, PA 19102

Pittsburgh Public Theatre
1 Allegheny Square, #230
Pittsburgh, PA 15212

Players State Theatre
3500 Main Highway
Coconut Grove, FL 33133

Playmakers Repertory Co.
206 Graham Memorial
052-A, UNC
Chapel Hill, NC 27514

The Repertory Theatre of St. Louis
Box 28030
St. Louis, MO 63119

Roundabout Theatre Co.
333 W. 23rd Street
New York, NY 10011

Seattle Repertory Theatre Co.
P.O. Box B
Queen Anne Station
Seattle, WA 98109

South Coast Repertory
655 Town Center Drive
Costa Mesa, CA 92626

Stage West
1511 Memorial Avenue
West Springfield, MA 01089

Studio Arena Theatre
710 Main St.
Buffalo, NY 14202

Syracuse Stage
820 E. Genesee St.
Syracuse, NY 13210

Theatre By the Sea
125 Bow Street
Portsmouth, NH 03801

Trinity Square Repertory Co.
201 Washington St.
Providence, RI 02903

Virginia Museum Theatre
Boulevard & Grove Avenue
Richmond, VA 23211

Virginia Stage Company
108-114 E. Tazewell St.
Norfolk, VA 23510

Yale Repertory Company
222 York St.
New Haven, CT 06520

ASSOCIATE MEMBERS
Alabama Shakespeare Festival
Box 141
Anniston, AL 36202

Great Lakes Shakespeare Festival
Bulkley Bldg. Suite 250
1501 Euclid Avenue
Cleveland, OH 44115

Missouri Repertory Theatre
5100 Rockhill Road
Kansas City, MO 64110

Tacoma Actors Guild
1323 South Yakima Street
Tacoma, WA 98405

The People's Light and Theatre Company
39 Conestoga Road
Malvern, PA 19355

Custom Costume Shops

Young designers who have just arrived in New York City often look for work in one of the shops that build costumes on order for commercial plays, ballet, opera, films, and television. The shops vary enormously in size and quality of work but most produce beautifully built and meticulously finished costumes. Finding work in a custom costume shop will depend largely on your skill level.

The majority of the people employed by custom costume shops are members of the IL-GWU (International Ladies Garment Worker's Union) but the shops may take on non-union workers for specific periods of time, a few days or, sometimes, several weeks. If you work in a shop for any great length of time, you may be required to join the union, depending on your position.

A young designer is most apt to find work as a shopper, a milliner's assistant, a craft assistant, or an assistant to the draper. Machine stitchers are usually high-speed union employees with a great deal of experience. So are hand stitchers, although sometimes additional, less experienced hand stitchers may be jobbed in.

Shopping for a custom costume shop is excellent experience for young designers. A shopper will swatch fabrics, compare prices, and buy yardage, trim, and all manner of accessories. Being a shopper is a great way to learn where to go and what to pay. Any young designer employed as a shopper is well advised to keep a notebook of addresses and the names of people who were especially helpful.

Apply for a job in a custom costume shop by sending a letter and resume when you are settled in New York. Make sure to include a reliable phone contact number. Ask if you may visit the workroom and show examples of your work. Follow up your visit with a phone call to check on work availability. Continue to phone periodically since labor may be added at any time and you may be fortunate enough to phone on the very day the shop is hiring extra help.

Costume Rental Houses

A job as a costume rental assistant, responsible for pulling together a set of costumes for a customer, can provide useful experience for a beginning designer. There are costume rental houses all over the country. Some concentrate on operas and musicals, some on fancy dress balls, Halloween and Christmas. The former would probably be more interesting than the latter. Before you apply for a position with a rental house, take a look at the catalogue to see what sorts of costumes they rent. Send a letter and resume and follow up with a phone call.

Rental houses also hire stitchers to make alterations and, sometimes, to construct new costumes. A stitching job might turn out to be less interesting than one dealing directly with assembling a costume or a set of costumes.

The Costume Collection, a unique rental organization discussed in some detail in Chapter 6, has a full-time staff and also offers several paid internships each year to beginning designers. It is the stated hope of Whitney Blausen, administrator, that The Collection can help introduce newcomers into the costume design community.

Free-Lance Design Assistants

Assisting an established designer on a show is one of the very best ways of learning a designer's process; all young designers should have some experience assisting.

A full-time, free-lance designer will often use one or more assistants on each large project. Duties will vary greatly and may range from swatching and shopping to doing a bit of library research, shipping fabrics and accessories to an out-of-town theatre or taking charge of some fittings. Assistants may or may not attend production conferences and dress rehearsals.

When the designer is working under certain United Scenic Artists contracts, the designer's assistant must also be a union member and signed to a union contract.

Designers tend to use the same assistants over and over again. The best assistant is one with whom the designer shares basic design taste and one who can see costume choices through the designer's eyes. Once a designer finds such an assistant, that person is apt to be engaged over and over again, and a professional relationship is established that may only be broken when the assistant strikes out and begins to design on his or her own.

If you want to assist a particular designer, write and send a resume. Don't be hurt if you don't get a reply. Be sure to tell every costume designer you know and meet that you are looking for work as an assistant. Costume designers tend to know other costume designers and you may eventually be referred to someone who will hire you.

Your First Professional Design Job

Most young designers do their first professional work in regional theatre, summer stock, summer Shakespeare festivals, or Off-Off Broadway. Both fees and budgets may be minimal but this is where you get your feet wet and show what you can do.

Designing an Off-Off Broadway show will test your imagination and resources to the utmost. The budget will be small; it may even be non-existent. The backstage facilities will leave a lot to be desired and you will probably work out of your own home with little or no help. You may be called on to borrow, beg, and scavenge. You may even be limited to picking and choosing from what the actors have available in their own wardrobes.

FIGURE 8-5. Costume sketch by Susan A. Cox for Shakespeare's *Much Ado About Nothing,* produced by the Alabama Shakespeare Festival. *Photograph by Frances Aronson.*

FIGURE 8-6. Jennifer von Mayrhauser's sketch for Sally Talley in *Talley's Folly* on Broadway, a show that moved to Broadway, with designer, from a smaller theatre. Sketch rendered in acrylics and Ebony pencil. *Photograph by Frances Aronson.*

Make the best possible use of your opportunity, however, and learn from it. Many of the plays done Off-Off Broadway are new scripts which give you a chance to design costumes for a totally uncharted and unexplored play. Every now and then an Off-Off Broadway production of a new play will excite enough interest to warrant an uptown production and, if your work has been good, you may have the opportunity to do it again—with budget, help, and a living wage!

When your first opportunity comes, no matter how remote the location or obscure the theatre, always be sure to do your very best work. The theatre community is, by comparison to most professions, very small and intricately interconnected. People with whom you work in the boondocks may be the very ones who will hire you again, in much more prestigious circumstances. You will be amazed how quickly you can acquire a reputation for doing consistently excellent work and for being a pleasant co-worker; or, for doing sloppy work and being ill-humored. Wherever you go, your reputation will precede you; make sure it's the reputation you want.

Resident Designer

Some regional theatres, usually the smaller ones, hire a full-season resident designer who is respon-

195

FIGURE 8-7. David Murin's sketch for *He Who Gets Slapped* at the Hartman Theatre. Sketch rendered in acrylics, felt-tip pen, and Dr. Martin's watercolor. *Photograph by Frances Aronson.*

For some of you, a resident design job will be deeply satisfying, offering personal and geographic stability rare for theatre people. For others, it is another step toward surviving as a full-time, free-lance designer.

Free-Lance Designer

Free-lancing is being in business for yourself. Your product is your design ability and you

FIGURE 8-8. Design for an Estee Lauder print advertisement by Lowell Detweiler. Rendered in colored pencil and colored inks. *Photograph by Frances Aronson.*

sible for designing most, or even all, of the shows. A resident designer works closely with the costume shop and often with the same directors and actors.

Security is an important advantage of a resident design position: the security of knowing you have many shows to do from different periods, the security of a season's employment, the security of a community of people with whom to work. A disadvantage which may surface over a long period of time is that some designers, working with the same people, may find themselves repeating their style and quality of work over and over again, not trying new approaches or experimenting with different techniques.

market it job by job. As a free-lance designer, you have a lot of freedom and not much security. You may work wherever you want and whenever you are offered a job that fits into your schedule. You contract only for short-term responsibility and negotiate each fee individually. You neither make lengthy commitments nor do you often find yourself on a weekly payroll.

Not everybody who wants to be a free-lance designer will succeed. Some lack talent but most simply find they don't have a desire equal to the anxieties, insecurities, and frustrations of never quite knowing what the next day will bring

or the stamina to keep up the hectic pace necessary to make an adequate income.

Successful free-lance designers are unusually energetic people who thrive on solving problems. They enjoy meeting and working with new people in unfamiliar situations. They travel at the drop of a hat, can tolerate hotel decor, and respond readily to early morning wake-up calls. They can work anywhere. They are the people, one young designer remarked, "who have a special gleam in their eye, something that tells you they're crazy about what they do."

FIGURE 8-9. David Murin's costume design for the television series, *Ryan's Hope*. Rendered with Dr. Martin's watercolor, felt-tip pen, and Magic Marker spray. *Photograph by Frances Aronson.*

Letter and Resume

What do you say in the letter you write to inquire about design positions? To whom do you send it? What should accompany it?

The letter should be short, to the point, and appropriate to the situation. Example: You have heard from an acquaintance who is a stage manager at Theatre A that the artistic director of Theatre A is looking for a guest costume designer for production number four in the season. You ask your acquaintance if you may mention his or her name (which is the same thing as saying, "Will you put in a good word for me?") and send off a brief letter:

Dear (director's name)
I have heard from (friend's name), a member of your stage management staff, that you are looking for a costume designer for (name of play). Please consider me for the job. I have enclosed a resume and am available at your convenience to show you my work.

That's all. State your business and stop. Don't waste words saying how great you are. Don't flatter the artistic director or the theatre. The letter is the polite introduction to your resume. The information in the resume—what you've done, where you've done it, and who you've done it for—will determine whether or not the director is interested enough in you to talk with you.

A general inquiry letter to a regional theatre, sent off in the spring for the following season, might read:

Dear (director's name):
I would like to be considered for a guest costume design position with your theatre next season. Enclosed is a resume. I can meet with you at your convenience and show you my work.

Don't expect too much from general inquiry letters. More than two-thirds of the time directors and producers hire designers:

1. with whom they have worked before;
2. who are recommended by a friend;
3. whose work they have seen and liked.

If you aren't famous and don't fit into any of the above categories, you may not even receive an answer to your letter of inquiry. Don't despair and don't give up writing. There is always the possibility that your letter will arrive at just the right moment, your resume will be found interesting, and you will end up landing a job. Luck should never be discounted in the theatre.

Always type job inquiry letters. Make sure your grammar is correct. Use good quality paper. When you design a professional letterhead for yourself, make sure it is simple and tasteful.

Address job inquiry letters to the appropriate person. Spell the name correctly and append the proper title. Never resort to "To Whom It May Concern." Letters so headed seldom concern anyone and usually wind up in wastecans. When you are inquiring about design jobs with a company, address your letter to the artistic director. Check the TCG *Theatre Directory* for the name or call the theatre and ask to whom you should write.

Your resume should be arranged to fit on one page. A second page is likely to go unread. Use your design sense and lay out the resume information to your best advantage. Focus on your most impressive work.

When you're just beginning, include everything you have done that is at all relevant to the work you are seeking. Include your educational background, your student design assignments, and significant part-time jobs. Later on you will omit some of these in favor of professional design experiences. Also, in the beginning, add three or four professional references who can be contacted about your work. Be sure to check with these people and obtain their permission to be so listed. Choose people who will say positive things about you. You can't be expected to please everyone but it's foolish to solicit a reference

SUSAN TSU – Costume Designer

AFFILIATIONS: USA Local #829
DEGREES: BFA, MFA Carnegie-Mellon University

AWARDS:
New York Drama Desk
New York Drama Critics
New York Young Film Critics
Los Angeles Distinguished Designer

BROADWAY:
Godspell
Elizabeth I

OFF- and OFF-OFF BROADWAY:
Alfred Dies – by Israel Horowitz, with Michael Moriarty – Actor's
        Studio
Still Life – Susan Yankowitz – Interarts Theatre
Quail Southwest – by Larry Ketron – Manhattan Theatre Club

REGIONAL THEATRE:
CINCINNATI PLAYHOUSE IN THE PARK:
Tartuffe – dir. Dan Sullivan, with Austin Pendleton
That Championship Season – dir. John Dillon, with Reid Shelton
Arsenic and Old Lace – dir. Tony Stimeck
Oh Coward! – dir. Garland Wright, with Bonnie Franklin and
        Leonard Frey

GREAT LAKES SHAKESPEARE FESTIVAL:
The Tempest – dir. Vincent Dowling
Ah, Wilderness! – dir. John Dillon
The Devil's Disciple – dir. Vincent Dowling

PITTSBURGH PLAYHOUSE:
A Streetcar Named Desire – dir. Maria ley Piscator
Alfred the Great – by Israel Horowitz, dir. Jimmy Hammerstein, with
        John Cazale

INDIANA REPERTORY THEATRE:
Arms and the Man – dir. Vincent Dowling
Three-Penny Opera – dir. Arne Zaslove
The Seagull – dir. Ed. Stern

FOLGER THEATRE GROUP:
Richard III – dir. Louis Scheeder

LIBRARY OF CONGRESS:
An Independent Woman – by Dan Stein, dir. Chuck Maryan

MILWAUKEE REPERTORY THEATRE:
Long Day's Journey into Night – dir. Irene Lewis
Ah, Wilderness! – dir. Irene Lewis
Romeo and Juliet – dir. John Dillon
Fighting Bob – by Tom Cole, dir. John Dillon
Taming of the Shrew – dir. John Dillon
The Recruiting Officer – dir. Bill Ludel

NATIONAL TELEVISION:
WHA-TV/PBS – Wilder Wilder! – dir. Rudy Goldman

FIGURE 8-10. A free-lance designer's resume.

Resumé:
Michael J. Cesario

Costume Designer
United Scenic Artists
NY Local 829

THEATRE

MUSICAL CHAIRS
Broadway
Rudy Tronto, Director

JULIUS CAESAR
Amer. Shakespeare Theatre, Stratford
Gerald Freedman, Director

1959 PINK THUNDERBIRD
McCarter Theatre Co.
Nagle Jackson, Director

CHERRY ORCHARD
Alley Theatre
Lou Criss, Director

MARY STUART
Alley Theatre, Houston
Nina Vance, Director

IMPORTANCE OF BEING EARNEST
Alley Theatre
Leslie Yeo, Director

THREEPENNY OPERA
Alley Theatre
Pat Brown, Director

ABSURD PERSON SINGULAR
Alley Theatre
Robert Symonds, Director

SCAPIN,
THE GOODBYE PEOPLE
Indiana Rep.
Ed Stern, Artistic Director

SHAY, THE RIVALS,
STAGE DOOR, MOUSETRAP
Playwrights Horizons
Bob Moss, Artistic Director

FAUST, THE COUNTRY WIFE,
FALSTAFF, HOUSE OF BLUE LEAVES
Krannert Center/Perform'g Arts

BUTLEY,
SCENES FROM AMERICAN LIFE
Illinois Rep. Festival

CARAVANSERAI
Ballet Hispanico of New York
Talley Beatty, Choreographer

SHAKERS, NIGHTSPELL
Illinois Dance Theatre
Doris Humphreys, Recr.

Productions for: Louisville Shakespeare Festival, Milwaukee Rep., Lake George Opera
Theatre, Illinois Opera Theatre, Nebraska Rep., Stage Co., NY, Actors Theatre Co., NY,
National Arts Club, Monomoy Theatre, Wisconsin Arts Council

TELEVISION, FEATURE, COMMERCIAL, PRINT

VINTON SPECIAL	CBS; Krofft Productions	Assistant to Madeline Graneto
ABC '78 SEASON INTRO SPECIAL	ABC	Assistant to Madeline Graneto
MUSIC WORLD AWARDS	Syndicated; H/R Productions	Costume Designer
GRANDSTAND DADS	CBS Pilot	Costume Designer
OHIO; WHAT MIGHT HAVE BEEN	Cannon Films	Costume Designer
MERCURY INTRO; VANISH	Mike Nebbia Productions	Costume Designer
NEW YORK MAG.; MENNIN; AMBIANCE MAG.	A&A Graphic Arts	Stylist/Make-up
J.C. PENNY CATALOG; LANE BRYANT	Mort Hyatt Studio	Stylist

MEMBERSHIPS

The Costume Society (England)
The Costume Society of America

PROFESSIONAL TRAINING

B.A., University of Wisconsin (Whitewater)
M.F.A., Ohio University

FIGURE 8-11. A free-lance designer's resume.

from someone who might give you a poor report. Until you are a well-known designer, you may be sure your references will be checked.

When you first enter the design field you will not have a great deal of experience. Accept this and never be tempted to pad out or lie about what you have done. Quite frankly, the theatre community is too small for you to be able to get away with it.

The Theatre Communications Group, already mentioned in connection with *ArtSEARCH* and the *Theatre Directory*, also helps young designers advertise themselves. You can put your resume and a small slide portfolio on file with TCG. Producers and directors who hire designers may contact TCG and examine these files. As a further service to beginning designers, TCG holds regular portfolio reviews conducted by a panel of prominent designers. All positive comments are placed in the young designer's file. For further information about the portfolio review contact Arthur Bartow at TCG (the address is on page 191).

Portfolios

A portfolio of your work should illustrate your process and the finished product. It is your most important advertisement. Assemble it with care; include things that you especially like and show it with pride. The following suggestions about choosing sketches and photographs for your portfolio were assembled from conversations with directors. As you might expect, there was little unanimity of opinion.

There was agreement, however, on form of presentation: Directors tend not to like slide shows. Photographs are preferable, in color if possible and, ideally, alongside the original sketches.

Limit the number of sketches in your portfolio to three or four dozen at the most. Choose designs from two or three shows to make up the bulk of the work and fill in with individual sketches from other shows that illustrate different styles and a broader range of your work.

Select designs that show off your work to its best advantage, ones that are clear and easy to read. Be sure each sketch has the name of the show, the character's name, the act and scene for which it was designed and, if you wish, the actor's name. Be prepared to answer questions about the sketches, particularly questions relating to the interpretation of the play.

Select work from plays that are familiar rather than from obscure plays. It is difficult for the person looking at your work to judge the aptness of your ability to interpret character unless he or she has at least a nodding acquaintance with the script.

Whenever it is possible to do so, include photographs of the final costumes to show how the designs were realized. Point out changes that occurred during the rehearsal and in the shop. Most directors will be glad to know you are flexible enough to make changes. No matter how wonderful your sketches are, if there is no evidence of the finished product you are not presenting a complete picture of your work.

All costume designers would be well advised to take their own costume record shots or, if lacking the skills, to get a friend to do them. Photographs taken by theatre photographers seldom include exactly what you want and prints are often prohibitively expensive.

Avoid using color photocopies unless the reproduction is especially good. As a rule they never show off the costume to best advantage, tending to be blurred and inaccurately colored.

If you know in advance what sort of play you are being interviewed to design, adjust and rearrange your portfolio accordingly. Pick work related to the appropriate style and period. If it is a contemporary work, don't take only Elizabethan and medieval sketches. You should always show a wide range of periods but you should also alter the balance and tailor your choices to the occasion.

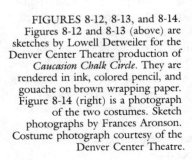

FIGURES 8-12, 8-13, and 8-14.
Figures 8-12 and 8-13 (above) are
sketches by Lowell Detweiler for the
Denver Center Theatre production of
Caucasion Chalk Circle. They are
rendered in ink, colored pencil, and
gouache on brown wrapping paper.
Figure 8-14 (right) is a photograph
of the two costumes. Sketch
photographs by Frances Aronson.
Costume photograph courtesy of the
Denver Center Theatre.

FIGURE 8-15. Colleen Muscha's sketch of Curley's Wife from *Of Mice and Men* for the Milwaukee Repertory Theater production. Rendered in pencil and watercolor. *Photograph by Frances Aronson.*

Interviews

First impressions are important; they may also be lasting. In an interview it is most important that you be as relaxed, as comfortable, and as natural as possible. Never put on airs or pretend to be anything you are not. You are there to present yourself, show your work, and sell your ability to do what you do as well as you know how to do it.

Dress appropriately without going to extremes. Theatre people tend to dress more casually than the business community or other professional groups. Casual is all right; sloppy is not. Most directors who were interviewed for this book said they were not very influenced by what designers wore to interviews. One did remark, however, that if he interviewed a designer who was expensively dressed, he might assume that person to be an expensive designer who would not be sufficiently budget conscious!

Some interviews are long and some are short. Some directors spend a good deal of time chatting before turning to the portfolio, others are interested in seeing your work right away. Some know a good deal about costumes and others know very little. Respond to individual situations and don't be surprised when each one is different.

It is not out of place for you to ask questions during the interview. Before you arrive, think about what you want to know. Ask about the stage, production dates, the acting company, the costume shop staff, and location. Ask for information that might influence your decision to take or not take the job if it is offered to you. Your enthusiasm for designing at that theatre may well be dampened when you discover the costume shop has two straight stitch sewing machines, one stitcher, and no cutter.

United Scenic Artists

In order to accept design jobs with some theatrical organizations, free-lance costume designers must join a union called United Scenic Artists. There are two USA locals, 829 in New York City and 350 in Chicago. Both are affiliated with the International Brotherhood of Painters and Allied Trades (IBPAT) of the AFL-CIO and both are subject to the same Brotherhood constitution. (The almost-parallel union on the West Coast is local 816, the Scenic and Title Artists Union which is affiliated with the International Alliance of Theatrical Stage Employees (IATSE), the "stagehands" union. Local 816 represents scenic, costume and lighting designers, and scenic artists

FIGURES 8-16, 8-17, and 8-18. A sketch from Andrew B. Marlay's union exam project in New York, *The Critic* (above left). *Photograph by Frances Aronson.* A sketch from Arnold S. Levine's union exam project in Chicago, *A Midsummer Night's Dream* (above right). *Photograph by Frances Aronson.* A sketch from Colleen Muscha's union exam project in New York, *Albert Herring* (right). *Photograph by Frances Aronson.*

for the stage in Los Angeles. Locals 705 and 891 also represent costume designers and technicians in various capacities within the film industry.)

Membership in USA is usually gained by way of an exam for the beginning designer or by portfolio review for the more experienced designer. The exam is given each spring. It includes a design project to be done at home and assignments to be completed on the day and at the place of the exam. Exams are reviewed by a panel of USA designers.

Theatrical organizations who have entered into contract agreements with United Scenic Artists may not hire a non-union costume designer except in special situations when they are also required to hire a union design supervisor. The prospect of hiring two designers for the same project usually prohibits the producing group from hiring non-union people.

Some of the large producing organizations that have hiring agreements with USA are Broadway theatres, Off-Broadway theatres, ABC, NBC, and CBS television, the Metropolitan Opera, and feature film producers. Some regional and dinner theatres, some regional opera and ballet companies, and some free-lance television producers are also contracted to USA.

United Scenic Artists exists to protect the interests of designers on the job. A union contract sets minimum fees for the designs and states that travel and out-of-pocket expenses must be reimbursed. It requires producers to pay into pension and welfare funds. It protects the designer's rights in cases of subsequent productions either of the original designs or the design concepts. It establishes rules for billing and prohibits the producing group from altering the designs after opening night without the express permission of the designer.

A union contract also clarifies the designer's responsibilities to the producer. The following broad statement describing a costume designer's duties on a production was taken from the February 1980 General Information handbook for USA Local 829:

1. design the costumes;
2. provide a costume plot listing the costume changes by scene for each character;
3. provide color sketches of all designed costumes and a visual representation for selected costumes;
4. provide complete color sketches or outline sketches with color samples, including necessary drawings or descriptions of detail and its application for the contracting shop, including selection of all necessary fabrics and trims;
5. be responsible for selection and coordination of contemporary costumes, including selection from performer's personal wardrobe;
6. supervise fittings and alterations of costumes;
7. design, select and/or approve all accessories: headgear, gloves, footwear, hose, purses, jewelry, umbrellas, canes, fans, bouquets, masks, etc.;
8. supervise and/or approve makeup and hairstyling, selection of wigs, hair pieces, moustaches and beards.

There are fringe benefits to union membership such as group health insurance and life insurance coverage. Perhaps the most important benefit is being part of a professional community. United Scenic Artists is a relatively small group (a few hundred members in Chicago; slightly over a thousand in New York City) of free-lance designers who have, in their organization, a means through which they can discuss and try to solve the common problems of their work.

What union membership does *not* do is find work for designers. It may protect you once you are on the job but securing that job remains entirely up to you.

Some costume designers choose to work for a long time in non-union contract situations without approaching United Scenic Artists for membership. Others rush to take the exam right away. The road to becoming a successful free-lance costume designer is about the same length for both groups. Membership in USA does not prevent you from accepting non-union design jobs yet it is no secret that the highest-paying design opportunities, especially on the East Coast, are with producing organizations that have hiring agreements with the union. Sooner or later union membership becomes a necessary step for self-supporting free-lancers.

Contracts

Designers' contracts range from the very simple to the relatively complex. Some contracts come in the form of a letter while others are set up along more formal lines. Certain points are always included while many others may or may not be present.

It goes without saying that you should always read your contract carefully and never sign it until you are satisfied with the agreement into which you are entering.

All contracts state the fee to be paid to the designer and the date on which completed costumes are expected. Beyond these two major points, a contract may state the materials budget, provisions for transportation, housing and per diem expenses, production dates, residence dates, and program billing. The contract will detail royalty terms if they apply. There may be a clause that promises the designer first refusal rights to design the production again if it moves to another theatre, an important clause in Off-Off Broadway theatre contracts.

The following four contracts, from regional and Off-Off Broadway theatres, will give you some idea of possible variations:

Contract #1

Dear _____ :

This letter, when signed by you, will constitute an agreement with the (name of theatre) .

We hereby engage you as Costume Designer for our production of _____ _____ opening _____. For your services you will receive a fee of _____ and a per diem of _____ for up to seven days. We also agree to reimburse your transportation from _____ to _____. Your fee will be payable in thirds: on receipt of a signed agreement, on receipt of designs, and on opening. The costume budget is _____.

Billing will be "Costumes by _____" and will appear with the Director in the same size and boldness.

Please sign and return the copy to me as soon as possible.

Contract #2

This agreement is made by and between the (name of producer) and (name of designer) . (designer) agrees to design the costumes for the (producer) production of (name of play) by (playwright) . In return for these services, the (producer) will pay (designer) the sum of (fee) on the (date) , the first performance of the production.

In addition, (designer) will be given the right of first refusal to design the costumes should the (producer) produce (play) at another theatre.

Contract #3

Dear _____:

The following shall constitute our entire agreement:

1. We hereby hire you as Costume Designer for the ___(producer)___ 's productions of
    ___(production #1)___ and ___(production #2)___ in its _____
    season.

2. For the design of these productions, you shall receive as compensation the amount
    of _____ per show, to be paid in the following manner:
    50 percent upon presentation of renderings for each show
    50 percent on the opening day of each show.

3. The following dates shall prevail for the productions you are designing:

___(Production #1)___		___(Production #2)___	
1st Rehearsal	_____	1st Rehearsal	_____
Opening	_____	Opening	_____
Closing	_____	Closing	_____

4. As Costume Designer your duties shall be determined in consultation with the
    Artistic Director and the Producing Director.

5. For the design of these productions, you agree to furnish the theatre with color
    sketches, material swatches; and if necessary, to assist in the shopping of supplies
    and materials. You will also be available to supervise construction and fittings of all
    costumes. Full renderings and swatches shall be presented to the management of
    the _____on the following dates:

___(Production #1)___	___(date)___
___(Production #2)___	___(date)___

6. You shall be available for design conferences, and if necessary shall travel to
    _____ prior to submission of renderings for such
    consultation. The expense of this shall be borne by the ___(producer)___.

7. For the duration of this contract, and while in residence at
    _____, your services are exclusive to the theatre. You
    will not accept any outside employment without prior consent from the
    _____. Such consent shall not be unreasonably
    withheld.

8. During the period from _____ through
    _____, and during the period of
    _____ through _____, your respon-
    sibilities shall call for you to be in _____ to execute the duties
    outlined in Paragraph 5, also, that during each of these periods, you shall be
    allowed to return to New York for a period of one week upon proper notice to the
    _____.

9. You agree to consult the _____'s Resident Costume
    Designer ___(name)___ regarding the theatre's inventory, and
    where possible to use items which are compatible with your designs from that
    inventory.

10. All designs, working drawings, color renderings and other material supplied under
    this contract may be used by the _____ in whatever

manner it deems necessary, but shall remain your property exclusive. The
_____ however, shall be entitled to reproductions of all
working drawings, color renderings, etc.

11. It is agreed between you and the _____ that you shall
be billed as follows: "Costumes Designed by _____"
to be placed directly under the Set Designer credit.

12. The theatre agrees to provide you with round trip air transportation for both
residencies between New York/_____/New York.

13. It is understood that either you or the _____ may
terminate this contract with four weeks written notice.

14. This Agreement cannot be changed orally. _____

Contract #4

Letter of agreement between _____(designer)_____ and _____(producer)_____.

This letter, when signed, will constitute an agreement between you (the "Artist")
and _____ (the "Theatre") and will confirm the terms
of your employment.

The Artist will be employed by the Theatre as Costume Designer for the Theatre's
production of _____.
                    (name of play)

The Artist agrees to the Theatre's schedule of production as follows:

1. Design conferences, to be held in _____, on
_____ and _____, at mutually acceptable
times.

2. Completed and approved designs, in sketch form, due in the shop by
_____.

3. Photo Call for selected costumes, scheduled for _____.

4. First Dress Rehearsal, scheduled for _____.

5. First Preview performance, scheduled for _____.

For such services rendered, the Theatre agrees to compensate the Artist with a fee
of _____, to be paid as follows:

1. $_____ on return of completed agreement.

2. $_____ on _____ (beginning of construction).

3. $_____ on _____ (opening performance).

The Theatre will provide two (2) round trip air fares from
_____, one for the design conference, and one for the
engagement. The Theatre will also provide housing for the Artist during the
engagement.

Changes in this agreement may be made only by written consent of both the Artist
and the Theatre.

If you accept this agreement, please sign and return two copies to the Theatre.

No contract is carved in marble. Alteration is easy. If you have special contractual requests, make them known at the time you are hired so they can be negotiated, agreed upon, and written in. If the contract comes to you with clauses that you feel were not agreed upon, call the producer and ask for changes. When you sign a contract, you have made a legal commitment to live up to the terms of the agreement. Never enter such agreements lightly.

Many designers dislike dealing with the business side of free-lancing and/or feel that they cannot assess or negotiate a contract effectively. Some of these designers engage agents to represent them and find their services well worth the agents' percentage. Others, who find they need contract assistance only some of the time, engage a lawyer to negotiate contracts on a one-time, one-fee basis.

Taxes

As an independent business person you are responsible for running your financial affairs in an orderly and legal manner. This includes filing annual or quarterly tax returns and paying the appropriate federal, state, and social security taxes.

Some designers manage to make their way through the intricacies of Department of Internal Revenue publications on their own while others gladly pay a tax accountant to do it for them. If you opt for a tax accountant, make sure you choose one who understands the nature of your work.

Don't forget to report *all* your earnings, even if they were fees from which no withholding tax or social security contributions were withheld.

Whether you do your own tax accounting or hire someone to do it for you, you will come out better in the end and save yourself a great deal of grief if you keep all expense receipts and cancelled checks and file them regularly into appropriate categories. Some of the tax deductible expenses for free-lance costume designers are: art supplies, professional stationery, film and theatre tickets, unreimbursed out-of-town expenses, entertaining for the purpose of getting work, work-related book and magazine purchases, union dues, assistant fees paid by you, rent and utilities paid for work space. In order to deduct these expenses, however, you have to be able to substantiate the expenditures. Get in the habit of putting receipts into individually labelled envelopes or file folders. Do your sorting regularly and save yourself the horror of facing a year's worth of miscellaneous paper scraps at tax time.

A Last Word

This book began with a designer reading and analyzing a playscript; it ends with paying income tax. The progression is not incongruous. Between starting and finishing you can count on being incomparably busy as you meet with other members of the production group, haunt museums and libraries, draw, paint, shop, and work shoulder-to-shoulder with costume technicians.

You have chosen a demanding profession, the pursuit of which will require prodigious amounts of energy. It also will require you to be brave, tough, and flexible. It asks you to be both artistic and practical—usually at the same time. It insists on the presence of humor in the face of anything.

Yet few other professions offer the variety, the potential for meeting interesting and gifted people, or the many opportunities to find personal and professional satisfaction. Every play is different, every production situation is unique, and every time you set out to design costumes for the theatre you may be sure you are in for an adventure.

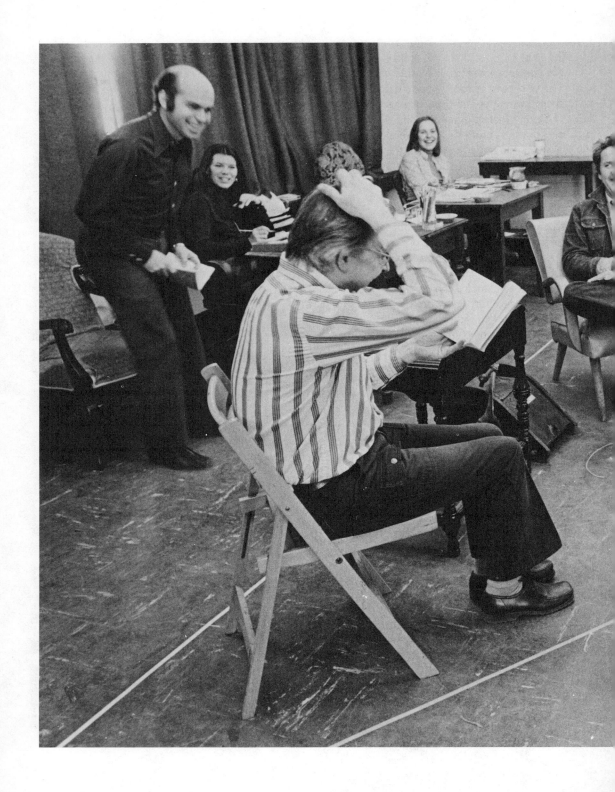

REFERENCE

Bibliography

Costume Accessories

Armstrong, Nancy, *The Book of Fans*. New Malden, Surrey, England: Colour Library International, 1978.
All illustrations in color.

Black, J. Anderson, *A History of Jewels*. London: Orbis Publishing, 1974.
Prehistory to twentieth century. Excellent glossary of techniques and technical terms. Over 500 color plates.

Braun-Ronsdorf, Dr. M., *The History of the Handkerchief*. Leigh-On-Sea, England: F. Lewis Publishers, Ltd., 1967.
Subject fully explored. Well illustrated.

Colle, Doriece, *Collars Stocks Cravats: A History and Costume Dating Guide to Civilian Men's Neckpieces 1655–1900*. Emmaus, Pa.: Rodale Press, Inc., 1972.
Good information. Line drawings not always clear.

Corson, Richard. *Fashions in Eyeglasses from the 14th Century to the Present Day*, second impression with supplement. London: Peter Owen, Ltd., 1980.
Fascinating, comprehensive and well illustrated.

Crawford, T. S., *History of the Umbrella*. Newton Abbot: David & Charles, 1970.
A wealth of information, well-illustrated.

Gostelow, Mary, *The Fan*. Dublin: Gill and Macmillan Ltd., 1976.
114 monochrome photographs and drawings; 15 color plates.

Laver, James, intro., *The Book of Public School, Old Boys, University, Navy, Army, Airforce and Club Ties*. London: Seeley Service, 1968.
Delightful little book. Many color plates.

Wilcox, R. Turner, *The Mode in Footwear*. New York: Charles Scribner's Sons, 1948.
Illustrated with line drawings. Glossary of shoe leathers.

Wilson, Eunice, *A History of Shoe Fashion*. New York: Theatre Arts Books, 1974.
Illustrated with line drawings and some monochrome photographs from primary sources.

Costume Patterning, Construction, Crafts, and Textiles

Alcega, Juan de, *Tailor's Pattern Book*, 1589 facsimile. Carlton, Bedford, England: Ruth Bean, 1979.
Reprint, with translations and explanations, of

213

Libro de Geometria, first published in 1589. A research source, not a manual for pattern drafting in modern costume shops.

American Fabrics & Fashions Magazine, eds., *Encyclopedia of Textiles*, 3rd ed. Englewood Cliffs, N.J.: Prentice-Hall, Inc., 1980.
Huge and comprehensive.

Arnold, Janet, *Patterns of Fashion 1 c. 1660–1860, English women's dresses and their construction*. New York: Drama Book Specialists, 1977.
Detailed drawings of period dresses with scaled patterns and construction instructions. Excellent book.
Patterns of Fashion 2 c. 1869–1940, Englishwomen's dresses and their construction. New York: Drama Book Specialists, 1977.
Detailed drawings of period dresses with scaled patterns and construction instructions. Excellent book.

Bradfield, Nancy, *Costume in Detail: Women's dress 1830–1930*. Boston: Plays, Inc., 1968.
Line drawings of extant period garments with details of inside and outside construction. Each page, though crowded at first glance, offers a wealth of information.

Burnham, Dorothy K., *Cut My Cote*. Toronto: Royal Ontario Museum, 1973.
28 line drawings with metric scale patterns for shirts, chemises, smocks, surplices and cotes.

Croonborg, Frederick T., *The Blue Book of Men's Tailoring*. New York: Van Nostrand Reinhold Co., 1977.
Reprint of a 1907 book. Line drawings and patterns with drafting instructions. Not for the inexperienced.

Doblin, Frank C., *The Modern Mitchell System of Men's Designing*. Chicago: The Master Designer, n.d.
Good basic pattern drafting information. Useful section on figure problems and measurements.

Dryden, Deborah M., *Fabric Painting and Dyeing for the Theatre*. New York: Drama Book Publishers, 1982.
Valuable and comprehensive book. Beautiful color illustrations.

Edson, Doris & Lucy Barton, *Period Patterns*. Boston: Walter H. Baker Co., 1942.
Supplement to *Historic Costume for the Stage*. Patterns taken from extant garments and period pattern sources and adapted to modern sizes. Selection restricted to very basic silhouettes.

Finch, Karen and Greta Putnam, *Caring for Textiles*. New York: Watson-Guptill Publications, 1977.
Useful and practical.

Gostelow, Mary, *The Complete International Book of Embroidery*. New York: Simon and Schuster, 1977.
Excellent both for research and how-to-do.

Hill, Margot Hamilton and Peter A. Bucknell, *The Evolution of Fashion: Pattern and Cut from 1066–1930*. New York: Drama Book Specialists, 1968.
Simplified patterns for period garments, not taken directly from period sources. Absence of fine detail.

Kohler, Carl, *A History of Costume*. New York: Dover Publications, Inc., 1963.
Over 600 illustrations and patterns; photographs of actual costumes and line drawings in text. Very valuable research source.

Lawson, Joan and Peter Revitt, *Dressing for the Ballet*. London: Adam and Charles Black, 1958.
Line drawings and scale patterns. Includes knitting patterns. Construction instructions.

McCunn, Donald H., *How to Make Sewing Patterns*. San Francisco: Design Enterprises of San Francisco, 1977.
A useful, straightforward approach to pattern drafting. Instructions are not always complete, however, and the illustrations are sometimes unclear.

Miller, Edward, *Textiles: Properties and Behaviour*. New York: Theatre Arts Books, 1969.
A good overview.

Motley, *Designing and Making Stage Costumes*. New York: Watson-Guptill Publications, 1974.
An informal, chatty book with lots of practical instructions. Excellent illustrations.

———, *Theatre Props*. New York: Drama Book Specialists, 1975.
Clear, concise instructions, well illustrated.

Smith, C. Ray, ed., *The Theatre Crafts Book of Costume*. Emmaus, Pa.: Rodale Press, 1973.
Selection of costume articles from *Theatre Crafts Magazine 1967–72*.

Tilke, Max, *Costume Patterns and Designs: A Survey of Costume Patterns and Designs of all Periods and Nations from Antiquity to Modern Times*. New York: Hastings House, 1974.
Garments displayed flat and in color. Excellent source for ethnic costumes based on geometric shapes. Beautiful trim details.

Vogue, *The Vogue Sewing Book*. New York: Vogue Patterns, 1981.
The best sewing instruction book available.

Waugh, Norah, *The Cut of Men's Clothes 1600–1900*. New York: Theatre Arts Books, 1964
17 scale patterns of actual period garments. Excellent text including many quotes from primary sources. An invaluable book.
———, *The Cut of Women's Clothes 1600–1930*. New York: Theatre Arts Books, 1968.
Scale patterns of actual period garments and period dressmaker's and tailor's patterns. Excellent text including many quotes from primary sources. An invaluable book.
Wingate, Dr. Isabel B., *Fairchild's Dictionary of Textiles*, 6th ed. New York: Charles Scribner's Sons, 1975.
Listings and definitions. No illustrations.

Decorative Design

Bakst, Leon, *The Decorative Art of Leon Bakst*. New York: Dover Publications, 1981.
Beautiful illustrations, 44 in color.
Christie, Archibald H., *Pattern Design: An Introduction to the Study of Formal Ornament*. New York: Dover Publications, Inc., 1969.
Originally published in 1910 as *Traditional Methods of Pattern Designing*. Lots of illustrations, all in black and white. A standard reference work.
Gillon, Edmund V., Jr., *Art Nouveau: An Anthology of Design and Illustration from The Studio*. New York: Dover Publications, Inc., 1969.
Pictures from an English publication, *The Studio*. Mostly graphic arts, black and white.
Loeb, Marcis, *Art Deco Designs and Motifs*. New York: Dover Publications, Inc., 1972.
Designs redrawn from primary sources. Black and white. Sources listed.
Meyer, Franz Sales, *Handbook of Ornament*. New York: Dover Publications, Inc., 1957.
300 plates and numerous illustrations in the text. No designer should be without it.
Mucha, Alphonse, Maurice Verneuil, and Georges Auriol, *Art Nouveau Designs in Colour*. New York: Dover Publications, Inc., 1974.
Reprint of a portfolio, *Combinations Ornamentales*, published in Paris c. 1900. Wonderful designs.
Seguy, E. A., *Full-Color Floral Designs in the Art Nouveau Style*. New York: Dover Publications, Inc., 1977.
40 plates; 166 motifs in full color.

Verneuil, M. P., et al, *Art Nouveau Floral Ornament in Colour*. New York: Dover Publications, Inc., 1976.
197 designs and motifs. 41 original art nouveau plates in color.

Dictionaries, Bibliographies, and Encyclopaedias

Anthony, P. and J. Arnold. *Costume: A Bibliography of Costume Books*, revised edition. London: The Victoria and Albert Museum, 1974.
Not comprehensive but one of the best.
Arnold, Janet, *A Handbook of Costume*. New York: S. G. Phillips, 1974.
An invaluable book for costume study. Includes extensive information on costume collections in Great Britain. Excellent bibliographies.
Cunnington, C. W., P. E. Cunnington and Charles Beard, *A Dictionary of English Costume*. London: Adam & Charles Black, 1960.
Concise accurate information with clear line drawings. Useful glossary listing fabric, textile and obsolete color names.
Evans, Hilary, Mary Evans, and Andra Nelki. *Picture Researcher's Handbook: An International Guide to Picture Sources—And How to Use Them*. Newton Abbot, London and Vancouver: David & Charles, 1975.
It does what it says it does.
Huenefeld, Irene Pennington, *International Directory of Historical Clothing*. Metuchen, N.J.: The Scarecrow Press, Inc., 1967.
Tells where to find actual garments in museums and in private collections.
Kesler, Jackson, *Theatrical Costume: A Guide to Information Sources*. Detroit: Gale Research Co., 1979.
Excellent, comprehensive bibliography. Subject, title and author indices.
Kyblova, Ludmila, Olga Herbenova, and Milene Lamarova, *The Pictorial Encyclopedia of Fashion*. New York: Crown Publishers, Inc., 1968.
Illustrated with photographs of primary sources, many of which are undated.
Snowden, James, *European Folk Dress: A Bibliography*. London: The Costume Society, 1973.
A thorough and comprehensive list of 555 titles available in libraries and private collections in Britain and Europe.

Whalon, Marion K., ed. *Performing Arts Research: A Guide to Information Sources*. Detroit: Gale Research Co., 1976.
A broad theatre arts bibliography.
Wilcox, R. Turner, *The Dictionary of Costume*. New York: Charles Scribner's Sons, 1969.
Illustrated with line drawings. Information is sometimes sketchy and generalized.

A collection of articles from *Theatre Crafts* magazine.
Wilcox, R. Turner, *The Mode in Hats and Headdress: Including Hair Styles, Cosmetics and Jewelry*. New York: Charles Scribner's Sons, 1959.
Brief descriptions illustrated with line drawings. The material is well presented.

Film Costume

Leese, Elizabeth, *Costume Design in the Movies*. New York: Frederick Ungar Pub. Co., 1977.
Illustrated with sketches and scenes from the movies. Very few in color.
McConathy, Dale and Diana Vreeland, *Hollywood Costume: Glamour! Glitter! Romance!*. New York: Harry N. Abrams, Inc., 1976.
Largely a record of the 1975 Metropolitan Museum of Art exhibit, "Romantic and Glamorous Hollywood Design." Lavishly illustrated.

Hats, Hair, and Make-Up

Corson, Richard, *Stage Makeup*, 6th ed. Englewood Cliffs, N.J.: Prentice-Hall, 1981.
Clearly written, well illustrated. Widely used as a text.
————, *Fashions in Makeup From Ancient to Modern Times*. New York: Universe Books, 1972.
Illustrated with drawings and photographs of primary sources. a fascinating book.
————, *Fashions in Hair, The First Five Thousand Years*. London: Peter Owen, 1971.
A very comprehensive research work.
Couldridge, Alan, *The Hat Book*. Englewood Cliffs, N.J.: Prentice-Hall, Inc., 1980.
A how-to book. Well illustrated and good for beginners.
Courtais, Georgine de, *Women's Headdress and Hairstyles in England from A.D. 600 to the present day*. New Jersey: Rowman and Littlefield, 1973.
Illustrated with drawings.
Dreher, Denise, *From the Neck Up, An Illustrated Guide to Hatmaking*, Minneapolis, Minn.: Madhatter Press, 1981.
Especially for theatrical costume shops.
Smith, C. Ray, ed., *The Theatre Crafts Book of Makeup, Masks and Wigs*, Emmaus, Penn.: Rodale Press, Inc., 1974.

Historical Costume

AMERICAN COSTUME

Baxter, Annette K. with Constance Jacobs, *To Be A Woman in America 1850–1930*. New York: The New York Times Book Co., Inc., 1978.
237 black and white photographs. All walks of life.
Beam, Philip C., *Winslow Homer's Magazine Engravings*. New York: Harper & Row, 1979.
220 Homer's magazine engravings. Many subjects including sports and bathing.
Blum, Daniel, *A Pictorial History of the American Theatre 1860–1970*. New York: Crown Publishers, Inc., 1969.
5000 photographs of actors and of productions.
Blum, Stella, ed., *Victorian Fashions and Costumes from Harper's Bazaar 1867–1898*. New York: Dover Publications, Inc., 1974.
Over 1000 illustrations including underwear, accessories, hairstyles, and children's fashions.
Copeland, Peter F., *Working Dress in Colonial and Revolutionary America*. Westport Conn. and London: Greenwood Press, 1977.
Drawings from original sources. Comprehensive and informative.
Daniel, Pete and Raymond Smock, *A Talent for Detail: The Photographs of Miss Frances Benjamin Johnston: 1889–1910*. New York: Harmony Books, 1974.
A small but useful book.
De Pauw, Linda Grant and Conover Hunt, *Remember the Ladies: Women in America 1750–1815*. New York: The Viking Press, 1976.
Well illustrated. Contains a wide range of information.
Earle, Alice Morse, *Two Centuries of Costume in America 1620–1820*, in two volumes. Rutland, Vt.: Charles E. Tuttle Co., 1971.
Reprint of 1903 publication. 255 illustrations, black and white, from primary sources. Pertinent contemporary quotations throughout.

Gehret, Ellen J., *Rural Pennsylvania Clothing: Being a Study of the Wearing Apparel of the German and English Inhabitants In the Late 18th and Early 19th Century*. York, Pa.: George R. D. Shumway, 1973.
Excellent.

Gibson, Charles Dana, *The Gibson Girl and Her America*. New York: Dover Publications, Inc.,
A collection of his illustrations.

Gummere, Amelia Mott, *The Quaker, A Study in Costume*. New York & London: Benjamin Blom, 1968.
Originally published in 1901. Very informative.

Jensen, Oliver, *America's Yesterdays: Images of Our Lost Past Discovered in the Photographic Archives of The Library of Congress*. New York: American Heritage Publishing Co., Inc., 1978.
Late nineteenth and early twentieth century. Excellent selection for costume research.

Jensen, Oliver, Joan Paterson Kerr and Murray Belsky, *American Album: How We Looked and Lived in a Vanished U.S.A.* New York: American Heritage/Ballantine Books, 1968.
226 rare and beautiful photographs.

Kunhardt, Dorothy Meserve and Philip B. Kunhardt, Jr., *Mathew Brady and His World*. Alexandria, Va.: Time-Life Books, 1977.
Photographs from the Meserve Collection. Many portraits.

Lee, Sarah Tomerlin, ed., *American Fashion. The Life and Lives of Adrian, Mainbocher, McCardell, Norell, Trigere*. New York: The Fashion Institute of Technology, 1975.

McClelland, Elisabeth, *History of American Costume 1607-1870*. New York: Tudor Publishing Co., 1969.
Originally published in two parts as *Historic Dress in America in 1904 and 1910*. Includes contemporary quotations. Uniforms, religious and legal dress.

Mills, Betty, *Flashes of Fashion 1830–1972*. Lubbock, Texas: West Texas Museum Association, 1973.
Color photographs of models wearing period costumes from the collection of the Texas Tech University Museum. Everyday clothing.

Rinhart, Floyd and Marion. *Summertime: Photographs of Americans at Play 1850–1900*. New York: Clarkson N. Potter, Inc., 1978.
A delightful book.

Sann, Paul, *The Lawless Decade: A Pictorial History of a Great American Transition: From the World War I Armistice and Prohibition to Repeal and the New Deal*. New York: Bonanza Books, 1957.
1920–1930. Well illustrated. Very detailed.

Sears, Stephen W., Murray Belsky, and Douglas Tunstell, *Hometown U.S.A.* New York: American Heritage Publishing Co., Inc., 1975.
Nineteenth- and twentieth-century photographs. Good for costume research.

Simpson, Jeffrey, *The American Family: A History in Photographs*. New York: The Viking Pess, 1976.
Beautiful book. Very useful for costume research.

Time-Life, *The Old West*, multiple volumes. New York: Time-Life Books, 1973–76.
Many illustrations. A wealth of information.

Trachtenberg, Alan, ed., *The American Image: Photographs from the National Archives, 1860–1960*. New York: Pantheon Books, 1979.
Excellent photographs. Very useful book.

Warwick, Edward, Henry C. Pitz, and Alexander Wyckoff, *Early American Dress: The Colonial and Revolutionary Periods*. New York: Outlet Book Co., Inc., 1977.
Originally published in 1929. Illustrated with black and white photographs of primary sources and line drawings.

Wilcox, R. Turner, *Five Centuries of American Costume*. New York: Charles Scribner's Sons, 1963.
An overview; not comprehensive. Illustrated with line drawings.

ANCIENT COSTUME

Brooke, Iris, *Costume in Greek Drama*. Westport, Conn.: Greenwood Press, Inc., 1973.
Originally published in 1962. Illustrated with line drawings made from primary sources.

Laver, James and Erhard Klepper, *Costumes in Antiquity*. New York: C. N. Potter, 1964.
Illustrated with line drawings redrawn from primary sources. Some armor. No text.

Hope, Thomas, *Costumes of the Greeks and Romans*. New York: Dover Publications, Inc., 1962.
Originally published in 1812 as *Costumes of the Ancients*. Illustrated with line drawings from primary sources. Good decorative detail but some very questionable draping.

Houston, Mary G., *Ancient Greek, Roman and Byzantine Costume and Decoration*. London: Adam and Charles Black, 1947.
2100 BC to twelfth century. Eastern church vestments. Diagrams to show shape and drape.

Houston, Mary G., *Ancient Egyptian, Mesopotamian & Persian Costume and Decoration*. London: Adam and Charles Black, 1954.
Originally published in 1920. Scale patterns and draping instructions.

BRITISH COSTUME

Blum, Stella, ed., *Ackermann's Costume Plates: Women's Fashions in England, 1818–1828*. New York: Dover Publications, Inc., 1978.
Fashion plates of the period.

Bott, Alan, *Our Fathers (1870–1900) Manners and customs of the ancient Victorians: A Survey in pictures and text of their history, morals, wars, sports, inventions and politics*. New York, Benjamin Blom, Inc., 1972.
Originally published in 1931. Excellent social history, well illustrated.

Bott, Alan and Irene Clephane, *Our Mothers: A Cavalcade in Pictures, Quotation and Description of Late Victorian Women 1870–1900*. New York: Benjamin Blom, Inc., 1969.
Originally published in 1932. Excellent social history, well illustrated.

Buck, Anne, *Dress in Eighteenth Century England*. London: B. T. Batsford, 1979.
Illustrated from primary sources. Broad range of clothing represented, court to peasantry. Servant dress well covered.

Buck, Anne M., *Victorian Costume and Costume Accessories*. New York: Universe Books, 1970.
1837–1900. Interesting and detailed. Good text.

Byrde, Penelope, *The Male Image: Men's Fashion in England 1300–1970*. London: B. T. Batsford, Ltd., 1979.
Good book. Well illustrated from primary sources.

Clinch, George, *English Costume From Prehistoric Times to the End of the Eighteenth Century*. Totowa, N.J.: Rowman and Littlefield, 1975.
Originally published in 1909. Information on military, civic, legal, ecclesiastic, coronation, academic and monastic dress.

Cunnington, C. Willett and Phillis E., *Handbook of English Costume in the 16th Century*, 2nd ed. Boston: Plays, Inc., 1970.
All the Cunnington books are authorative, well organized and very detailed. Many contemporary quotations. Illustrated with line drawings from primary sources.

———, *Handbook of English Costume in the 17th Century*, 3rd ed. Boston: Plays, Inc., 1973.

———, *Handbook of English Costume in the 18th Century*, 3rd ed. Boston: Plays, Inc., 1972.

———, *Handbook of English Costume in the 19th Century*, 3rd ed. Boston: Plays, Inc., 1970.

———, *Handbook of English Medieval Costume*, 2nd ed. Boston: Plays, Inc., 1969.

Dunbar, J. Telfer, *History of Highland Dress*. London: B. T. Batsford, Ltd., 1962.
Definitive. Civil and military dress, including weapons. Interesting appendix on early Scottish dyes.

Gibbs-Smith, Charles H., *The Fashionable Lady in the 19th Century*. London: Her Majesty's Stationery Office, 1960.
Handsome fashion plates. Each five years through century.

Munro, R. W., *Highland Clans and Tartans*. New York: Crescent Books, 1977.
Ancient to present day. Useful information and well illustrated.

Shesgreen, Sean, ed. *Engravings by Hogarth*. New York: Dover Publications, Inc., 1973.
101 plates. Everyday life in England; all classes and types of folks.

Stevenson, Sara and Helen Bennett, *Van Dyck in Check Trousers: Fancy Dress in Art and Life. 1700–1900*. Scottish National Portrait Gallery, 1978.
Exhibition catalogue. Interesting and unusual.

Broad Surveys of Costume

Barton, Lucy, *Historic Costume for the Stage*, new ed. Boston: Walter H. Baker Co., 1961.
Somewhat dated but very comprehensive. Illustrated with line drawings.

Batterberry, Michael and Ariane, *Mirror, Mirror: A Social History of Fashion*. New York: Holt, Rinehart and Winston, 1977.
A serious work written with style and humor. Well illustrated, much in color.

Black, J. Anderson and Madge Garland, *A History of Fashion*. New York: William Morrow & Co., Inc., 1975.
Lavishly illustrated, much in color. A good survey.

Boehn, Max von, *Modes and Manners*, 4 vols in 2, Joan Joshua, trans., 1932 reprint. New York: Benjamin Blom, Inc., 1971.
Very valuable, comprehensive source. Many primary source illustrations.

Boucher, Francois, *20,000 Years of Fashion*. New York: Harry N. Abrams, Inc., 1967.
Extensive coverage of the subject but quite generalized. Primary source illustrations exceptionally valuable.

Braun & Schneider Publishers, *Historic Costume in Pictures*. New York: Dover Publications, 1975. Reprint of 1907 book, *Costumes of all Nations*. Plates done between 1861 and 1900. Not always well dated. Good for European folk costume.

Bruhn, Wolfgang and Max Tilke, *A Pictorial History of Costume*. New York: Hastings House Publishers, 1973. 200 plates, mostly by Tilke. Particularly good for detail and decorative motifs. Eastern European costume well represented.

Contini, Mila, *Fashion from Ancient Egypt to the Present Day*. New York: Outlet Book Co., 1977. Originally published in 1965. Excellent photographs from primary sources; not, however, well dated.

Davenport, Milia, *The Book of Costume*. New York: Crown Publishers, Inc., 1948. The most detailed of all the surveys. Three thousand illustrations in black and white.

Hansen, Henny Harald, *Costumes and Style*. New York: E. P. Dutton & Co., 1956. Illustrations redrawn, in color, from original sources. Brief, general text.

Kemper, Rachel H., *Costume*. New York: Newsweek Books, 1979. Well illustrated. Interesting text.

Laver, James, *A Concise History of Costume and Fashion*. New York: Charles Scribner's Sons, 1974. Originally published in 1974. Excellent source for quick reference.

———, *Costume in the Theatre*. New York: Hill and Wang, 1964. Excellent source.

Laver, James and Erhard Klepper, illus., *Costume Through the Ages*. New York: Simon and Schuster, 1963. Brief introduction by Laver but no text. Illustrated with line drawings.

Molinari, Cesare, *Theatre Through the Ages*, Colin Hamer, trans. New York: McGraw-Hill Book Co., 1975. Excellent text, valuable illustrations.

Payne, Blanche, *History of Costume:From the Ancient Egyptians to the Twentieth Century*. New York: Harper & Row, 1965. Broad and relatively thorough survey. Illustrated with photographs of primary sources and line drawings. Interesting pattern information.

Russell, Douglas A., *Period Style for the Theatre*. Boston: Allyn and Bacon, Inc., 1980. Western culture divided into 18 periods. Clothing, architecture, decor and major artists of each period surveyed. A good place to start research.

———, *Stage Costume Design: Theory, Techniques and Style*. Englewood Cliffs, N.J.: Appleton-Century-Crofts, 1973. The only book that sets out to cover all facets of the costume design and construction process between two covers.

Squire, Geoffrey, *Dress and Society 1560–1970*. New York: The Viking Press, 1974. Interesting theorizing about the whys of fashion. Well written and beautifully illustrated.

Wilcox, R. Turner, *The Mode in Costume*. New York: Charles Scribner's Sons, 1948. Illustrated with line drawings. Not comprehensive but useful.

Children's Costume

Cunnington, Phillis and Anne Buck, *Children's Costume in England from the 14th to the End of the 19th Century*. New York: Barnes and Noble, 1965. Detailed, century-by-century survey. Photographs and excellent drawings based on primary sources.

Ewing, Elizabeth, *History of Children's Costume*. London: B. T. Batsford, Ltd., 1977. Illustrated with photographs of primary source material. Valuable book.

Martin, Linda, *The Way We Wore: Fashion Illustrations of Children's Wear 1870–1970*. New York: Charles Scribner's Sons, 1978. No text but a wealth of visual information.

Pierce, A. J. and D. K., *Victorian and Edwardian Children from Old Photographs*. London: B. T. Batsford, Ltd., 1980. 137 photographs with commentary. Excellent.

Costume from Other Countries and Periods

Appelbaum, Stanley, ed., *Scenes from the Nineteenth-Century Stage in Advertising Woodcuts*. New York: Dover Publications, Inc., 1977. Amusing and interesting.

Bentley, Nicolas, *The Victorian Scene: A Picture Book of the Period 1837–1901*. New York: Spring Books, 1968.

Thorough and beautifully illustrated study of manners, customs and social institutions.

Birbari, Elizabeth, *Dress in Italian Painting 1460–1500*. London: John Murray, 1975.
Thorough, detailed study. Patterns, fabrics and construction details.

Boehn, Max von and Max Fischel, *Modes and Manners of the Nineteenth Century as Represented in the Pictures and Engravings of the Time*, 4 vols in 2, M. Edwards, trans. New York: Benjamin Blom, Inc., 1970.
Reprinted from 1927 edition. Covers 1790–1914. Extremely detailed. Valuable source.

Brooke, Iris, *Medieval Theatre Costume: A Practical Guide to the Construction of Garments*. New York: Theatre Arts, 1967.
More useful for research detail than for patterning and construction.

Cappi Bentivegna, Ferruccia, *Abbigliamento e Costume Nella Pittura Italiana* (Clothing and Costume in Italian Painting), 2 vols. Rome: Edizioni d'Arte, 1964.
Renaissance in vol. 1; Baroque in vol. 2. Carefully chosen and dated photographs of paintings with many close-up details. Text in Italian.

Ducharte, Pierre Louis, *The Italian Comedy*. New York: Dover Publications, Inc., 1966.
Originally published in 1929. History of *Commedia dell' Arte*, well illustrated. Standard research work.

Ford, Colin, ed., *An Early Victorian Album: The Photographic Masterpieces (1843–1847) of David Octavius Hill and Robert Adamson*. New York: Alfred A. Knopf, 1976.
An excellent selection of period photographic portraits. Covers a very small period in great detail.

Houston, Mary G., *Medieval Costume in England and France, the 13th, 14th and 15th Centuries*. London: Adam and Charles Black, 1939.
Covers many facets of the subjects including ecclesiastical and academic dress, textiles, accessories and notes on cut and construction. Excellent.

Jones, Michael Wynn, *The World 100 Years Ago*. New York: David McKay Co., Inc., 1976.
A selection of very useful photographs.

Kelly, F.M., *Shakespearian Costume for Stage and Screen*, revised by Alan Mansfield. London: Adam and Charles Black, 1970.
Originally published in 1938. General survey and specific considerations of costumes for each play. Illustrated with period portraits and line drawings.

Larkin, David, ed., *The Paintings of Carl Larsson*. London & New York: Peacock Press/Bantam Books, 1976.
Paintings done by Carl Larsson of his home and family between 1894 and 1914. Lovely detail. Full color. Sweden.

Laver, James, *17th and 18th Century Costume*. London: His Majesty's Stationery Office, 1951.
English, French and Flemish clothing for the period. Well illustrated with descriptive notes.

Lucie-Smith, Edward and Celestine Dars, *How the Rich Lived: The Painter as Witness*. New York and London: The Paddington Press, Ltd., 1976.
A wonderful book. Beautifully illustrated with photographs of paintings, many unusual and little-known.

Newton, Stella Mary, *Renaissance Theatre Costume and the Sense of the Historic Past*. New York: Theatre Arts Books, 1975.
A study of the theatre and its costumes in the 15th and 16th centuries. Unique and valuable.

Noma, Seiroku, *Japanese Costume and the Textile Arts*. New York and Tokyo: Weatherhill, 1965.
Illustrated with photographs of primary source material. Noh, Kyogen and Kabuki costume. A good discussion of the kimono.

Rubens, Alfred, *A History of Jewish Costume*. New York: Crown Publishers, 1973.
Excellent text, well illustrated with primary source materials.

Oblensky, Chloe, *The Russian Empire, A Portrait in Photographs*. New York: Random House, 1979.
A wonderful book. Photograph selection made by a theatre designer.

Onassis, Jacqueline, ed., *In the Russian Style*. New York: The Viking Press, 1976
Presentation arranged by rulers: Peter I, 1682 to Alexander II, 1882. Many photographs in color. Some peasants but mostly upper class Russians.

Scott, Margaret, *The History of Dress Series: Late Gothic Europe, 1400–1500*. Atlantic Highlands, New Jersey: Humanities Press, 1980.
First volume in a projected history of dress series. Beautifully illustrated from primary sources.

Snowden, James, *The Folk Dress of Europe*. New York: Mayflower Books, Inc., 1979.
Illustrated with drawings and photographs from primary sources. Useful source.

Strong, Roy, *Festival Designs by Inigo Jones: An Exhibition of Drawings for Scenery and Costumes for the Court Masques of James I and Charles I*. London: Victoria and Albert Museum, 1969.
Good exhibition catalogue. Some drawings reproduced in color.

Vecellio, Cesare, *Vecellio's Renaissance Costume Book*. New York: Dover Publications, 1977.
Reprint of original five hundred woodcuts from the 1598 edition. Italian Renaissance costume.

Vreeland, Diana, ed., *The Imperial Style: Fashions of the Hapsburg Era*. New York: The Metropolitan Museum of Art, 1980.
Exhibition catalogue: Fashions of the Hapsburg Era: Austria-Hungary. Interesting articles, well illustrated.

Worswick, Clark and Jonathan Spence, *Imperial China: Photographs 1850–1912*. New York: Pennwick Publishing, Inc., 1978.
Very interesting selection of photographs.

Mansfield, Alan, *Ceremonial Costume*. London: Adam & Charles Black, 1980.
Parliamentary dress, coronation robes, court uniforms, women's court dress, various orders of chivalry, royal bodyguards, etc.

McGowan, Alan, *Sailor: A Pictorial History*. New York: David McKay Co., Inc., 1977.
Photographs, twentieth century. Useful and interesting.

Oakes, Alma and Margot Hamilton Hill, *Rural Costume: Its Origin and Development in Western Europe and the British Isles*. New York: Van Nostrand Reinhold Co., 1970.
A generalized survey illustrated with line drawings.

Stevenson, Pauline, *Bridal Fashions*. London: Ian Allan, Ltd., 1978.
Mostly nineteenth and twentieth centuries. Excellent text and illustrations.

Special and Occupational Costume

Cunnington, Phillis and Catherine Lucas, *Charity Costumes of Children, Scholars, Almsfolk, Pensioners*. London: Adam and Charles Black, 1978.
Very useful book for specific research.

———, *Occupational Costume in England From the Eleventh Century to 1914*. London: Adam and Charles Black, 1967.
Valuable book. Well illustrated.

———, *Costumes for Births, Marriages and Deaths*. London: Adam and Charles Black, 1972.
Medieval to 1900. Interesting text with many contemporary quotations. Well illustrated.

Cunnington, Phillis, *Costumes of Household Servants From the Middle Ages to 1900*. New York: Barnes & Noble, 1974.
Expansion of chapters on servants' costume in *Occupational Costume in England*. Very useful.

Ewing, Elizabeth, *Women in Uniform Through the Centuries*. London: B.T. Batsford, Ltd., 1975.
Interesting book, well-illustrated.

Hiley, Michael, *Victorian Working Women: Portraits from Life*. London: Gordon Fraser, 1979.
Photographs and some engravings. Unusual source: women working in mines, dairies, circuses, etc. British Isles and Belgium.

Twentieth-Century Costume

Bernard, Barbara, *Fashion in the 60's*. New York: St. Martin's Press, 1978.
A small, interesting book. Black and white illustrations.

Blum, Stella, *Designs by Erte: Fashion Drawings and Illustrations from 'Harper's Bazaar.'* New York: Dover Publications, Inc., 1976.
A beautiful selection. Eight color illustrations, the rest black and white.

Carter, Ernestine, *20th Century Fashions: A Scrapbook, 1900 to Today*. London: E. Methuen, 1975.
Interesting information. Black and white illustrations.

Dars, Celestine, *A Fashion Parade: The Seeberger Collection*. London: Blond & Briggs, 1979.
High fashion from 1909–1950. Black and white photographs taken by the Seeberger brothers in Paris. Excellent.

Dorner, Jane, *Fashion in the Twenties and Thirties*. London: Ian Allan, Ltd., 1973.
Illustrated from many sources: original fashion drawings, photographs, advertisements from fashion magazines, etc.

———, *Fashion in the Forties and Fifties*. London: Ian Allan, Ltd., 1975.
Well illustrated with photographs and sketches. The emphasis is on women's clothing. Good source.

Eckardt, Wolf von and Sander L. Gilman, *Bertolt Brecht's Berlin: A Scrapbook of the Twenties*. Garden City, N.Y.: Anchor Press/Doubleday, 1975.
Many photographs. Very useful book.

Erte, *Erte Fashions*. New York: St. Martin's Press, Inc., 1972. Erte fashions created between 1911 and 1972, clothing, jewelry and accessories.

Ewing, Elizabeth, *History of 20th Century Fashion*. New York: Charles Scribner's Sons, 1975.
Women's fashion, couture and mass produced. Interesting book.

Glynn, Prudence with Madeline Ginsburg, *In Fashion: Dress in the Twentieth Century*. London: George Allen & Unwin, 1978.
Illustrations include photographs, line drawings, fashion drawings and paintings. Some color. The emphasis is on women's clothing.

Hennessy, Val, *In the Gutter*. London/Melbourne/New York: Quartet Books, 1978.
Compares punk dress with the costumes of primitive tribes. Great photographs.

Horan, James D. *The Desperate Years: From Stock Market Crash to World War II: A Pictorial History of the Thirties*. New York: Bonanza Books, 1962.
Interesting text and many good photographs.

Horsley, Edith, *The 1950's*. London: Domus Books, 1978.
Good photographs, some in color. Useful book.

Jenkins, Alan, *The Forties*. New York: Universe Books, 1977.
Interesting text, many good photographs, some color.

———, *The Thirties*. New York: Stein and Day, 1976.
Lively and informative text, well illustrated, some color.

———, *The Twenties*. New York: Universe Books, 1974.
As good as the other two.

Mansfield, Alan and Phillis Cunnington, *Handbook of English Costume in the 20th Century 1900–1950*. Boston: Plays, Inc., 1973.
Detailed, informative text. Illustrated with line drawings that are not as good as those in previous handbooks.

Peacock, John, *Fashion Sketchbook 1920–1960*. New York: Avon Books, 1977.
No text. Illustrated with line drawings that are crisp and easy to read.

Robinson, Julian, *Fashion in the 30's*. London: Oresko Books, Ltd., 1978.

Small, interesting book, well illustrated with some color.

———, *Fashion in the 40's*. New York: St. Martin's Press, 1976.
Photographs and fashion drawings. Useful.

Sann, Paul, *The Angry Decade: The Sixties, A Pictorial History*. New York: Crown Publishers, Inc., 1979.
Over 400 black and white photographs. A useful source.

Schoeffler, O. E. and William Gale, *Esquire's Encyclopedia of 20th Century Men's Fashions*. New York: McGraw-Hill Book Co., 1973.
Comprehensive, detailed and beautifully illustrated. A must for costume libraries.

Stevenson, Pauline, *Edwardian Fashion*. London: Ian Allen, Ltd., 1980.
Men, women and children. Illustrated with photographs, line drawings and pages from old store catalogues. Excellent book.

Thompson, Paul and Gina Harkell, *The Edwardians in Photographs*. London: B.T. Batsford, Ltd., 1979.
Men, women and children of all classes. Useful book.

Time-Life, *This Fabulous Century* (8 vols.). New York: Time-Life Books, 1969–70.
Each volume covers one decade of the twentieth century. Lively text, well illustrated. Endlessly useful series.

Torrens, Deborah, *Fashion Illustrated*. New York: Hawthorn Books, Inc., 1975.
Material from French, English and American fashion magazines, 1920–1950. Many illustrations; 23 color plates. A few original patterns.

Underwear

Caldwell, Doreen, *And All Was Revealed: Ladies' Underwear 1907–1980*. New York: St. Martin's Press, 1981.
Fascinating book. Text is brief but illustrations are excellent.

Colmer, Michael, *Whalebone to See Through: A History of Body Packaging*. London and Edinburgh: Johnston & Bacon, 1979.
Emphasis is on this century. Interesting book.

Cunnington, C. Willett and Phillis, *The History of Underclothes*. London: Michael Joseph, 1951.
Comprehensive, detailed and well illustrated.

Ewing, Elizabeth, *Dress and Undress: A History of Women's Underwear*. New York: Drama Book Specialists, 1978.
Based, in part, on her earlier book, *Fashions in Underwear*. Good general survey, 3000 BC to present.

Gray, Mitchel, *The Lingerie Book*. New York: Quartet Books, 1980.
Text by Mary Kennedy. Illustrated with photographs of lingerie from 1900 to 1980 on models. Black and white and color. Beautiful book.

Morel, Juliette. *Lingerie Parisienne*. New York: St. Martin's Press, 1976.
Fashionable Parisienne lingerie in the 1920's. Very little text. Interesting illustrations from a variety of sources.

Waugh, Norah, *Corsets and Crinolines*. New York: Theatre Arts Books, 1970.
Comprehensive and detailed. Scale period patterns and many contemporary quotations. Covers sixteenth through early twentieth centuries. The major work in this area.

Uniforms, Arms and Armor

Ashdown, Charles Henry, *British and Continental Arms and Armour*. New York: Dover Publications, Inc., 1970.
Survey, ancient times to seventeenth century. Some chapters more detailed than others. Good illustrations. Fairly useful.

Blair, Claude, *European Armour circa 1066 to circa 1700*. New York: Crane, Russak & Co., Inc., 1971.
Reprint from 1958 publication. Brief survey. Illustrated with line drawings and photographs of primary sources.

Blakeslee, Fred Gilbert, *Uniforms of the World*, New York: E. P. Dutton & Co., Inc., 1929.
Excellent and informative book that covers military, police, civil servant, and diplomatic costumes for most major countries. Well and carefully illustrated.

Cassin-Scott, Jack and John Fabb, *Ceremonial Uniforms of the World*. New York: Arco Publishing Co., Inc., 1977.
Illustrated with 80 color plates redrawn from original sources. By country, alphabetically.

Davis, Brian Leigh and Pierre Turner, *German Uniforms of the Third Reich 1933–1945*. New York: Arco Publishing Co., Inc., 1980
Excellent detail. Color illustrations.

David, Brian L., *German Army Uniforms and Insignia 1933–1945*. New York: Arco Publishing Co., Inc., 1977.
Comprehensive. Over 350 illustrations, photographs and line drawings. Some color.

Elting, John R., ed., *Military Uniforms in America: The Era of the American Revolution, 1755–1795*. San Rafael, Ca.: Presidio Press, 1974.
Very detailed. Illustrated with color illustrations redrawn from original sources.

———, *Military Uniforms in America, Vol. 11: Years of Growth, 1796–1851*. San Rafael, Ca.: Presidio Press, 1974.
Same format as above.

Fox-Davies, A. C., *A Complete Guide to Heraldry*. New York: Bonanza Books, 1978.
An excellent, well-illustrated book.

Hoffschmidt, E. J. and W. H. Tantum, IV, eds., *German Army and Navy Uniforms and Insignia 1871–1918*. Old Greenwich, Conn.: WE, Inc., 1968.
Detailed and well-illustrated.

Katcher, Philip, *Armies of the American Wars 1753–1815*. New York: Hastings House, Publishers, 1975.
Good coverage of subject. Informative and well-illustrated.

Kelly, Francis M. and Randolph Schwabe, *A Short History of Costume and Armour 1066–1800*. New York: Arco Publishing Co., Inc., 1973.
Reprinted from 1931 edition. A good source, somewhat general.

Knotel, Herbert Jr. and Herbert Steig, *Uniforms of the World: A Compendium of Army, Navy and Air Force Uniforms, 1700–1937*. New York: Charles Scribner's Sons, 1980.
Originally published in 1956 in German as *Handbuch der Uniformkunde*. Excellent source. 1,600 illustrations.

Koch, H. W., *Medieval Warfare*. Englewood Cliffs, N.J.: Prentice-Hall, 1978.
Very informative and beautifully illustrated from primary sources. Covers dress, weapons and ways of making war.

Martin, Paul, *Arms and Armour: From the 9th to 17th Century*. Rutland, Vt.: Charles E. Tuttle Co., Inc., 1967.
Good survey. Well illustrated, some color.

———, *European Military Uniforms: A Short History*. London: Spring Books, 1967.
Originally published in 1963 in German as *Der Bunte Rock*. Illustrated with color plates and line drawings.

Mollo, Andrew, *The Armed Forces of World War II, Uniforms, Insignia and Organisation.* New York: Crown Publishers, Inc., 1981.
Thoroughly comprehensive. 365 color drawings; 160 photographs and 53 plates of insignia. Includes an excellent glossary and table of ranks. The best to date.

Mollo, Andrew and Pierre Turner, *Army Uniforms of World War I.* New York: Arco Publishing Co., Inc., 1978.
Good general information. Well illustrated in color.

Robinson, H. Russell, *The Armour of Imperial Rome.* New York: Charles Scribner's Sons, 1975.
Comprehensive study of the subject, first century BC to third century AD. Over 700 illustrations.

Sietsema, Robert, *Weapons and Armor.* New York: Hart Publishing Co., Inc., 1978.
A collection of 1400 pictures, black and white. Useful.

Smith, Digby and Michael Chappell, *Army Uniforms Since 1945.* Pool, Dorset, England: Blandford Press, 1980.
Very useful book. Covers Malaya, Korea, Africa, Israel, Vietnam, etc. Illustrations redrawn from original sources, black and white and color.

Stone, George Cameron, *A Glossary of the Construction, Decoration and Use of Arms and Armor in All Countries and in All Times, Together With Some Closely Related Subjects.* New York: Jack Brussel, 1961.
Useful book. Black and white illustrations.

WE, *German Military Uniforms and Insignia 1933–1945.* Old Greenwich, Conn.: WE, Inc., 1967.
Good detail. Black and white photographs and line drawings.

Windrow, Martin, ed. *Men-At-Arms Series.* London: Osprey Publishing Co., 1972–77.
A series that includes 68 small books, each dealing with a specific military encounter. Many periods and many countries represented. Informative texts. Illustrated with photographs and color plates redrawn from primary sources. Excellent.

Windrow, Martin and Gerry Embleton, *Military Dress of North America 1665–1970.* New York: Charles Scribner's Sons, 1973.
Quite detailed. Information on accessories, insignia and weapons. 20 color plates, many photographs.

Wise, Arthur, *Weapons in the Theatre.* New York: Barnes & Noble, Inc., 1968.
Manual for stage fighting. Many periods considered.

Period Catalogues

All the following are reprints of period originals and all are valuable sources.

Langbridge, R. H., ed. *Edwardian Shopping: A Selection From the Army & Navy Stores Catalogues 1898–1913.* Newton Abbot/London/Vancouver: David & Charles, 1975.

Montgomery Ward & Co., *Catalogue No. 57 1895 Spring and Summer.* New York: Dover Publications, Inc., 1969.

Sears, Roebuck & Co., *Catalogue: 1897.* New York: Chelsea House Publishers, 1968.

——, *Catalogue: 1906.* Secaucus, N.Y.: Castle Books, n.d.

——, *Catalogue: 1908.* Northfield, Ill.: Digest Books, Inc., 1971.

——, *Catalogue: 1902.* New York: Bounty Books, 1969.

——, *Catalogue: 1927.* New York: Bounty Books, 1970.

——, *Catalogues of the 1930's.* New York: Nostalgia, Inc., 1978.
Selected pages from the decade.

Miscellaneous

Hodge, Francis, *Play Directing Analysis Communication and Style.* Englewood Cliffs, N.J.: Prentice-Hall, Inc., 1971.

Hornby, Richard, *Script Into Performance: A Structuralist View of Play Production.* Austin, Texas & London: University of Texas Press, 1977.

Russell, Douglas A., *Theatrical Style: A Visual Approach to the Theatre.* Palo Alto, Cal.: Mayfield Publishing Co., 1976.
Explores similarities between theatre and other visual arts. Classical period to present day. Interesting text and illustrations.

Wilson, Angus, *The World of Charles Dickens.* New York: The Viking Press, Inc., 1970.
Excellent social history, 1812–1870. Beautiful illustrations, many in color.

Sketching and Rendering

Birren, Faber, *Creative Color: A Dynamic Approach for Artists and Designers*. New York: Van Nostrand Reinhold Co., 1961.
An interesting and practical color theory.

Edwards, Betty, *Drawing on the Right Side of the Brain*. Los Angeles: J.P. Tarcher, Inc., 1979.
Readily accessible text that relates how we see to what we draw. Fascinating and useful.

Itten, Johannes, *The Art of Color*. New York: Reinhold Publishing Corp., 1961.
Good theory. Beautiful book.

Loomis, Andrew, *Figure Drawing For All It's Worth*. Cleveland, Ohio: The World Publishing Co., 1943.
An excellent book for costume designers. Clear presentation, good illustrations.

Mugnaini, Joseph, *The Hidden Elements of Drawing*. New York: Van Nostrand Reinhold Co., 1974.
An interesting investigation of figure drawing.

Raynes, John, *Human Anatomy for the Artist*. New York: Crescent Books, 1979.
Male and female anatomy. Clearly presented, illustrated from photographs and drawings.

Sloan, Eunice Moore, *Illustrating Fashion*. New York: Harper & Row, 1968.
An excellent fashion illustration book full of techniques useful to costume designers.

Walters, Margaret, *The Nude Male: A New Perspective*. New York: Penguin Books, 1979.
The male figure studied from artists' work over the centuries. Interesting text and very useful illustrations.

Theory and Psychology of Dress

Bell, Quentin, *On Human Finery*, 2nd ed. New York: Schocken Books, 1976.
First published in 1947. A lively and perceptive discussion of the pressures underlying our modes of dress. Nicely illustrated.

Cremers-van der Does, Eline Canter. *The Agony of Fashion*. Leo Van Witsen, trans. Poole, Dorset, England: Blandford Press, 1980.
A survey of fashion pressures, early times to present day. Well illustrated.

Hollander, Anne, *Seeing Through Clothes*. New York: Avon Books, 1975.
A delightful study of how the human image is revealed in changing fashion shapes. Illustrated with many black and white photographs of primary sources.

Lurie, Alison, *The Language of Clothes*. New York: Random House, 1981.
An amusing look at the way people dress through the eyes of popular psychology.

Newton, Stella Mary, *Health, Art and Reason. Dress Reformers of the 19th Century*. London: John Murray, 1974.
A study of the various movements toward less constricting, more comfortable clothing for nineteenth-century women, including bloomers and Grecian drapery. Adequately illustrated.

Rudofsky, Bernard, *The Unfashionable Human Body*. New York: Doubleday, 1974.
An amusing look at the ways in which humans have altered the body shape. Unusual and interesting illustrations from primary sources.

Booksellers

USA

NEW YORK CITY
Applause
100 W. 67th St.
New York, NY 10023
212–496–7511
A theatrical bookshop that carries costume books.

Dover Publications, Inc.
180 Varick St.
New York, NY 10014
212–255–3755
Bookstore on 9th floor.

The Drama Bookshop
723 7th Ave.
New York, NY 10019
212–944–0595

Large selection of theatre books including costume, stage design and allied subjects. Mail orders welcome.

Hacker Art Books, Inc.
54 W. 57th St.
New York, NY 10019
212–757–1450
Specialists in art books with a large selection of books on costume. Mail order catalogue of discount books available.

Military Bookman
29 E. 93rd St.
New York, NY 10028
212–348–1280
Military books including arms and uniform

Quinion Books
541 Hudson St.
New York, NY 10014
212–989–6130
Theatrical books; some costume books.

Sky Books International, Inc.
48 E. 50th St.
New York, NY 10022
212–688–5086
Military books including arms and uniform books.

The Soldier Shop, Inc.
1013 Madison Ave.
New York, NY 10028
212–535–6788
Military books including arms and uniform books.

Richard Stoddard
90 E. 10th St.
New York, NY 10003
212–982–9440
Theatrical books, some costume books, mostly out of print.

Strand Book Store
828 Broadway (at 12th St.)
New York, NY 10003
212–473–1452
"Eight miles of books." New and used, many at bargain prices. Large selection of art books. Many costume books, some used, at good prices. Catalogue of bargain books available.

Theatrebooks, Inc.
1576 Broadway
New York, NY 10036

212–757–2834
New, used and out of print books, a few on costume.

SEATTLE
R. L. Shep
Box C–20
Lopez, Washington 98261
206–468–2023
Catalogue on request.

WASHINGTON, D.C.
Smithsonian Bookstore
14th St. and Constitution Ave., N.W.
Washington, D.C. 20560

British Isles

LONDON

Foyles
119 Charing Cross Road
London WC2
01–437–5660
"The world's largest bookstore." Large selection of art and costume books as well as plays and general theatre books.

Hatchards
187 Piccadilly
London W1
01–734–3201
Art books.

Lesley Hodges
Queen's Elm Parade (off Fulham Rd.)
Old Church Street
Chelsea, London SW3 6EJ
01–352–1176
Antiquarian bookseller specializing in books on costume, fashion and related subjects. Also carries new publications. Catalogue available.

Ken Trotman
2–6 Hampstead High Street
London NW3 1PR
01–794–3277
Specializing in books on arms and armor, guns,
   weaponry and related subjects. Catalogues
   available.

A. Zwemmer
78 Charing Cross Road
London WC2
01–836–4710
Art and costume books.

SUFFOLK
Faith Legg
The Guildhall Bookroom
Church Street
Eye, Suffolk
(0379) 870193 and 870308
Open Fridays and Saturdays, other days by
   arrangement. Mostly used, some new books on
   costume, textile crafts, local and social history.

Costume Organizations

Costume Societies

The Costume Society of America
Suite 1702
330 W. 42nd St.
New York, NY 10036

The Costume Society of Ontario
P.O. Box 2044
Bramalea, Ontario, Canada L6T 353

The Costume Society
Membership secretary:
Mrs. T.A. Heathcote
Cheyne Cottage,
Birch Drive,
Hawley,
Camberley, Surrey
England

The Costume Society of Scotland
Hon. Treasurer:
Mrs. E.S. Melville,
24 Esplanade Terrace,
Edinburgh, Scotland EH15 2ES

Custom Costume Companies

NEW YORK CITY
Costume Arts, Inc.
345 W. 36th St.
New York, NY 10018
212–947–2105

Carelli Costumes
257 W. 38th St. (16th fl.)
New York, NY 10018
212–921–5260

Eaves–Brooks Costume Co., Inc.
21–07 41st Ave.
Long Island City
Queens, NY 11101
212–786–4956

Grace Costumes, Inc.
254 W. 54th St.
New York, NY 10019
212–586–0260

Karinska
16 W. 61st St.
New York, NY 10023
212–247–3341
Mainly dance costumes.

Marlene Kustesky
245 W. 74th St.
New York, NY 10023
212–873–3132

Barbara Matera Ltd.
890 Broadway
New York, NY 10011
212–475–5006

Michael–Jon Costumes, Inc.
39 W. 19th St.
New York, NY 10011
212–741–3440

Parsons–Meares, Ltd.
306 W. 38th St.
New York, NY 10018
212–736–0290

John Reid
49 W. 24th St. (7th fl.)
New York, NY 10010
212–242–6059

Schnoz & Schnoz Costume Shop
84 E. 7th St.
New York, NY 10003

212–260–1496
Sally Lesser.

The Studio
250 W. 14th St.
New York, NY 10011
212–924–4736
Betty Williams.

Vincent Costume, Inc.
39 W. 19th St.
New York, NY 10011
212–741–3423
Mainly tailoring.

Selected Painters for Costume Design Research

The following list of painters is organized into periods that roughly correspond with major changes in clothing silhouette. Since a painter's work may span many years, there are names that appear in more than one period. The first appearance of the painter's name is accompanied by dates and comments; subsequent appearances are limited to the name. Most dates are from:
Peter and Linda Murray, *The Penguin Dictionary of*

> *Art and Artists,* 4th ed. (Harmondsworth, Middlesex, England: Penguin Books Ltd., 1976).

1250–1350

ITALIAN

Cimabue (Cenni di Pepi) (1240–1302?)
Florentine. Believed to be Giotto's teacher.

Duccio (Duccio di Buoninsegna) (c. 1255/60–1318?)
Sienese. Blended Byzantine and Gothic elements.
Giotto (Giotto di Bordone) 1266/7–1337)
Florentine. Also sculptor and architect. Introduced, with Cimabue, a new naturalism into figures.
Martini, Simone (c. 1284–1344)
Sienese. Pupil of Duccio. Excellent sense of silhouette & good costume detail.
Orcagna, Andrea (Andrea di Cione) (c. 1308–1368)
Florentine. Also sculptor and architect.

During this period in Northern Europe artists did not sign their work and there was very little painting relevant to costume design. Sculpture from the great cathedrals such as Reims, Notre–Dame, Amiens, Naumburg, etc. offer excellent costume research. Secular manuscript illuminators appeared. The anonymously done illuminations from the *Psalter of St. Louis* (c.

1260) and those from the *Prayer Book of Philip the Fair* by Master Honoré of Paris are of particular interest.

1350–1450

FRENCH

Limbourg, Paul, Jean, and Herman de (all dead by end of 1416)

Three brothers, Flemish by birth but trained in Paris. Came under the protection of the Duke of Burgundy. Manuscript illuminators responsible for the extraordinarily beautiful *Les Tres Riches Heures du Duc de Berry* (1413) containing detailed examples of high fashion French clothing of the period.

ITALIAN

Gozzoli, Benozzo (c. 1421–1497)

His frescoes are secular in outlook.

Lippi, Fra Filippo (c. 1406–1469)

Florentine. Painted religious subjects with great attention to flowing drapery.

Masaccio, Tommaso Cassio (Tommaso di ser Giovanni di Mone) (1401–1428)

Florentine. Regarded as one of the founders of modern painting. See his frescoes in the Brancacci Chapel, especially *The Tribute Money.*

Piero della Francesca (c. 1410/20–1492)

From Tuscany. Painted strong, heroic figures. Very sensitive to clothing silhouette.

Pisanello, Antonio (c. 1395–1455/6)

Also medalist and draughtsman. His work includes costume sketches.

Uccello, Paolo (1397–1475)

Three *Battles* painted between 1454 and 1457 are of particular interest.

NETHERLANDISH

Eyck, Jan van (c. 1380?–1441)

Portraits and religious paintings with good costume detail. See particularly the *Ghent Altarpiece*. Also beautifully detailed drawings. Had a brother, Hubert, also a painter, about whom little is known.

Weyden, Roger van der (Rogier de le Pasture) (1399/1400–1464)

Settled in Brussels sometime after 1426. Painted many portraits for members of the Burgundian court. Sensitive costume detail.

1450–1550

FRENCH

Clouet, Jean II (d. 1540/1)

Court painter in France. Good costume detail especially in his portrait drawings.

Fouquet, Jehan (c. 1420–in or before 1481)

Paintings and miniatures with good costume detail.

GERMAN

Cranach, Lucas, the Elder (1472–1553)

Also etcher and designer of woodcuts. Designed propaganda woodcuts for Luther. Painted full-length portraits with fine costume detail.

Dürer, Albrecht (1471–1528)

Also produced woodcuts, engravings, drawings and watercolors. Wonderful costume detail. Good for peasant costume.

Grünewald (Mathis Neithardt–Gothardt) (c. 1470/80–1528)

Only a few paintings extant. Figures are highly dramatic with sensitively rendered clothing detail.

Holbein, Hans the Younger (1497/8–1543)

Penetratingly realist portrait painter. Settled in England and became court painter to Henry VIII. Meticulous costume detail. See drawings especially.

ITALIAN

Bellini, Giovanni (c. 1430–1516)

Venetian. Religious and mythological paintings as well as portraits. Good clothing silhouettes.

Botticelli, Sandro (c. 1445–1510)

Florentine. Favorite painter of the Medici circle. An individualist in painting style and color use. Many beautifully detailed hairstyles with classical overtones.

Carpaccio, Vittore (c. 1460/65–1523/6)

Venetian. Assistant to Giovanni Bellini. See his full-length portrait *Knight in a Landscape.*

Ghirlandaio, Domenico Bigordi (1449–1494)

Florentine. Executed religious frescoes and portraits with naturalistic detail. His son Ridolfo (1483–1561) was a portrait painter of great distinction.

Leonardo da Vinci (1452–1519)
>   Worked first in Milan then in Florence. The epitome of the "Renaissance man." The drawings especially have excellent clothing and hair details.

Michelangelo Buonarroti (1475–1564)
>   Florentine. Worked also in Bologna and Rome. Sculptor and architect. Most work heroic in nature. Drawings best for costume research.

Piero della Francesca
Raphael (Raffaello Sanzio) (1483–1520)
>   Born in Perugia; worked in Florence and Rome. The central painter of the High Renaissance. Exceptionally fine portraits in which both realism and idealism are present.

Signorelli, Luca (c. 1441/50–1523)
>   Religious frescoes and altarpieces. Vividly realistic, detailed figures.

Titain (Tiziano Vecellio, (c. 1487/90–1576)
>   Venetian. After Raphael's death, the most sought-after portraitist of the age. Splendid clothing detail.

NETHERLANDISH

Bruegel (Brueghel, Breughel), Pieter I (c. 1525/30–1569)
>   Wonderful paintings of local peasant life.

Goes, Hugo van der (d. 1482)
>   Highly dramatic, intricately detailed work. See *The Portinari Altarpiece* for exquisite costume details.

Memling, Hans (c. 1430/40–1494)
>   German-born but pure Netherlandish painter. Pupil of Roger van der Weyden. Religious paintings and fine portraits with superb costume detail. See drawings also.

1550–1625

ENGLISH

Hilliard, Nicholas (c. 1547–1619)
>   Goldsmith and miniaturist. Wonderful clothing detail, including footwear. See doublet with peascod belly in *A Young Man Among Roses* and several portraits of Queen Elizabeth.

Jones, Inigo (1573–1652)
>   Architect and designer of court masques. There are 450 extant drawings for stage scenery and costumes.

Oliver, Isaac (d. 1617)
>   Miniaturist. History paintings and portraits. Student of Hilliard.

FLEMISH

Brouwer, Adriaen (c. 1605/6–1638)
>   Worked in Holland. Good for realistic low life, especially sordid tavern scenes.

Gheeraerts, Marcus, the younger (c. 1561–1636)
>   Huguenot refugee who settled in England. Member of a large family of painters. Full and half-length portraits, formal, heraldic, bright in color.

Rubens, Sir Peter Paul (1577–1640)
>   From Antwerp. The great Baroque painter. Court painter to the Spanish Governors of the Netherlands. Early portrait work best for costume detail.

FRENCH

Clouet, Francois (d. 1572)
>   Son of Jean Clouet whom he succeeded as French court painter. Specialized in portrait drawings and paintings.

ITALIAN

Bronzino, Agnolo (1503–1572)
>   Florentine. Court painter to Cosimo I de Medici. One of the most important Mannerist portrait painters. Elegant clothing and fabric detail.

Caravaggio, Michelangelo (1571–1610)
>   Milanese. Dramatic work. Wealth of clothing detail. Many peasant figures.

Moroni, Giovanni Battista (c. 1525–1578)
>   Venetian. Quiet family portraits with good costume detail and delicate grayed colors.

Reni, Guido (1575–1642)
>   Bolognese. Painter and etcher.

Tintoretto, Jacopo (1518–1594)
>   Venetian. Mannerist painter of religious themes. Figures in exaggerated poses. Good garment silhouettes.

Veronese, Paolo Caliari (1528–1588)
>   Trained in Verona; worked in Venice after 1553. Huge pictures crowded with fashionably dressed figures including courtiers, musicians and soldiers.

SPANISH

El Greco (Domenikos Theotocopoulos) 1541–1614)
 Cretan by birth; trained in Venice and worked in Spain. Mannerist painter. Ecstatic and passionate style. Eerie use of color and unusual clothing.

Mor, Anthonis (Antonio Moro) (c. 1517/21–1576/7)
 Portrait painter from Utrecht who became Court Painter of the Spanish Netherlands. Combined an acute sense of character with Titian-like grand style.

1625–1700

DUTCH

During this period the prosperous Dutch acquired a prodigious taste for being painted and for acquiring paintings. There is probably no other place or period where the population's appearance is so widely recorded. The most prolific of the following Dutch painters left several hundred works each.

Hals, Frans (c. 1581/85–1666)
 The great portrait painter of Haarlem. Executed both individual and group portraits of middle- and lower-class life. Painted large lively groups of Archers and Musketeers during the Dutch Wars with Spain.

Helst, Bartholomeus van der (1613–1670)
 Amsterdam. Fashionable portrait painter.

Honthorst, Gerrit van (1590–1656)
 Born and trained in Utrecht; later Court Painter at The Hague. Genre scenes and elegant portraits.

Hooch (Hoogh) Pieter de (1629–after 1689)
 Delft. Like Vermeer, his pictures are often of interiors with two or three figures engaged in some household task. Clothing rendered in sensitive detail.

Ostade, Adriaen van (1610–1681)
 Haarlem genre painter. Student of Hals. Many peasant scenes.

Rembrandt van Rijn (1606–1681)
 Leyden and Amsterdam. Enormous body of work includes etchings and drawings. Individual portraits, pairs and groups. See especially *The Night Watch* and *Staal Masters*.

Steen, Jan (1626–1679)
 Tavern keeper in Leyden. Painted humorous subjects from peasant and middle-class life. Unusual clothing details; see children's garments in *The Eve of St. Nicholas*.

Ter Borch (Terborgh, Terburg, Terborch), Gerard (1617–1681)
 Painted genre subjects and portraits, many full length. Beautiful fabric rendering. Note exquisite costume detail in the *Brothel Scene*.

Vermeer, Jan (1632–1675)
 From Delft. Painted mostly domestic interiors with figures engaged in ordinary work. Jewel-like color.

ENGLISH

Hollar, Wenceslaus (1607–1677)
 Born in Prague, worked in England. Illustrator and topographer. Etchings and watercolors of everyday, middle-class life have superb costume detail.

Jones, Inigo

Jordaens, Jacob (1593–1678)
 Born and died in Antwerp. Assistant to Rubens. Executed portraits of the House of Orange and large genre scenes of drinking bouts.

Kneller, Sir Godrey (c. 1646/9–1723)
 Born in Lubeck, trained in Amsterdam. Arrived in England around 1776 and became a leading portrait painter.

Lely, Sir Peter (1618–1680)
 Born in Germany, studied in Haarlem. Arrived in London in 1640's. Became the most influential English painter of his period and left hundreds of portraits.

FLEMISH

Brouwer, Adriaen

Rubens, Sir Peter Paul

Teniers, David II, the Younger (1610–1690)
 Predominantly genre scenes of peasant life. Over 2,000 pictures are attributed to him. His father, David Teniers, the Elder, painted religious pictures and landscapes.

Van Dyck, Sir Anthony (1599–1641)
 From Antwerp. Best work done during the nine years he lived in England executing portraits at the Court of Charles I. These are excellent costume research. See, for example, *Portrait of Charles I Hunting*.

FRENCH

Berain, Jean (1640–1711)
Designer of court masques.
Bosse, Abraham (1602–1676)
Illustrator, etcher and engraver. Son of a tailor. Superb source for detailed middle-class clothing.
Callot, Jacques (c. 1592/3–1635)
Illustrator, etcher and engraver. Beautifully drawn clothing detail for the middle and upper classes.
Champaigne, Philippe de (1602–1674)
Born in Brussels; settled in Paris in 1621. Many excellent middle-class portraits.
Largillierre (Largillière) Nicholas de (1656–1746)
Born in Paris, trained in Antwerp. Settled in Paris in 1682. Executed portraits of the wealthy middle classes.
La Tour, Georges de (1593–1652)
Painter of religious subjects with figures dressed in superbly detailed contemporary clothing. Wonderful use of light.
Le Brun (Lebrun), Charles (1619–1690)
A powerful and influential artist who was chief decorator to Louis XIV. Left many drawings of interest to costume researchers.
Le Nain, Antoine (c. 1588–1648)
Louis (c. 1593–1648)
Mathieu (c. 1607–1677)
Three brothers whose work is difficult to assign positively. Louis generally credited with a group of large scale paintings in cool grey tones of peasant families. See, for example, *Peasant Family* (c. 1640).
Mignard, Pierre (1612–1695)
Lebrun's rival. Important court portrait painter. Did many allegorical portraits.
Rigaud, Hyacinthe (1659–1743)
Principal official painter to court of Louis XIV. Also worked under Louis XV. The state portraits done with great pomp; nonofficial portraits are more natural. Particularly good for wig and hairstyle research.

SPANISH

Murillo, Bartholomé Esteban (c. 1617–1682)
Seville. Early paintings of beggar-children are naturalistic; later ones become idealized, "fancy-dress" rags. Many religious paintings with peasant figures which tend to be sentimentalized.
Ribera, Jusepe or Jose de (1591?–1652)
From Valencia; settled and worked in Naples.

Painted life around him with great vigor and human reality.
Velasquez, Diego Rodriguez de Silva (1599–1660)
Born in Seville. Became Court Painter in Madrid in 1623. Beautiful portraits with good costume detail.
Zubarán, Francisco de (1598–1664)
Studied and settled in Seville. Executed devotional pictures, many of saints, with figures of massive solidity and solemnity.

1700–1790

AMERICAN

Blackburn, Joseph (c. 1730–? After 1774)
Active portrait painter 1754–1763. Excellent clothing detail.
Copley, John Singleton (1738–1815)
Excellent American portraits done in the early part of his career. See, for example, portrait of *Joseph Sherburne* (1767). Spent the latter half of his life in England doing chiefly history paintings.
Feke, Robert (c. 1705–c. 1750)
New England portrait painter, both individuals and groups. Excellent examples of dress during the Colonial Period.
Peale, Charles Willson (1741–1827)
Painted the leading citizens of Philadelphia and Annapolis. Also executed excellent miniatures of Revolutionary War officers; several of George Washington.
Pratt, Matthew (1734–1805)
Portrait painter in Philadelphia and New York. Good clothing detail.
Stuart, Gilbert (1755–1828)
Painted nearly every prominent American of his day. Excellent clothing detail. The Metropolitan Museum owns 22 Stuart portraits.
Theiis, Jeremiah (c. 1719–1774)
Painted the important social and political leaders in Charleston, South Carolina.
Trumbull, John (1756–1843)
Painter of portraits and historical subjects. Of particular interest are his many portraits of Revolutionary generals.

ENGLISH

Bigg, William Radmore (1755–1828)
Genre painter. An interesting example of his work is *Shipwrecked Sailor Boy*.

Gainsborough, Thomas (1727–1788)

Regarded landscape painting as his real bent but did many portraits of great elegance. See, for example, the beautiful painting of *Mrs. Siddons*. Look out for his tendency in some portraits to costume his subject in clothing of an earlier period, such as *Blue Boy*.

Hogarth, William (1697–1764)

Also goldsmith and engraver. Great success with several series of paintings on "modern moral subjects" such as *Harlot's Progress* (1731–32), *Rake's Progress* (1735) and *Marriage a la Mode* (1733–35). The paintings and engravings in these series are full of excellent costume detail, both dress and undress.

Kneller, Sir Godrey

Morland, George (1763–1804)

Executed picturesque rustic genre paintings. Modelled himself on Brouwer. The paintings were popularized through engravings. See particularly *Industry, Idleness* and *The Stable*.

Raeburn, Sir Henry (1756–1823)

Jeweller and miniaturist. Early portraits of local Scottish dignitaries. See, for example, the *Rev. Robert Walker Skating* (1784). Portraits after 1790 are less detailed.

Reynolds, Sir Joshua (1723–1792)

Painted almost every notable man and woman in the 2nd half of the eighteenth century. Also history works. Good costume detail, especially men. Painted some women in loose-fitting gowns especially made for use in his studio.

Romney, George (1734–1802)

Shared popularity with Reynolds and Gainsborough but artistically inferior to both. Many prosaic portraits with uninspired but accurate rendering of clothes.

Smith, Joseph R. (1752–1812)

Wheatley, Francis (1747–1801)

Early work consists of small detailed portraits. After 1884 turned to genre subjects. See, especially, *Cries of London* (1795).

West, Benjamin (1738–1812)

Born in Philadelphia but left America to study in Rome and settle in London. Maintained a long and highly profitable relationship with George III. Portraits and history paintings.

Zoffany, Johann (1725–1810)

German born, Italian trained painter who settled in England in 1761. Portraits and theatrical scenes. Several portraits of Garrick. Superb clothing and costume detail.

FRENCH

Boucher, François (1703–1770)

Began as Watteau's engraver. The most typical Rococo decorator. Painted charming mythological scenes; clothing beautiful and romantic.

Chardin, Jean–Baptiste–Siméon (1699–1779)

Best known as still-life painter. Also did small genre scenes, unsentimentalized and unidealized. Some pastel portraits.

Drouais, François–Hubert (1727–1775)

Portrait painter. Subjects included actresses and members of the royal family. Particularly successful with children.

Fragonard, Jean–Honoré (1732–1806)

Painted beautiful and sentimental subjects during reign of Louis XV. See especially the *Progress of Love* series done for Mme. du Barry. No work after the Revolution.

Greuze, Jean–Baptiste (1725–1805)

Narrative genre painting with superbly detailed middle and lower class clothing. Portraits also. No work of note after the Revolution.

Lancret, Nicholas (1690–1743)

Imitator of Watteau. Painted chiefly *fetes galantes*.

Largillierre, Nicholas de

Latour, Maurice-Quentin de (1704–1788)

With Perronneau, most celebrated 18th C. French pastellist. Vigorous portraits of French royalty and high society.

Liotard, Jean–Etienne (1702–1789)

Swiss pastellist who worked in Paris from 1725. Travelled widely as a successful portraitist.

Nattier, Jean–Marc, the Younger (1685–1766)

Painter of the ladies in Louis XV's court. Good costume detail.

Rigaud, Hyacinthe

Vigeé–Le Brun (Lebrun), Marie-Louise Elisabeth (1755–1842)

Highly successful portrait painter. Subjects included Marie Antoinette and members of the court. Fled France at the outbreak of the Revolution. Travelled widely painting excellent portraits in several countries. Her *Memoirs* are fascinating.

Watteau, Jean–Antoine (1684–1721)

His paintings of Italian comedy characters and country scenes and his beautiful crayon drawings in black, red and white are all superb costume research material.

IRISH
Buck, Adam (1759–1833)

ITALIAN
Longhi, Alessandro (1733–1813)
Well known portraitist and son of Pietro Longhi.

Longhi, Pietro (1702–1785)
Venetian genre painter. His scenes of quiet domestic life in patrician or wealthy merchant households are rich in clothing detail.

Teipolo, Giovanni Battista (1696–1770)
Venetian. Great decorator of palaces and churches. Purest exponent of the Italian Rococo.

SPANISH
Goya, Francisco Jose de (1746–1828)
Painted scenes of Spanish life and many unflattering portraits of Charles IV and his family. Graphic artist also; etched plates of the Napoleonic invasion. Good costume detail.

1790–1815

AMERICAN
Copley, John Singleton
Peale, Charles Willson
Pratt, Matthew
Stuart, Gilbert
Trumbull, John

ENGLISH
Beechey, Sir William (1753–1839)
Named Portrait Painter to the Queen in 1793. Truthful eye for detail.

Bigg, W.R.
Gillray, James (1757–1815)
Caricaturist. Good costume detail.

Hoppner, John (c. 1758–1810)
A principal follower of Reynolds. Named Portrait Painter to the Prince of Wales in 1793.

Lawrence, Sir Thomas (1769–1830)
Enormously successful portrait painter. Appointed Painter to the King in 1792. Commissioned by George IV to paint portraits of all the great personalities of the struggle against Napoleon.

Moreland, George
Opie, John (1761–1807)
Portraits and historical subjects. Best at painting peasants, particularly children and old men.

Raeburn, Sir Henry
Romney, George
Rowlandson, Thomas (1756–1827)
Brilliant caricaturist and graphic artist. Portrayed English life and manners with exuberance and humor.

West, Benjamin
Wheatley, Francis
Zoffany, Johann

FRENCH
Boilly, Louis–Leopold (1761–c. 1830/45)
Printmaker and painter of genre scenes. Many grotesque or tragic pictures of the Revolution.

David, Jacques–Louis (1748–1825)
Principal painter of French Republican virtues. Clothing beautifully rendered in all his pictures.

Gerard, Baron Francois (1770–1837)
Student of David. Popular portrait painter during the 1st Empire.

Gros, Baron Antoine Jean (1771–1835)
Pupil of David. Executed large pictures illustrating the Napoleonic saga. Brilliant battlepieces.

Ingres, Jean Auguste Dominique (1780–1867)
Student of David. French portraits until 1806 when he went to Italy. Work in Italy includes wonderful drawings of visitors to Rome. Great clothing detail.

Isabey, Jean–Baptiste (1767–1855)
Portrait painter and miniaturist.

Vigeé–Le Brun, Marie-Louise Elisabeth

IRISH
Buck, Adam

ITALIAN
Longhi, Alessandro

SPANISH
Goya, Francisco Jose de

1815–1840

AMERICAN

Ingham, Charles Cromwell (1796–1863)
Born in Dublin, settled in New York in 1816. Elegant portraits with intricately rendered details. See full-length portrait of *Amelia Palmer* (1830).

Morse, Samuel Finley Breese (1791–1872)
Born in Massachusetts, studied in London. Painted many portraits in New England and the South. See, for example, the full-length portrait of his eldest daughter (1835). Also inventor of, among other things, the telegraph.

Peale, Charles
Stuart, Gilbert
Sully, Thomas
Trumbull, John
Waldo and Jewett William Jewett (1795–1873) and *Samuel Waldo* (1793–1861)
Two painters who produced joint portraits from 1818 to 1854. Clothing details always carefully rendered. See *The Knapp Children* painted about 1849.

AUSTRIAN

Waldmüller, Ferdinand George (1793–1865)
Portrait and landscape painter who worked in the simple, unaristocratic Biedermeier style. Superb costume detail.

ENGLISH

Cruikshank, George (1792–1878)
Leading caricaturist of his day, illustrator and cartoonist. Illustrated books by Charles Dickens and Harrison Ainsworth.

Beechey, Sir William
Lawrence, Sir Thomas
Raeburn, Sir Henry
Rowlandson, Thomas

FRENCH

Corot, Jean–Baptiste–Camille (1796–1875)
Travelled widely and made many drawings to record his journeys. The late portraits are particularly strong and forthright. Many rural subjects.

David, Jacques–Louis

Delacroix, Ferdinand–Victor Eugene (1798–1863)
Major painter of the Romantic movement in France. Subjects include scenes from North African Arab and Jewish life, battles, hunts and portraits of close friends. See his rendering of Chopin (1838). Also illustrated Byron's work.

Gros, Baron Antoine–Jean.
Ingres, Jean–Auguste–Dominique
Isabey, Jean Baptiste
Vigeé–Le Brun, Marie-Louise Elisabeth
Vernet, Emile–Jean–Horace (1789–1863)
Paintings and lithographs include excellent battle scenes.

IRISH

Buck, Adam

1840–1865

AMERICAN

Bingham, George Caleb (1811–1879)
Painted scenes from everyday life in the American West.

Healy, George Peter Alexander (1813–1894)
Boston painter. Portraits include many of the great political and social figures of his time.

Ingham, Charles Cromwell
Morse, Samuel Finley Breese
Mount, William Sidney (1807–1868)
New York painter. Portraits and genre paintings of rural life on Long Island. Exquisite clothing detail.

Nast, Thomas (1840–1902)
Cartoonist.

Waldo and Jewett

AUSTRIAN

Waldmüller, Ferdinand George

BELGIAN

Stevens, Alfred (1828–1906)
Also sculptor and decorator. Some good portraits and many drawings with excellent clothing detail.

ENGLISH

Burne-Jones, Sir Edward (1833–1898)
One of the painters in the circle around William Morris and Rossetti. Dreamy romantic paintings; tapestry and stained-glass designs.

Cruikshank, George

Du Maurier, George (1834–1896)
Caricaturist. Illustrator for *Punch*.

Frith, William Powell (1819–1909)
Portrait painter until 1840 when he turned to costume history and genre painting. Intricate Victorian scenes. Costume of all social classes. Examine the wealth of detail in *The Railway Station*.

Hunt, William Holman (1827–1910)
Founded the Pre-Raphaelite Brotherhood with Millais and Rossetti. His paintings in Egypt and the Holy Land have particularly interesting rustic costume detail.

Keene, Charles Samuel (1823–1891)
Graphic artist. Many drawings in *Punch*. Pen studies of figures and landscapes.

Leech, John (1817–1864)
Caricaturist.

Millais, Sir John Everett (1829–1896)
Founded the Pre-Raphaelite Brotherhood with Hunt and Rossetti. Fashionable, technically brilliant painter. Portraits, costume history and genre pieces.

Morris, William (1834–1896)
Became a painter under the influence of Rossetti. Turned to "art for use" and founded a design firm in 1861 to produce wallpaper, furniture, tapestries, stained-glass windows, carpets, etc.

Rossetti, Dante Gabriel (1828–1882)
Poet as well as painter. Founder of the Pre-Raphaelite Brotherhood with Hunt and Millais. Highly aesthetic and self-conscious work.

FRENCH

Chassériau, Théodore (1819–1856)
Born in the West Indies. Subject matter includes Biblical and Shakespearean illustration, scenes from North African life, religious and allegorical decorations. Pencil portraits are beautifully detailed.

Corot, Jean-Baptiste-Camille

Courbet, Gustave (1819–1877)
Vivid naturalism. Excellent research materials in his everyday scenes from French middle-class and peasant life.

Daumier, Honoré (1808–1879)
Also lithographer and cartoonist. Strong watercolor scenes of everyday life and in the Court of Justice; straightforward and untouched by Romanticism.

Degas, Hilaire Edgar Germain (1834–1917)
Also sculptor. Early works include family portraits and history pictures in the academic manner. His own Impressionist style appears after 1860. Ballet girls, working girls, models and cabaret artists among his favorite subjects. Later work almost entirely in pastels.

Delacroix, Ferdinand-Victor Eugene

Gavarni (1804–1866)
Lithographer and caricaturist.

Manet, Édouard (1832–1883)
Early works included beautiful paintings of Spanish visitors to Paris. After 1870 adopted the Impressionist technique and palette. Always good costume detail.

Millet, Jean-François (1814–1875)
Son of a peasant. Painted genre scenes of peasants and their labors that are excellent for costume research.

PRUSSIAN

Winterhalter, Franz (1806–1873)
Painted in Paris. Portraits of royalty and aristocracy. Also genre subjects.

1865–1890

AMERICAN

Abbey, Edwin Austin (1852–1911)
Illustrator for periodicals, genre painter and watercolorist.

Bingham, George Caleb

Cassatt, Mary Stevenson (1844–1926)
Lived in Paris. Influenced by Degas. Exhibited with the Impressionists. Beautiful paintings and pastels of women and children with sensitive clothing detail.

Eakins, Thomas Cowperthwaite (1844–1916)
Also photographer. Portraits and paintings are realistic and detailed.

Healy, George Peter Alexander

Homer, Winslow (1836–1910)
Early career as magazine illustrator includes record of the Civil War with good uniform details. After 1875 devoted himself to painting

American country life. Adopted a quasi-Impressionist style.

Johnson, Eastman (1824–1906)
Genre scenes. Pictures of American life, many set in New England.

Nast, Thomas

Pennell, Joseph (c. 1857/60–1926)
Printmaker and illustrator.

Pyle, Howard (1853–1911)
Popular illustrator of chivalric tales. Teacher and founder of the Brandywine School where artists like N. C. Wyeth and Maxfield Parrish studied.

Sargent, John Singer (1856–1925)
American portrait painter who settled in London and painted High Society in Edwardian and Georgian times. Huge output of work. Some larger-than-life portraits.

Whistler, James Abbott McNeill (1834–1903)
From Massachusetts. Cartographer and etcher as well as portraitist. Good costume detail.

BELGIAN

Stevens, Alfred

ENGLISH

Burne–Jones, Edward
Cruikshank, George
Du Maurier, George
Frith, William Powell
Greenaway, Kate (1846–1901)
Illustrator, painter and author of children's books. Rendered exquisite children's clothing.
Hunt, William Holman
Keene, Charles Samuel
Millais, Sir John Everett
Morris, William
Orchardson, Sir William Quiller (1832–1910)
Scottish genre and portrait painter. Painted scenes from Shakespeare.
Rossetti, Dante Gabriel

FRENCH

Béraud, Jean (1849–1935)
Genre scenes and portraits.

Cézanne, Paul (1839–1906)
One of the greatest painters of the last 100 years. Many landscapes and still lifes. Portraits have dramatic, beautifully rendered but not particularly detailed clothing.

Corot, Jean–Baptiste–Camille

Daumier, Honoré
Degas, Hilaire Edgar Germain
Doré, Gustave (1832–1883)
Brilliant graphic artist and sculptor as well as painter. His engravings of the squalor of London life are of particular interest.

Gervex, Henri (1852–1929)
History and genre painter. Mythological scenes.

Goubie, Jean Richard (1842–1899)
Hunting scenes.

Manet, Édouard

Millet, Jean–François

Renoir, Pierre Auguste (1841–1919)
One of the greatest of the painters affected by Impressionism. Early works include portraits and figure groups with nice costume details.

Tissot, James Joseph Jacques (1836–1902)
French by birth but worked in England much of his life. Produced charming illustrations of Victorian life in paintings and etchings. Superb costume details.

Toulouse–Lautrec, Compte Henri Marie Raymond de (1864–1901)
All his paintings, prints and drawings have lovely costume details. Subject matter reflected his own haunts: dance halls and cafes in Montmartre, cabarets, the circus, brothels.

SWEDISH

Larsson, Carl (1853–1919)
Paintings of his own home and family provide beautiful costume research.

1890–1900

AMERICAN

Abbey, Edwin Austin
Cassatt, Mary Stevenson
Eakins, Thomas Cowperthwaite
Frost, A.B. (1851–1928)
Illustrator. Good examples of rustic costume.

Gibson, Charles Dana (1867–1944)
From Massachusetts. Illustrator who created the famous "Gibson Girl," an attractive, athletic, outdoor woman. His work is an excellent source for costume research.

Homer, Winslow
Johnson, Eastman
Nast, Thomas

Pennell, Joseph
Pyle, Howard
Remington, Frederic (1861–1909)
> Beautiful paintings and sculptures of life in the American West.
Russell, Charles (1864–1926)
> Genre paintings of the American West. Excellent clothing detail for both white and Indian populations.
Sargent, John Singer
Smith, Francis Hopkinson (1838–1915)
> Also novelist and engineer.
Whistler, James McNeill

BELGIAN
Stevens, Alfred

ENGLISH
Beardsley, Aubrey Vincent (1872–1898)
> Illustrator. His work is the perfect expression of Art Nouveau. Often represents highly fanciful clothing.
Burne–Jones, Edward
Greenaway, Kate
Orchardson, Sir William Quiller

FRENCH
Aublet, Albert (B. 1851)
> Also sculptor. History scenes and portraits. Great attention to costume detail.
Béraud, Jean
Bonnard, Pierre (1867–1947)
> Subjects of paintings and lithographs were usually quiet interiors with a woman bathing, dressing, or sleeping and family scenes.
Cézanne, Paul
Degas, Hilaire Edgar Germain
Gervex, Henri
Goubie, Jean Richard
Jeanniot, Pierre George (1848–1934)
> Landscapes, genre subjects and portraits.
La Touche, Gaston (1854–1913)
> Genre painter and illustrator. Favorite subject, life in Paris. See *The Casino* for evening dress.
Prinet, Rene Francois Xavier (1861–1946)
Renoir, Pierre Auguste
Tissot, James Joseph Jacques
Toulouse–Lautrec, Compte Henri de

NORWEGIAN
Munch, Edvard (1863–1944)
> Worked in German expressionist style. Graphic works and paintings are powerful. Figures have strong silhouettes but little detailed clothing.

SWEDISH
Larsson, Carl

Twentieth Century

In the twentieth century, photographs become the primary material for clothing research. Candid family pictures, newspaper and magazine photos and the work of photographic artists record exactly what people wore, when and under what circumstances. Fashion illustrators remain important sources for high fashion clothing. Painters turn, for the most part, to subjects other than the realistically rendered, clothed human form. The following artists are some of those who continue to provide useful examples of clothing well into this century.

AMERICAN
Abbey, Edwin Austin
Cassatt, Mary Stevenson
Eakins, Thomas Cowperthwaite
Flagg, James Montgomery (1877–1960)
> Illustrator. Concentrated on urban American life. Well known for his World War I posters.
Frost, A.B.
Gibson, Charles Dana
Homer, Winslow
Hopper, Edward (1882–1967)
> Foremost twentieth century American realist. Good source for everyday, ordinary dress of the thirties and forties. See drawings for greatest detail.
Leyendecker, Joseph Christian (1874–1951)
> Illustrator. Produced 321 *Saturday Evening Post* covers. In 1905 created the "Arrow Collar Man" symbol of fashionable American manhood. Excellent resource for well dressed men of the period.
Pennell, Joseph
Phillips, Coles (1880–1927)
> Illustrator.

Pyle, Howard
Rockwell, Norman (1894–1980)
> Noted magazine illustrator. Many examples of everyday American life, detailed and somewhat romanticized.

Russell, Charles
Sargent, John Singer
Smith, Jessie Wilcox (1863–1935)
> Painter and magazine illustrator. Did many covers for *Good Housekeeping*. Beautifully rendered women and children.

ENGLISH
Orchardson, Sir William Quiller

FRENCH
Aulet, Albert
Avy, Joseph Marius (B. 1871)
> Illustrator and painter of genre scenes. Active 1900–1941.

Barbier, George (1882–c. 1940)
> Fashion illustrator, 1910's and 1920's.

Béraud, Jean
Bónnard, Pierre
Cézanne, Paul
Erté (b. 1893)
> Fashion designer and illustrator. Associated with *Harper's Bazaar* from 1915–1935.

Gervex, Henri
Jeanniot, Pierre George
La Touche, Gaston
Prinet, Rene Francois Xavier

NORWEGIAN
Munch, Edvard

SWEDISH
Larsson, Carl

Shopping Guide

Boston Area

ACCESSORIES
Dorothy's Boutique
190 Massachusetts Ave.
Boston, MA 02115
617-262-9255
Jewelry

ARTISTS' SUPPLIES
Charrette
95 Mt. Auburn St.
Cambridge, MA 02138
617-935-6000
and
1 Winthrop Square
Boston, MA 02110
617-935-6000

Catalogue and discount membership available.

Johnson's Artists' Supplies
355 Newbury St.
Boston, MA 02115
617-536-4065

Lambert Co.
920 Commonwealth Ave.
Boston, MA 02215
617-232-8551
Catalogue available.

Utrecht's
333 Massachusetts Ave.
Boston, MA 02115
617-262-4948

BOXES AND PLASTIC TAPE
Carter, Rice, Storrs and Bement Co.
273 Summer St.
Boston, MA 02210
617-542-6400

Perry Box Co.
95 Chapel St.
Newton, MA 02158
617-964-3220
Boxes to order.

CANVAS AND GROMMETS
New England Canvas and Tent
150 W. 4th St.
Boston, MA 02127
617-268-5010

CELASTIC AND HOT GLUE
Warren Electric and Hardware Supply
470 Tremont St.
Boston, MA 02116
617-426-7525

CLOTHING—USED

Bluefingers
101 Charles St.
Boston, MA 02114
617-532-8774

C&S Talking Machine
864 Massachusetts Ave.
Cambridge, MA 02139
617-547-4424

The Closet
739 Boylston St.
Boston, MA 02116
617-536-1515

Forever Flamingo
285 Newbury St.
Boston, MA 02115
617-267-2547

Great Eastern Trading Co.
49 River St. (Central Sq.)
Cambridge, MA 02139
617-354-5279

Hadassah Bargain Spot
1121 Commonwealth Ave.
Boston, MA 02215
617-254-8300

High Society
273 Newbury St.
Boston, MA 02116
617-266-8957

Jim's Clothing Store
1240 Washington St. (near
  Dover Station)
Boston, MA 02118
617-542-2617
Good work boots.

Keezer's
221 Concord Ave.
Cambridge, MA 02138
617-547-2455
Men's wear.

*Morgan Memorial Goodwill
  Industries*
436 Moody St.
Waltham, MA 02154
617-893-0400

Dartmouth St.
Boston, MA 02116

Davis Square
Somerville, MA

Oona's
1210 Massachusetts Ave.
  (near Harvard Sq.)
Cambridge, MA 02138
617-497-1533
Lots of leather jackets.

Rags
Main St. (near Central Sq.)
Cambridge, MA 02139
$1 lb. clothing.

Reddog
1737 Massachusetts Ave.
Cambridge, MA 02138
617-354-9676
Good selection of 30's,
  40's, and 50's men's and
  women's; medium to
  high prices.

RFG Antiques
195 Harvard St.
Brookline, MA 02146
617-734-2226
Good, but expensive.

Rowan & McGeough
11 Marion St.
Brookline, MA 02146
617-566-8126

Salvation Army
61 Brookline Ave.
Boston, MA 02215
617-536-7540

Silver Threads
189 North St.
Boston, MA 02113
617-523-2360

Vintage, Etc.
2014a Massachusetts Ave.
  (1 block past Porter Sq.)
Cambridge, MA 02140
617-497-1516
30's, 40's and 50's.

COSTUME RENTALS

Hooker-Howe
46 S. Main St.
Haverhill, MA 01830
617-373-3731

Tracey Music
429 Boylston St.
Boston, MA 02116
617-266-2730

DANCEWEAR

Capezio
28 Cottage Ave.
Quincy, MA 02169
617-479-1717

59 Temple Place
Boston, MA 02111
617-482-5825

Taffy's Dancewear
5566 Washington St.
Wellesley, MA 02181
617-237-5526

475 Commonwealth Ave.
Boston, MA 02215
617-267-8525
Carries all major brands.

DECORATIVE ITEMS

Koplow Trimming Co.
29 Kneeland St.
Boston, MA 02111
617-426-8549
Bulk.

Metro Trim
80 Bedford St.
Boston, MA 02111
617-542-7900

Windsor Button
36 Chauncy St.
Boston, MA 02111
617-482-4969

FABRICS

The Bargain Center
6 Washington St.
Quincy, MA 02169
617-472-1414

Beaconway Fabrics
47 Temple Place
Boston, MA 02111
617-426-3877

Clement Textiles
54 Kneeland St.
Boston, MA 02111
617-542-9511

Dicarlo Fabrics
15 Temple Place
Boston, MA 02111
617-426-5749

The Fabric Place
136 Howard St.
Framingham, MA 01701
617-237-9675

Fabric Showroom
319 Washington St.
Brighton, MA 02135
617-782-3169

Fabrications
1740 Massachusetts Ave.
Cambridge, MA 02138
617-661-6276

General Rubber Fabric Co.
131 Portland St.
Boston, MA 02114
617-523-0958
Upholstery fabrics and
  supplies.

Harrison/North End Fabrics
31 Harrison Ave.
Boston, MA 02111
617-426-2116

Ralph Jordan Textiles
332 Washington St.
Brighton, MA 02135
617-254-5852

New England Textiles
50 Essex St.
Boston, MA 02111
617-426-1965

Sewlow Discount Fabrics
473 Cambridge St.
Cambridge, MA 02141
617-661-8361

Slesinger
30 Chauncy St.
Boston, MA 02111
617-542-1805

Winmil Fabrics
111 Chauncy St.
Boston, MA 02111
617-542-1815

MUSLIN

Sparrow Chisholm
120 Kingston St.
Boston, MA 02111
617-426-0360
Bulk muslin.

FELT

Commonwealth Felt
76 Summer St.
Boston, MA 02111
617-423-3445
Industrial felt.

LEATHER

Beacon Leather
106 South St.
Boston, MA 02111
617-542-7158
Magix.

Berman Leather
147 South St.
Boston, MA 02111
617-426-0870

Siegel Leather
120 Pond St.
Ashland, MA 01721
617-881-5200

MAKE-UP

Make-Up Center
80 Boylston St.
Boston, MA 02111
617-542-7865

A&A Beauty Supply
1255 River St.
Hyde Park, MA 01960
617-361-6606
Retail and wholesale.

MILLINERY SUPPLIES

Exclusive Wholesale Millinery
90 Chauncy St.
Boston, MA 02111
617-426-7202
Cash only.

PLEATING

State Pleating Co.
35 Kneeland St.
Boston, MA 02111
617-426-1986

PRESSING EQUIPMENT

D.&R. Steam
45 A St.
S. Boston, MA 02127
617-268-5633
Sales and service.

REWEAVING

Invisible Mending Service
26 Little Bldg.
Boston, MA
617-542-7806

SCISSORS

Stoddard's
50 Temple Place
Boston, MA 02111
617-426-4187
Scissors and sharpening.

SEWING MACHINES AND REPAIR

Mor Real Sewing Machine Co.
126-132 High St.
Framingham, MA 01701
617-891-5333

Reliable Sewing Machine
72 Kneeland St.
Boston, MA 02111
617-426-1080

Seidel's Sewing Machine Repair Shop
1411 Dorchester Ave.
Dorchester, MA 02122
617-825-0746

Singer Sewing Center
280 Elm St. (Davis Sq.)
Somerville, MA 02144
617-625-6668

SEWING SUPPLIES

Pacific Paper Products
0 Broadway
Lawrence, MA 01840
617-683-8771
Dotted pattern paper.

Pam Tailor Supply
625 Adams St.
Dorchester, MA 02122
617-265-8500

Sewing Notions Division, Scoville Manufacturing Co.
90 Hatch St.
New Bedford, MA 02745
Box c-903
617-999-6431
Elastic.

Solo Slide Fasteners, Notions
77 Tosca Dr.
Box 528
Stoughton, MA 02072
Toll free: 1-800-343-9670
In Massachusetts:
  617-828-6110

SURGICAL AND MEDICAL SUPPLIES, PLASTER BANDAGES

Phillips Drugs
155 Charles St.
Boston, MA 02114
617-532-1028

Sparr's Drugs
635 Huntington Ave.
Boston, MA 02115
617-738-9737

UNIFORMS

Boston Uniform
78 Essex St.
Boston, MA 02111
617-542-2635

Stern Uniform
100 VFW Parkway
Revere, MA 02151
617-284-8700

WIGS

Dorothy's Boutique
190 Massachusetts Ave.
Boston, MA 02115
617-262-9255

Wigwam
59 Temple Place
Boston, MA 02111
617-426-8709

Chicago Area

ACCESSORIES

Haren Hosiery
4 S. State St.
Chicago, IL 60603
312-346-0094

1123 Lake St.
Oak Park, IL 60301
312-386-9400

ADHESIVES AND TAPES

Iroquois Paper Co.
2220 W. 56th St.
Chicago, IL 60636
312-436-7000
3-M glue system.

Swift's Adhesives & Coatings
3649 Chase Ave.
Skokie, IL 60076
312-761-0100

Tapes Unlimited
2310 Main St.
Evanston, IL 60202
312-273-4111

Joseph Weil & Sons
1401-43 S. Clinton
Chicago, IL 60607
312-738-7800
Tapes.

ARMOR

Tobin's Lake Studios, Inc.

2650 Seven Mile Road
South Lyon, MI 48178
313-449-4444
Vacuum-formed armor
pieces. Catalogue
available.

ARTIST AND CRAFT SUPPLIES

Brudno Art Supply Co.
601 N. State St.
Chicago, IL 60610
312-787-0030

Lee Ward's Creative Crafts Center
1200 St. Charles
Elgin, IL 60120
312-888-5800
Branches through U.S.
Catalogue available.

SS Artists Materials, Inc.
712 N. State St.
Chicago, IL 60610
312-787-2005

BOOK SHOPS AND PUBLICATIONS

Contemporary Drama Service
Box 457, Dept. CAP
Downers Grove, IL 60515
312-969-4988

Oak St. Book Shop, Inc.
54 E. Oak St.
Chicago, IL 60611
312-642-3070

Chicago Resource Directory for the Performing Arts
Chicago Alliance for the
Performing Arts (CAPA)
176 W. Adams, Suite 1810
Chicago, IL 60603
312-372-5178

CELASTIC

Maharam Fabric Corp.
420 N. Orleans
Chicago, IL 60610
312-527-2580

CLOTHING—USED

Follies
6981 N. Sheridan
Chicago, IL 60626
312-761-3020

S. Hirsh & Sons
621-23 W. Randolph
Chicago, IL 60606
312-263-5213

George Stotis
5308 N. Clark
Chicago, IL 60640
312-878-8525

COSTUME RENTAL

Broadway Costumes, Inc.
932 W. Washington Blvd.
Chicago, IL 60607
312-829-6400
Sales, rentals, make-up,
accessories.

Costumes Unlimited
(Main Office)
814 N. Franklin
Chicago, IL 60610
312-642-0200

New York Costume Co., Inc.
20 W. Hubbard
Chicago, IL 60610
312-644-6644
Make-up, costumes,
accessories, and sewing
supplies.

DANCEWEAR

Capezio Dance/Theatre Shop
116 E. Walton
Chicago, IL 60602
312-236-1911

Dance Centre of London, Inc.
936 N. Michigan Ave.
Chicago, IL 60611
312-649-0525

Kling Theatrical Shoe Co.
218 S. Wabash
Chicago, IL 60604
312-427-2028

Leo's Advance Theatrical Co.
125 N. Wabash
Chicago, IL 60602
312-772-7150

Also carries own line of
dancewear and shoes.
Mail Order:
2451 N. Sacramento
Chicago, IL 60647

DECORATIVE ITEMS

Leonard Adler & Co.
190 N. State St. (3rd fl.)
Chicago, IL 60601
312-332-5454
Dressmakers' and furriers'
supplies, trims, and
feather boas.

International Importing Bead & Novelty Co.
17 N. State St.
Chicago, IL 60602
312-332-0061
Beads, rhinestones, sequins,
pearls, jewels, etc.

R. Nyren & Co.
2222 W. Diversey
Chicago, IL 60647
312-276-5515
Braid, cord, tassels, tape,
fringe, etc.

Progress Feather Co.
657 W. Lake
Chicago, IL 60606
312-726-7443

A. Robbin & Co.
321 W. Jackson
Chicago, IL 60606
312-939-2240
Bridal fabrics, laces,
sequins, rhinestones.

DYESTUFFS

Almore Dye House
4422 S. Wentworth
Chicago, IL 60609
312-268-5000

Keystone Aniline Dye
321 N. Loomis
Chicago, IL 60607
312-666-2015

J.C. Larson Co.
Triarco Arts & Crafts
110 W. Carpenter
Wheeling, IL 60090
312-547-2210

Versatex, Paintex, Dylon,
cold water dyes.

Western Solvents & Eaton Chemical Co.
13395 Huron Drive
Romulous, MI 48174
313-941-4800
Aniline dyes by the pound.

ECCLESIASTICAL

Norbert J. Daleiden, Inc.
212 W. Adams
Chicago, IL 60606
312-332-3893
Manufacturer of
ecclesiastical furnishings.

FABRICS

Dazian's Inc.
400 N. Wells St.
Chicago, IL 60610
312-467-1991

Fishman's Fabrics
1101 S. Des Plaines
Chicago, IL 60607
312-922-7250

Vogue Fabrics
718-732 Main St.
Evanston, IL 60202
312-864-9600

FELT

Metric Felt Co.
135 S. Peoria
Chicago, IL 60607
312-733-0037
Industrial felt.

MAKE-UP

Perle Roland Perfume Shop
946 Rush
Chicago, IL 60611
312-944-1432
Max Factor and Mehron.

Syd Simons Cosmetics, Inc.
2 E. Oak
Chicago, IL 60611
312-943-2333
Make-up artists and make-
up lessons and cosmetic
sales.

Tech Theatre, Inc.
4724 Main
Lisle, IL 60532
312-971-0855
Ben Nye, Stein, Max
Factor. Prosthetic
appliances and fabrics.
Catalogue available.

SEWING SUPPLIES
Lapham Hickey Steel Corp.
5500 W. 73rd St.
Chicago, IL
312-496-6111
Spring steel for corsets,
hoops, etc. 1000 ft. rolls.

David Kaplan & Co., Inc.
210 S. Des Plaines
Chicago, IL 60606
312-454-1610
Thread.

B.L. Marder Co.
9543-59 S. Cottage Grove
Chicago, IL 60628
312-221-1111
Hy-Mark thread.

Troy Thread & Textile Corp.
2300 W. Diversy Ave.
Chicago, IL 60625
312-227-1711
Catalogue available.

Velcro Corp.
34 Plaza Dr.
Westmont, IL 60559
312-887-1450

WIGS AND HAIR SUPPLIES
Chicago Hair Goods Co.
428 S. Wabash
Chicago, IL 60605
312-427-8600

Herman Leis & Son
6729 W. North
Oak Park, IL 60302
312-524-0424
Custom-made wigs.

Selan's
32 N. State
Chicago, IL 60602
312-782-0331
Wigs.

MISCELLANEOUS
Thunderbird Products Co.
1042 W. Van Buren
Chicago, IL 60607
312-733-2340
Western novelties, square
dance, etc.

Wayne's Trick Shop
5413 Hohman
Hammond, IN 46320
219-933-9322

Los Angeles Area

ACCESSORIES
Hammer
7210 Melrose Ave.
Los Angeles, CA 90046
213-938-0288
Custom-made gloves.

ARTIST AND CRAFT SUPPLIES
Cane and Basket Supply
1283 Cochran Ave.
Los Angeles, CA 90018
213-939-9644
Raffia, reeds, bamboo,
rush, etc.

Crescent Bronze Powder Co.
Western Division
1841 S. Flower St.
Los Angeles, CA 90015
213-748-5285
Color chart, price list
available. Colors
matched.

Daniel's Co.
2543 W. Sixth St.
Los Angeles, CA 90057
213-387-1211

Michael's Artist Crafts & Drafting Supplies
1518 N. Highland Ave.
Hollywood, CA 90028
213-466-5195

Standard Brand Paint Co., Inc.
124 W. Pico Blvd.
Los Angeles, CA 90015
213-748-2933

BOOK SHOPS
B. Dalton
6743 Hollywood Blvd.
Los Angeles, CA 90028
213-469-8191

Doubleday
9477 Santa Monica Blvd.
Beverly Hills, CA 90210
213-274-8706

Hunter's Books
463 N. Rodeo Dr.
Beverly Hills, CA 90212
213-274-7301

CLOTHING—USED
Aardvark's Odd Ark
7579 Melrose
Los Angeles, CA 90046
213-655-6769
Antique clothing.

Crystal Palace
8457 Melrose
Los Angeles, CA 90069
213-653-6148
Antique clothing and
accessories.

Donna's Olde Clothes
1523 N. Le Brea Ave.
Hollywood, CA 90028
213-874-8119

Hollywood Used Clothing Store
7836 Santa Monica Blvd.
Los Angeles, CA 90046
213-654-4232

COSTUME RENTALS
*California Costume
(Norcostco)*
2101 W. Garvey Ave. No.
West Covina, CA 91790
213-960-4711

Tuxedo Center
7360 Sunset Blvd.
Hollywood, CA 90046
213-874-4200
Spats, rent parts of period
tuxedos, top hats, etc.

Western Costume Co.
5335 Melrose Ave.
Hollywood, CA 90038
213-469-1451

DANCEWEAR
Albert's Hosiery
6332 Hollywood Blvd.
Los Angeles, CA 90028
213-465-2834

Capezio Dance Shoe Co.
1777 N. Vine
Hollywood, CA 90028
213-465-3744/9704

DECORATIVE ITEMS
Berger Specialty Co., Inc.
413 E. 8th St.
Los Angeles, CA 90014
213-627-8783
Glass and wood beads,
shells, pearls, sequins,
etc.

Colby Feathers, Inc.
7923-1/2 W. Third St.
Los Angeles, CA 90048
213-653-3054

Handy Button Machine Co.
1315 Maple Ave.
Los Angeles, CA 90015
213-747-5349
Grommets and dyes, durable snaps.

Hyman Hendler & Sons, Inc.
763 S. Los Angeles St.
Los Angeles, CA 90014
213-627-9348

Hollywood Fancy Feathers Co.
512 S. Broadway
Los Angeles, CA 90013
213-625-8453

Klein Bead Box
314 N. King's Rd.
Los Angeles, CA 90048
213-651-3595

Pacific Coast Commercial, Inc.
745 San Julian
Los Angeles, CA 90014
213-624-3982
Floral supplies.

DYESTUFFS
Calusa Chemical Co.
11641 Pike St.
Santa Fe Springs, CA 90670
213-695-0761
Caldye.

FABRICS
Beverly Hills Silks and Woolens
417 N. Canon Drive
Beverly Hills, CA 90028
213-272-2565

Dazian's, Inc.
165 S. Robertson Blvd.
Beverly Hills, CA 90211
213-655-9691
Novelty fabrics, muslin.

Home Silk Shop
330 S. La Cienega Blvd.
Los Angeles, CA 90048
213-655-7513

International Silks and Woolens
8347 Beverly Blvd.
Los Angeles, CA 90048
213-653-6453
Also boas, beads, and buttons.

Left Bank Fabric Co.
8354 W. Third St.
Los Angeles, CA 90048
213-655-7289
Imported and designer fabrics.

Levine Bros.
530 South Los Angeles St.
Los Angeles, CA 90013
213-624-6541
Woolens and trims.

Oriental Silk Import & Export Co.
8377 Beverly Blvd.
Los Angeles, CA 90048
213-651-1212

FELT
George B. Tewes Co., Inc.
2619 E. 8th St.
Los Angeles, CA 90023
213-269-0435

Standard Felt Co.
115 S. Palm Ave.
Alhambra, CA 91801
213-282-1106
Industrial and decorative felt.

FOOTWEAR
The Folk Motif
2752 E. Broadway
Long Beach, CA 90803
213-439-7380
Mid-Eastern shoes, imported and custom-made, catalogue.

LEATHER
Macpherson Leather Co.
200 S. Los Angeles St.
Los Angeles, CA 90012
213-626-4831
Skins, dyes, sprays, buckles, etc.

MAKE-UP
Columbia Drug Co.
6098 W. Sunset Blvd.
Hollywood, CA 90028

213-464-7555
Make-up supplies.

Ben Nye, Inc.
11571 Santa Monica Blvd.
Los Angeles, CA 90025
213-477-0443
Brochure and price list available, kits.

MILLINERY SUPPLIES
Leon Berlin Milliners Supplies
707 S. Broadway
Los Angeles, CA 90014
213-622-7064
Flowers, veiling, long hat pins, buckram, etc.

California Millinery Supplies
718 S. Hill St.
Los Angeles, CA 90014
213-622-8746
Hat blocks, new and used, millinery supplies, flowers, felts, straws, buckram shapes, trims, etc.

PLEATING
A-1 Pleating & Button Service
8426-1/2 W. 3rd St.
Los Angeles, CA 90048
213-653-5557
Pleating, covered buttons, and buckles.

SEWING MACHINES AND REPAIR
Bernina Distributors
2401 S. Hill
Los Angeles, CA
213-383-4761

Kennedy Sewing Machine Co.
106 E. 17th St.
Los Angeles, CA 90021
213-748-3192 & 748-3194

SEWING SUPPLIES
B. Black & Son
548 S. Los Angeles St.
Los Angeles, CA 90013
213-624-9451

Fine Brand, Inc.
411 Wall St.
Los Angeles, CA 90013
213-629-1446
Catalogue available, corset bones, velcro, etc.

Keller Tailor's Trimmings Co., Inc.
8455 Beverly Blvd.
Los Angeles, CA 90048
213-655-5577
Scissors, chalk, seam tape, etc.

Levine Bros., Inc.
530 S. Los Angeles St.
Los Angeles, CA 90013
213-624-6541

STEAM IRONS
Sussman Automatic of California, Inc.
1907 2nd Ave.
Los Angeles, CA 90018
213-734-1129

SHOE REPAIR
Dandee Shoe Repair
1713 N. Vine St.
Hollywood, CA 90028
213-464-4082

Di Fabrizio
6276 W. 3rd St.
Los Angeles, CA 90036
213-936-6883

Willie's Shoe Service
5326 Melrose
Los Angeles, CA 90038
213-463-5011

WIGS AND HAIR SUPPLIES
Emil Corsillo
1343 N. La Brea Ave.
Hollywood, CA 90028
213-851-1700

Favian Hair, Inc.
6542 Greenbush Ave.
Van Nuys, CA 91401
213-785-8932 & 986-4541
Wigs.

Wilshire Wigs & Toupes, Inc.
13213 Saticoy St.
N. Hollywood, CA 91605
213-875-2260

New York Area

ACCESSORIES

Albert Hosiery
2113A Broadway
New York, NY 10023
212-595-5860

925 Lexington Ave.
New York, NY 10021
212-988-1195

20 W. 43rd St.
New York, NY 10036
212-564-5644
Seamed stockings.

Jonas Dept. Store
62 W. 14th St.
New York, NY 10011
212-675-5990
Inexpensive costume
jewelry, cufflinks, etc.

Marchele Co.
1123 Broadway
New York, NY 10010
212-568-3404
Walking sticks. Brochure
available.

Mitsu Novelties Inc.
36 W. 35th St.
New York, NY 10018
212-947-7892
Paper fans.

Parklane Hosiery
34th St. & Broadway
New York, NY 10001
212-868-0228

49 W. 57th St.
New York, NY 10019
212-838-1008
And other branches.

Sand & Siman, Inc.
34 W. 32nd St.
New York, NY 10001
212-564-4484
Gloves in quantity, all
types.

F.R. Tripler & Co.
366 Madison Ave. (46th
St.)
New York, NY 10017
212-922-1090
Wing collars, men's white
cotton gloves, collar
studs, etc.

Uncle Sam Umbrella Shop
161 W. 57th St.
New York, NY 10019
212-247-7163
Umbrellas, parasols, canes.

ADHESIVES

Beacon Chemical Co., Inc.
125 MacQuesten Parkway S.
Mount Vernon, NY 10550
914-699-4300
Adhesives for all purposes,
millinery sizings, etc.

H.G. Pasternak, Inc.
225 Lafayette
New York, NY 10012
212-925-4865

ARMOR AND WEAPONS

Costume Armor, Inc.
Shore Rd.
P.O. Box 325
Cornwall-on-Hudson
NY 12520
914-534-9120
Vacuum-formed armor
pieces.

Santelli
465 S. Dean St.
Englewood, NJ 07631
201-871-3105
Fencing equipment and
swords.

Weaponry, Inc.
P.O. Box 791
Cooper Station, NY 10003
212-621-9966
Fighting-quality theatrical
weapons for sale or rent.
Price list available.

ARTIST AND CRAFT SUPPLIES

Art Brown
2 W. 46th St. (off 5th
Ave.)
New York, NY 10036
212-575-5555

Charrette
212 E. 54th St.
New York, NY 10022
212-683-8822

215 Lexington Ave. (at
33rd St.)
New York, NY 10016
212-683-8844

*Eastern Artists & Drafting
Materials, Inc.*
352 Park Ave. S. (11th Fl.)
New York, NY 10010
212-725-5555

Sam Flax, Inc.
551 Madison Ave.
New York, NY 10022
212-620-3050

55 E. 55th St.
New York, NY 10022
212-620-3060

25 E. 28th St.
New York, NY 10016
212-620-3040

15 Park Row
New York, NY 10007
212-620-3030

A.I. Friedman, Inc.
25 W. 45th St.
New York, NY 10036
212-575-0200

Lee's Art Shop
220 W. 57th St.
New York, NY 10019
212-247-0110

New York Central Supply
62 3rd Ave.
New York, NY 10003
212-473-7705

Pearl Paint
308 Canal St.
New York, NY 10013
212-431-7932

CANVAS AND MUSLIN

*The Astrup Co. at Raritan
Center*
12 Parkway Pl.
Edison, NJ 08817
201-225-1776
Muslin and canvas.

John Boyle & Co.
112 Duane St.

New York, NY 10013
212-962-4770
Good prices on canvas.
Large quantities only.

Rose Brand Textiles
517 W. 35th St.
New York, NY 10001
212-594-7424 or
800-223-1624
Muslin, chintz, etc.

CELASTIC

Alcone Co., Inc.
575 8th Ave. (38th St.)
New York, NY 10018
212-594-3980

CLOTHING—NEW

Barney's
111 7th Ave. (at 17th St.)
New York, NY 10011
212-929-9000
Men's and women's
designer clothing.

Fowad
2554 Broadway (at 96th
St.)
New York, NY 10025
212-222-7000 and 8000
Inexpensive suits.

Moe Ginsburg
162 5th Ave. (7th fl.)
New York, NY 10011
212-242-3482
Men's discount designer
suits and coats.

Syms
45 Park Place
New York, NY 10013
212-791-1199
Discount suits and
clothing.

J. Wippell & Co., Ltd.
13-00 Plaza Rd.
Box 456
Fairlawn, NJ 07410
201-796-9421
Clerical and choir
garments.

CLOTHING—USED and ANTIQUE

Andy's Chee-Pee's, Inc.
14 St. Mark's Place
New York, NY 10003
212–674–9248
Used and some antique
clothing for men and
women.

Bogies Antique Furs and Clothing
201 E. 10th St.
New York, NY 10003
212–260–1199

Cheap Jack's
151 1st Ave.
New York, NY 10003
212–674-9718

167 1st Ave.
New York, NY 10003
212–473–9599
Used clothing, men's and
women's.

Church Street Surplus
327 Church St. (corner of
Canal)
New York, NY 10013
212–226–5280
Used clothing.

Early Halloween
180 9th Ave. (at 21st St.)
New York, NY 10011
212–691–2933
Antique clothing and
accessories.

Nostalgia Alley Antiques
380 2nd Ave.
New York, NY 10010
212–988–3949
Antique clothing and
accessories.

The Late Show
2 St. Mark's Place
New York, NY 10003
212–674–9823
Used clothing and
accessories for men and
women.

Unique Clothing Warehouse
718 Broadway (near 8th
St.)
and adjacent stores
New York, NY 10003
212–674–1767

Antique and used clothing
for men and women—
four stores.

CORSET SUPPLIES

E. Degrandmont, Inc.
50 W. 17th St.
New York, NY 10011
212–242–5122

L. Laufer & Co.
39 W. 28th St.
New York, NY 10001
212–685–2181–2

Nathan's Boning Co.
336 W. 37th St.
New York, NY 10018
212–244–4781
Continuous steel boning.

COSTUME RENTALS

The Costume Collection
601 W. 26th St.
New York, NY 10001
212–989–5855–6

David's Outfitters
36 W. 20th St.
New York, NY 10011
212–691–7388
Uniforms

Eaves-Brooks Costume Co., Inc.
21–07 41st Ave.
Long Island City
Queens, NY 11101
212–786–4956

Lillian Costume Company
226 Jericho Turnpike
Mineola, NY 11501
516–746–6060

Rubie's Costume Co.
1 Rubie Plaza
Richmond Hill, NY 11418
212–846–1008

Stivanello
66–38 Clinton Ave.
Maspeth, Queens, NY
11378
212–651–7715
Opera costumes.

DANCEWEAR

Capezio Dance-Theatre Shops
755 7th Ave. (at 50th St.)
New York, NY 10019
212–245–2130

177 MacDougal St. (at
8th St.)
New York, NY 10011
212–477–5634

16 W. 61st St. (at
Broadway)
New York, NY 10023
212–246–4944

136 E. 61st St.
New York, NY 10021
212–758–8833

Freed of London
108 W. 57th St.
New York, NY 10019
212–489–1055–6–7

Herbet Dancewear, Inc.
902 Broadway (at 20th St.)
New York, NY 10010
212–677–7606

Pavlova's Pointe Ltd.
35 W. 8th St.
New York, NY 10011
212–260–7855 and 2248

Taffy's
1776 Broadway (at 57th
St.) (2nd fl.)
New York, NY 10019
212–586–5140

DECORATIVE ITEMS

Abetter Cork Co.
262 Mott St.
New York, NY 10012
212–925–7755
Cork beads and balls.

A.&S. Button Co.
131 Essex St. (2nd fl.)
New York, NY 10002
212–647–0669

Sydney Coe, Inc.
65 W. 37th St.
New York, NY 10018
212–391–6960
Beads, jewels, etc.

Cinderella Flower & Feather Co.
57 W. 38th St.
New York, NY 10018
212–840–0644

Duplex Novelty Co.
575 8th Ave.
New York, NY 10018
212–564–1352
Wooden beads.

40th St. Trimmings
252 W. 40th St.
New York, NY 10018
212–354–4729

Gordon Button Co., Inc.
142 W. 38th St.
New York, NY 10018
212–921–1684–5

Joseph Hersh
1000 6th Ave. (at 37th St.)
New York, NY 10018
212–391–6615
Buttons.

Hyman Hendler & Sons
67 W. 38th St.
New York, NY 10018
212–840–8393
Ribbons.

K. Trimming Co.
519 Broadway
New York, NY 10012
212–431–8929
Laces, trimmings, thread,
zippers, buttons, etc.

La Bern Novelty Co., Inc.
1011 6th Ave.
New York, NY 10018
212–719–2131
Buttons.

M.&J. Trimming Co.
1008 6th Ave.
New York, NY 10018
212–391–9072
Ribbons, buttons,
trimmings, etc.

Lew Novik
45 W. 38th St.
New York, NY 10018
212–575–0850
Laces.

Ben Raymond
611 Broadway (near
Houston)
New York, NY 10012
212–777–7350
Laces and trimmings.
Good selection, excellent
prices.

Sheru
49 W. 38th St.
New York, NY 10018
212–730–0766
Beads, findings, etc.

So-Good Inc.
28 W. 38th St.
New York, NY 10018
212–398–0236
Ribbons.

*Star Buttonhole & Button
Works Co.*
242 W. 36th St.
New York, NY 10018
212–736–4960
Buttonholes made and
buttons covered to order

Tender Buttons
143 E. 62nd St.
New York, NY 10021
212–758–7004
Expensive but beautiful!

Tinsel Trading Co.
47 W. 38th St.
New York, NY 10018
212–730–1030
Antique trims.

DYESTUFFS

Aljo Mfg. Co.
450 Greenwich St.
New York, NY 10013
212–226–2878
Dyes for all types of
fabrics.

Gothic Color Co.
727 Washington St.
New York, NY 10014
212–929–7493
Aniline dyes, gold leaf.

Pearl Paint
308 Canal St.
New York, NY 10013
212–431–7932
Good variety of various
types in small amounts.

FABRICS
Upper East Side

Silk Surplus, Inc.
843 Lexington Avenue
New York, NY 10021
212–879–4708
223 E. 58th St.
New York, NY 10022
212–753–6511
Open Mon.–Sat. (closed
Sun.); swatches; will
ship: beautiful drapery
and upholstery fabrics,
many in silk. Expensive,
but worth it!

Regent Fabrics
122 E. 59th St.
New York, NY 10022
212–355–2039 and 2217
Open Mon.–Sat. (closed
Sun.); swatches; will
ship; good selection of
woolens, silks, velvets,
brocades, cottons,
novelty fabrics, on main
floor. Lots of great
buttons and trimmings
in basement. Reasonable
prices.

57th Street Between 5th and 6th Avenues

Weller Fabrics, Inc.
54 W. 57th St.
New York, NY 10019
212–247–3790
Open Mon.–Sat. (closed
Sun.); swatches; will
ship; printed and plain
silks and cottons,
woolens, laces, velvets,
metallics, some unusual
and imported fabrics.
Expensive.

*Jerry Brown Imported
Fabrics, Inc.*
37 W. 57th St.
New York, NY 10019
212–753–3626
Open Mon.–Sat. (closed
Sun.); no swatches (as a
rule); will ship; silks,
woolens, cottons, etc.
Very expensive—not
recommended unless you
have a huge budget!

57th Street Between 6th and 7th Avenues

Poli Fabrics
132 W. 57th St.
New York, NY 10019
212–245–7589
Open Mon.–Sat. (closed
Sun.); swatches; good
selection of silks,
woolens, brocades,
velvets, cottons,
imported and designer
fabrics. Reasonable prices
(sometimes negotiable).

Paron Fabrics
140 W. 57th St.
New York, NY 10019
212–247–6451
Open Mon.–Sat. (closed
Sun.); swatches; will
ship; good selection of
silks, woolens, brocades,
cottons, metallics, and
imported fabrics.
Reasonable prices
(sometimes negotiable).

Fe-Ro Fabrics
147 W. 57th St.
New York, NY 10019
212–581–0240
Open Mon.–Sat. (closed
Sun.); swatches; will
ship; good selection of
silks, woolens, brocades,
cottons, and imported
fabrics. Expensive.

56th Street Between 5th and 6th Avenues

Gladstone Fabrics
16 W. 56th St.
New York, NY 10019
212–765–0760 and
245–5950 and 664–9610
Open Mon.–Fri., some
Saturdays (closed Sun.);
swatches; will ship;
specialists in theatrical
fabrics, silks, some
woolens, cottons,
brocades, laces, velvets,
metallics, sequin fabrics,
and lots of unusual
theatrical fabrics.
Reasonable prices
(sometimes negotiable).

40th Street Between 7th and 8th Avenues

Rosen & Chadick
246 W. 40th St.
New York, NY 10018
212–869–0136
Open Mon.–Sat. (closed
Sun.); swatches; silks,
woolens, cottons,
brocades, laces, velvets,
metallics, synthetics and
imported fabrics.
Expensive.

Modlin Fabrics
240 W. 40th St.
New York, NY 10018
212–391–4130
Open Mon.–Sat. (closed
Sun.); swatches; cottons,
some woolens, blends,
synthetics, knits, some
silks. Inexpensive.

B&J Fabrics
263 W. 40th St.
New York, NY 10018
212–354–8150 and
221–9287
Open Mon.–Sat. (closed
Sun.); swatches; will
ship; good selection of
silks, woolens, cottons,
brocades, laces, imported
and designer fabrics.
Reasonable prices.

Felsen Fabrics
264 W. 40th St.
New York, NY 10018
212–398–9010 and 9011
Open Mon.–Sat. (closed
Sun.); swatches; will
ship; good selection of
silks, woolens, cottons,
brocades, laces, velvets,
metallics, unusual
imported and designer
fabrics. Expensive.

Art-Max Fabrics
250 W. 40th St.
New York, NY 10018
212–398–0755
Open Mon.–Sat. (closed
Sun.); swatches; will
ship; good selection of
silks, woolens, cottons,
brocades, laces, velvets,

metallics, synthetics and imported fabrics. Reasonable prices (sometimes negotiable).

39th Street Between 7th and 8th Avenues

C&F Fabrics, Inc.
250 W. 39th St.
New York, NY 10018
212–354–9360
Open Mon.–Sat. (closed Sun.); swatches; good selection of silks, woolens, cottons, prints, laces, velvets, metallics, unusual theatrical fabrics, some drapery and upholstery fabrics. Inexpensive.

Sutter Textile Co.
257 W. 39th St.
New York, NY 10018
212–398–0248
Open Mon.–Sat. (closed Sun.); swatches; some silks and woolens. cottons, brocades, velvets, linings, synthetics and blends, knits, drapery and upholstery fabrics. Inexpensive.

5th Avenue Near 39th Street

Maxine Fabrics Co.
417 5th Avenue (Room 1115)
New York, NY 10016
212–685–1790
Open Mon.–Fri. (closed Sat. and Sun.), large swatch book available for a deposit of $25, which is refundable for an order of over $500 (at time of writing); will ship. Prices are fairly expensive, but the swatch book, which comes out four times a year, has hundreds of silks, wools, cottons, brocades, prints, etc.—all dress fabrics and many are imported. A good source if you are stuck out in the

boondocks without a fabric source close by.

38th Street Between 5th and 6th Avenues

Mayer & Fisher, Inc.
15 W. 38th St.
New York, NY 10018
212–840–8438
Open Mon.–Fri. (closed Sat. and Sun.); swatches; will ship; imported fabrics, Swiss, German, French, etc. Specialty fabrics, some metallics. Reasonable prices.

35th Street at 11th Avenue

Rose Brand Textile Fabrics
517–27 W. 35th St.
New York, NY 10001
212–594–7424
Toll free: 800–223–1624
Open Mon.–Fri. (closed Sat. and Sun.); swatches; will ship; muslin in several different weights from light weight to heavy weight, scenery canvas, chincha (tobacco cloth), felt, velours, etc. Primarily scenery fabrics, but a good inexpensive source for muslin and chincha. Discount prices on quantity yardage.

Madison Avenue

Far Eastern Fabrics Ltd.
171 Madison Avenue (between 33rd and 34th Sts.)
New York, NY 10016
212–683–2623 and 2624
Open Mon.–Fri. (closed Sat. and Sun.); swatches; will ship; imported silks and cottons. This is a wholesale company that gives discount prices to theatres (on 2nd fl.).

East 29th Street Near Madison Avenue

Dazian's Inc.

40 E. 29th St.
New York, NY 10016
212–686–5300
Open Mon.–Fri. (closed Sat. and Sun.); swatches; will ship; theatrical fabrics. Nets, duck, muslin, canvas, metallics, burlap, etc. Reasonable to expensive prices. Discount on quantity yardage. Branches in Beverly Hills, Dallas, Chicago, Boston, and N. Miami.

Park Avenue South

Jacob and Meyer
234 Park Avenue South (at 19th St.)
New York, NY 10011
212–254–6237
Open Mon.–Fri. (closed Sat. and Sun.); swatches; good selection of suitings, woolens, worsteds, etc. Reasonable prices.

14th Street

Patterson Silks
36 E. 14th St. (at University Place)
New York, NY 10003
212–929–7861
Open 7 days; swatches; silks, woolens, blends, synthetics, knits, etc. downstairs; drapery and upholstery fabrics upstairs; remnants on the sidewalk. Reasonable prices.

Jonas Dept. Store
62 W. 14th St.
New York, NY 10011
212–242–9583
Open 7 days; swatches; prices are good, and it's worth a visit. Drapery and upholstery, as well as dress fabrics and remnants. Limited selection. Very inexpensive.

First Avenue

Diamond Discount Fabric Center
165 First Avenue (at 10th St.)
New York, NY 10003
212–228–8189 and 674–9612
Open 7 days; swatches; good selection of silks, woolens, blends, synthetics, cottons, prints, velvets, knits, drapery fabrics, etc. Very inexpensive (sometimes negotiable).

Lower Broadway

Ben Raymond
611 Broadway (at Houston Street)
New York, NY 10012
212–777–7350
Open Mon.–Sat. (closed Sun.); swatches; cottons, eyelets, linings. Fabric selection is limited, but very inexpensive.

Inter-Coastal Textile Corp.
480 Broadway (at Broome Street)
New York, NY 10013
212–925–9235
Open Mon.–Fri. (closed Sat. and Sun.); swatches; will ship; drapery and upholstery fabrics. Great selection at excellent prices. On two floors, but best selection is in the basement. Antique satins, velvets, cottons, brocades, sheers, etc. Very inexpensive (sometimes negotiable).

Orchard Street

Kordol Fabrics
194 Orchard St.
New York, NY 10002
212–254–8319 and 254–8364
Open Sun.–Fri. (closed Sat.); swatches; good selections of woolens, suitings and blends. Some synthetics. Reasonable prices.

Orchard Fabric Center
189 Orchard St.
New York, NY 10002
212–777–6457
Open Sun.–Fri. (closed
Sat.); swatches; some
woolens, blends,
synthetics, cottons,
velvets, drapery and
upholstery fabrics,
moires, antiques, satins,
etc. Inexpensive.

Weiss & Katz, Inc.
187 Orchard St.
New York, NY 10002
212–477–1130
Open Sun.–Fri. (closed
Sat.); swatches; good
selection of woolens and
suitings. knits, synthetics,
cottons, velvets, etc.
Inexpensive.

European Woolens, Inc.
177 Orchard St.
New York, NY 10002
212–254–1520
Open Sun.–Fri. (closed
Sat.); swatches; silks,
woolens, suitings,
velvets, knits, cottons,
some metallics, remnants,
laces, etc. Very
inexpensive.

The Woolen Closet, Inc.
167 Orchard St.
New York, NY 10002
212–674–0180
Open Sun.–Fri. (closed
Sat.); swatches; woolens,
worsteds, some
velveteens.

Modern Woolens
129 Orchard St.
New York, NY 10002
212–473–6780
Open Sun.–Fri. (closed
Sat.); swatches; good
selections of woolens,
worsteds, suitings, some
velvets. Fairly reasonable
prices (sometimes
negotiable).

S. Beckenstein, Inc.
130 Orchard St.
New York, NY 10002
212–475–4525

Open Sun.–Fri. (closed
Sat.); swatches
(sometimes!); will ship;
silks, woolens, cottons,
velvets, shirtings,
metallics downstairs;
drapery and upholstery
fabrics upstairs. You may
find some of the fabrics
cheaper elsewhere, but
their selection is good
and worth a visit. But
don't go on Sundays—
it's very crowded, and
they definitely will not
give swatches on
Sundays! Moderate to
expensive prices
(sometimes negotiable).

S. Beckenstein, Inc.
125 Orchard St.
New York, NY 10002
212–475–4525
Open Sun.–Fri. (closed
Sat.); swatches; devoted
to woolens, worsteds,
suitings, etc. of all
descriptions, mainly on
the second floor.
Reasonable prices.

Eldridge Street
(just north of Grand St.
between Allen & Forsyth)
Leratex Fabrics
110 Eldridge St.
New York, NY 10002
212–925–3678
Open Sun.–Fri. (closed
Sat.); swatches; will
ship; drapery and
upholstery fabrics only.
Store is small, so
selection is limited and
varies from time to time,
but prices are excellent.
Moires, antique satins,
velvets, chintzes, prints,
cottons, and sheers. Very
inexpensive.

M. Zupnik, Inc.
113 Eldridge St.
New York, NY 10002
212–226–4669
Open Sun.–Fri. (closed
Sat.); no swatches; will
ship; store is mostly

wholesale but does sell
retail, and prices are
excellent. You usually get
a break in price for
quantity yardage (more
than 10 or 12 yards of
same fabric); cottons,
prints, synthetics, blends,
corduroys, some
woolens, some brocades,
linings. Very inexpensive.

Grand Street
(at the corner of Essex Street,
close to Orchard St.)
Grand Silk House
357 Grand St.
New York, NY 10002
212–475–0114
Open Sun.–Fri. (closed
Sat.); swatches; will
ship; silks, woolens,
cottons, velvets,
imported and designer
fabrics. Reasonable
prices.

Hester Street
(between Allen and Orchard
Streets)
Listokin & Sons Fabrics, Inc.
87 Hester St.
New York, NY 10002
212–226–6111 and 6112
and 6113
Open Sun.–Fri. (closed
Sat.); swatches; some
silks, some woolens,
blends, synthetics,
cottons, laces, some
printed rayon crepes,
velvets, and trimmings
(mostly bridal!).
Reasonable prices.

Mendel Goldberg, Inc.
72 Hester St.
New York, NY 10002
212–925–9110
Open Sun.–Fri. (closed
Sat.); no swatches (as a
rule); silks, woolens,
cottons, velvets, some
metallics, printed rayon
crepes (good source)
imported and designer
fabrics. Reasonable
prices.

Harry Snyder
70 Hester St.
New York, NY 10002
212–925–0885
Open Sun.–Fri. (closed
Sat.); swatches; silks,
woolens, cottons,
imported and designer
fabrics at discount and
some unusual fabrics.
Fairly expensive to
reasonable prices.

FELT
Central Shippee, Inc.
Bloomingdale, NJ 07403
201–838–1100
Industrial and decorator
felts.

Continental Felt Co.
22 W. 15th St.
New York, NY 10011
212–929–5262
Industrial and display felts.

FOOTWEAR
Anania Bros.
46 W. 46th St.
New York, NY 10036
212–757–7189
Custom footwear, repairs.

Capezio's
See Dancewear

Custom Theatrical Shoes
4 W. 62nd St.
New York, NY 10023
212–265–3212

Eiser's
1304 N. Broad St.
Hillside, NJ 07205
201–352–6428
Riding equipment. Good
prices on boots, western
and riding. Carries riding
boots for wide calves.
Catalogue available.

Lynn Boot & Shoe Ltd.
20 W. 46th St.
New York, NY 10036
212–246–1492
Western Boots in wide
fittings.

McCreedy & Schreiber
37 and 55 W. 46th St.
New York, NY 10036
212–719–1552
Men's shoes and boots.

Montana Leather Works Ltd.
47 Greene St.
New York, NY 10012
212–431–4015
Custom theatrical footwear and leatherwork.

FORMAL WEAR

David's Outfitters
36 W. 20th St.
New York, NY 10011
212–691–7388
Rentals and sales.

Jack Silver
1780 Broadway (between 57th & 58th Sts.)
New York, NY 10019
212–582–3298 and 3389
Rentals and sales. Also has some period men's clothing.

HATS

A.B.C. Hatters (Modern Hatters)
313 3rd St.
Jersey City, NJ
201–659–1113 and 9300
Factory outlet—large selection of men's and some women's hats.

Jay Lord
30 W. 39th St.
New York, NY 10018
212–221–8941
Men's hats, including derbies.

Scott Hatters, Inc.
620 8th Ave.
New York, NY 10036
212–840–2130
Men's hats.

J.J. Hat Center, Inc.
(Stetson Hats)
1276 Broadway (33rd St.)
New York, NY 10001
212–244–8860

Van Dyke Hatters
848 6th Ave. (30th St.)
New York, NY 10001
212–683–6226
Men's hats, also reblocking and cleaning.

LEATHER AND LEATHER SUPPLIES

A.&B. Leather & Findings Co.
500 W. 52nd St. (10th Ave)
New York, NY 10019
212–265–8124
Supplies, tools, and Magix.

Leathercrafter's Supply Co.
25 Great Jones St.
New York, NY 10012
212–673–5460
Leather, tools, dyes, buckles, hardware, etc.

Leather Sales Corp.
78 Spring St. (near Broadway)
New York, NY 10012
212–925–6270

National Leather & Shoe Findings Co.
313 Bowery
New York, NY 10003
212–982–6227
Supplies, tools, and Magix.

MAKE-UP

Bob Kelly Cosmetics, Inc.
151 W. 46th St.
New York, NY 10036
212–819–0030

Leichner Cosmetics Ltd.
599 11th Ave.
New York, NY 10036
212–246–5543

The Make-Up Center Ltd.
150 W. 55th St.
New York, NY 10019
212–977–9494

Mehron, Inc.
250 W. 40th St.
New York, NY 10036
212–997–1011

Performer's Make-Up, Inc.
13 E. 47th St.
New York, NY 10017
212–752–6800

M. Stein Cosmetic Co.
430 Broome St.
New York, NY 10013
212–226–2430

MILLINERY SUPPLIES

Feldman Machine Works, Inc.
1032 6th Ave. (at 39th St.)
New York, NY 10018
212–947–1662
Millinery wire, hat steamers, sizings, etc.

Gampels Supply Corp.
33 W. 37th St.
New York, NY 10018
212–398–9222
Millinery wire.

Manny's Millinery Supply Co.
63 W. 38th St.
New York, NY 10018
212–840–2235
Wire, buckram, felts, buckram shapes, flowers, long hat pins, etc.

PLEATING

Raymond Miligi Pleating Co.
58 W. 56th St.
New York, NY 10019
212–247–3785

SEWING MACHINES AND REPAIR

American Trading Co.
599 6th Ave. (18th St.)
New York, NY 10011
212–691–3666

Continental Sewing Supply Co.
104 W. 25th St.
New York, NY 10001
212–255–8837
Machines, parts, and attachments.

Fox Sewing Machine, Inc.
307 W. 38th St. (between 8th and 9th)
New York, NY 10018
212–594–2438

Smith Bros. Sewing Machine & Elec. Co.
555 8th Ave. (near 37th St.)
New York, NY 10018
212–736–0022
Also has used tailor's dummies.

SEWING SUPPLIES

Greenberg and Hammer
24 W. 57th St.
New York, NY 10019
212–246–2836 and 586–6270

Joseph Hersh
1000 6th Ave. (at 37th St.)
New York, NY 10018
212–391–6615

Louis A. Lew Co., Inc.
108 5th Ave.
New York, NY 10011
212–242–1475

Steinlauf & Stoller
239 W. 39th St.
New York, NY 10018
212–869–0321

Wolf Form Co.
39 W. 19th St.
New York, NY 10011
212–255–4508
New tailor's dummies.

THEATRICAL SUPPLIES

Alcone Co., Inc.
575 8th Ave. (38th St.)
New York, NY 10018
212–594–3980

Gordon Novelty Co., Inc.
933 Broadway (22nd St.)
New York, NY 10010
212–254–8616–7

UNIFORMS

Budget Uniform
110 E. 59th St.
New York, NY 10022
212–593–0965
Nurse's, doctor's, etc.

David's Outfitters
36 W. 20th St.
New York, NY 10011
212–691–7388
All types, rental, and sales.

Kaufman's Surplus, Inc.
319 W. 42nd St.
New York, NY 10036
212–757–5670
Army surplus.

Leitner Uniforms, Inc.
26 Bowery (near Canal)
New York, NY 10002
212–267–8765 and 8740
Police, guards, etc.—new
and used.

Weiss & Mahoney, Inc.
142 5th Ave.
New York, NY 10011
212–675–1915
Military, police, etc.—new
and used.

WIGS AND HAIR SUPPLIES

Charles Elsen
170 W. 74th St.
New York, NY 10023
212–873–9337
Wig rentals only.

Paul Huntley Productions, Inc.
28 W. 82nd St.
New York, NY 10024

212–580–9063
Custom wigs; specializes in
movies only. Expensive.

Bob Kelly Wig Creations
151 W. 46th St., 9th Fl.
New York, NY 10036
212–819–0030
Wigs, custom and rentals,
facial hair, etc.

Charles Lo Presto Wig Productions
330 W. 38th St. (Room 1608)
New York, NY 10008
212–947–7281
Custom wigs, facial hair,
and rentals.

Ray Beauty Supply Co., Inc.
721 8th Ave.
New York, NY 10019
212–757–0175

United Beauty Supply, Inc.
49 W. 46th St.
New York, NY 10036
212–719–2324

Zauder Bros., Inc.
902 Broadway
New York, NY 10010
212–228–2600
Hair and wig supplies,
needles, netting, etc.

San Francisco Area

ARMS AND ARMOR
The Armoury
American Fencing Supply
1180 Folsom St.
San Francisco, CA 94103
415–863–7911

ARTIST AND CRAFT SUPPLIES
Douglas & Sturgess
730 Bryant St.
San Francisco, CA 94107
415–421–4456
Polyurethane foam
   compounds, slip mould,
   plastics, adhesives,
   moulage, fiber-glass, etc.

Flax
250 Sutter St.
San Francisco, CA 94108
415–391–7400

DYESTUFFS
Fibrec, Inc.
1154 Howard St.
San Francisco, CA 94103
415–431–8214

Screen Process Supplies
1199 E. 12th St.
Oakland, CA 94606
415–451–1048

Siphon Art
74-D Hamilton Dr.
Ignacio, CA 94947
415–883–9006
Versatex.

Straw into Gold
5533 College Ave.
Oakland, CA 94618
Weaving and dyeing
   supplies, catalogue
   available.

FABRICS
Britex Fabrics
146 Geary St.
San Francisco, CA 94108
415–392–2910

Fabriano's
5011 Telegraph Ave.
Oakland, CA 94609
415–658–3666

Home Yardage
3245 Geary
San Francisco, CA
415–221–3404

New York Fabrics
1519 San Pablo
Oakland, CA 94612
415–893–5633

Winne & Sutch Co.
The Showplace
2 Kansas St.
San Francisco, CA 94103
415–626–4113
Canvas and muslin, price
   letter available.

FELT
Pacific States Felt Co.
23850 Clawiter Rd.
Hayward, CA 94545
   415–783–0277

FOOTWEAR
Madrid Street Bootmakers
126 Pixley St.
San Francisco, CA 94123
415–921–9696

LEATHER AND LEATHER SUPPLIES
S.H. Frank & Co.
3075 17th St.
San Francisco, CA 94110
415–863–6244
Leather goods, buckles,
   dyes, etc.

Macpherson Bros.
730 Polk St.
San Francisco, CA 94101
415–771–1900

MAKE-UP
California Theatrical Supply
256 Sutter
San Francisco, CA 94108
415–957–1686

PLEATING
San Francisco Pleating Co.
425 2nd St.
San Francisco, CA 94107
415–982–3003

SEWING SUPPLIES

Lion Notions, Inc.
222 Harris Ct.
S. San Francisco, CA
94080
415–873–4693
Catalogue available.

THEATRICAL SUPPLIES

Bob Mandell's Costume Shop
834 Mission St.
San Francisco, CA 94103
415–391–0811
Danskin, wigs, costumes,
make-up, etc.

Lew Serbin
Dance Art Co.
222 Powell St.
San Francisco, CA 94102
415–392–4912
Findings, sewing supplies,
trimmings, costume
accessories, celastic, etc.;
catalogue available.

WIGS AND HAIR SUPPLIES

Mark Bernstein Co.
Western Wig Sales
332 Pine
San Francisco, CA 94104
415–391–8767
Ready-made wigs and wig
supplies.

Other Areas

ARMOR AND WEAPONS

Unique Imports, Inc.
Dept. MM 974
610 Franklin St.
Alexandria, VA 22314
703–549–0775
Weapons, uniforms,
militaria; catalogue
available.

Dixie Gun Works, Inc.
Gunpowder Lane
Union City, TN 38261
901–885–0700
Toll-free: 800–238–6785
Catalogue available.

COLLARS

Gibson Lee, Inc.
78 Stone Place
Melrose, MA 02176
617–662–6025
Disposable collars, collar
studs, cufflinks, shirts,
etc.; brochure available.

COSTUME RENTAL

Malabar
14 McCaul St.
Toronto, Ontario, Canada
M5T I26
416–362–6581
Opera and Operetta
costume rentals;
brochure available.

DANCEWEAR

Taffy's
701 Beta Dr.
Cleveland, OH 44143
216–461–3360
Has other branches;
catalogue available.

DECORATIVE ITEMS

Baer Fabrics Co.
515 E. Market
Louisville, KY 40202
502–583–5521
Flowers, feathers, beads,
buttons, jewels, trims,
etc., as well as fabrics;
catalogue available.

DYESTUFFS

Cerulean Blue, Ltd.
1314 N.E. 43rd St.
Seattle, WA 98105
Carries procion and
disperse dyes. Silk screen
and batik supplies;
catalogue available.

W. Cushing & Co.
Kennebunkport, ME
04046
207–967–3711

ICI Organics, Inc.
Wilmington, DE 19899
302–658–9311
Procion cold water dyes.

SPECIAL PRODUCTS

CPC North America
1437 W. Moues St.
P.O. Box 21070
Indianapolis, IN 46221
Bulk Rit Dye.

FABRICS

The Amluxen Co.
913 Nicollet Ave.
Minneapolis, MN 55402
612–333–6393
Silks, woolens, trims, etc.

See *Baer Fabrics Co.* under
Decorative Items.

Osgood Textile Co., Inc.
30 Magaziner Place
Springfield, MA
413–737–6488
Large selection of silks,
woolens, cottons,
drapery, etc.

Testfabrics, Inc.
200 Blackford Ave.
P.O. Box 0 Middlesex, NJ
08846
201–469–6446
Specializes in white,
untreated fabrics for
fabric dyers and printers.
Swatch book available.
Cottons, silks, blends,
linens, etc. Good prices.
Fast shipping.

FELT

A.B. Boyd Co.
6136 N.E. 87th Ave.
Portland, OR 97220
503–255–5405
Industrial felt.

Brady Felt Co.
2630 5th Ave.
Pittsburgh, PA 15213
412–683–5322
Industrial felt.

Rumpel Felt Co., Ltd.
Mfg. of Wool & Synthetic
Felts
P.O. Box 1283
Kitchener, Ontario, Canada
H2G 4G8
519–743–6341
Industrial felt, allow two
weeks for delivery.

FOOTWEAR

Anello & Davide Ltd.
Theatrical Footwear
30-35 Drury Lane
London WC2 England
01–836–6744
Make to order and some
stock. Catalogue
available.

Michael Bolubash
615 College St.
Toronto, Ontario, Canada
M6G 1B5
416–537–2986
Custom-made shoes and
boots.

HATS
Haentze Hatcrafters
20 N. Springfield Rd.
Clifton Hts. PA 19018
215–623–2620
Theatrical hats to order;
   catalogue available.

LEATHER AND LEATHER SUPPLIES
Macpherson Bros.
1309 2nd Ave.
Seattle, WA 98101
206–622–0855
Skins, leather supplies,
   dyes, etc.

Tandy Leather Co.
1001 Foch
Ft. Worth, TX 76107
817–335–4161
Other branches throughout
   country; catalogue
   available.

MILLINERY SUPPLIES
Milliner's Supply Co.
911 Elm St.
Dallas, TX 74202
214–742–8284
Millinery supplies, flowers,
   Jiffy steamers, and hat
   stretchers.

SEWING SUPPLIES
Henry Stuart Co., Inc.
108 W. Main St.
P.O. Box 551
Milford CT 06460
Inviso-boning, "rigid" steel
   enamel coated up to 2″
   wide from ⅟₁₆″, spiral
   boning, tipping fluid.
   Good prices.

THEATRICAL SUPPLY HOUSES
Atlanta Costume (Norcostco)
2089 Monroe Drive N.E.
Atlanta, GA 30324
404–874–7511
Catalogue available.

Eastern Costume (Norcostco)
375 Route 10
Whippany, NJ 07981
201–428–1177

Mask and Wig Theatrical
   Costume Co.
20 W. 5th St.
Dayton, OH 45402
513–228–9163
Catalogue available.

Northwestern Costume
   (Norcostco)
3203 N. Highway 100
Minneapolis, MN 55422
612–533–2791
Catalogue available.

Salt Lake City Costume Co.
1701 W. 11th St. E
Salt Lake City, UT 84105
801–467–9494
Catalogue available.

Texas Costume (Norcostco)
2125 North Harwood St.
Dallas, TX 75201
214–748–4581
Catalogue available.

Theatre House, Inc.
400 W. 3rd St.
P.O. Box 2090
Covington, KY 41012
606–431–2414
Catalogue available.

UNIFORMS
G. Gedney Gidwin, Inc.
Box 100
Valley Forge, PA 19481
215–783–0670
Eighteenth-Century
   military gear and
   accessories; catalogue
   available for purchase.

INDEX